Cornbread Nation 7

Cornbread Nation 7
The Best of Southern Food Writing

Edited by Francis Lam

General Editor, John T. Edge

Published in association with
the Southern Foodways Alliance
and the Center for the Study of Southern Culture
at the University of Mississippi

The University of Georgia Press ■ Athens and London

Publication of this work was made possible, in part, by a generous gift
from the University of Georgia Press Friends Fund.

■ ■

Published by the University of Georgia Press
Athens, Georgia 30602
www.ugapress.org
© 2014 by the Southern Foodways Alliance,
    Center for the Study of Southern Culture, University of Mississippi
All rights reserved
Designed by Anne Richmond Boston
Set in 10.5 Adobe Minion by Graphic Composition, Inc., Bogart, Ga.
Manufactured by Thomson-Shore
The paper in this book meets the guidelines for permanence and durability of
the Committee on Production Guidelines for Book Longevity of the Council
on Library Resources.

Most University of Georgia Press titles are available from popular e-book vendors.

Printed in the United States of America
18 17 16 15 14 P 5 4 3 2 1

ISBN: 978-0-8203-4666-3 (pbk. : alk. paper)
ISBN: 978-0-8203-4695-3 (e-book)
ISSN: 2333-4940 (print)
ISSN: 2333-4967 (e-book)

Contents

PROVISIONS AND PROVIDERS

FIVE WAYS OF LOOKING AT SOUTHERN FOOD

THE SOUTH, STEPPING OUT

SOUTHERNERS GOING HOME

Cornbread Nation 7

Introduction

Francis Lam

In my younger, more offensive years, I used to say that Michigan was the South's northernmost state, on account of the popularity of pickup trucks and country music. I also thought any state that started with a vowel was probably dispensable, and for proof, I would start with Alabama, Arkansas.

What enabled me to such opinions? A privileged, cosmopoli-vincial upbringing in . . . New Jersey.

We were, of course, "normal." And our normalness was modern, urban, and worldly. By the 1980s, our shopping malls had Japanese sushi! (Made by Chinese people.) And Greek gyros! (Made by machines.) I thought then that the South was backward and closed minded and in love with Billy Ray Cyrus.

I lived in my actively ignorant state for years, blithely casting aspersions on places and people I knew nothing about. I grew up some, eventually, and did the equally-abstract-180 thing: "Wait, I don't know anything about the South. How can I hate it? Um . . . now I should love it!" I fetishized soul food and barbecue; I talked about the greatness of rock-and-roll bands from Chapel Hill. I went around self-righteously shaming anyone who talked disparagingly of "rednecks" before I had met anyone who could have reasonably been called one.

And here I am, many more years after that, welcoming you to an anthology of Southern food writing. Past editions of *Cornbread Nation* have been edited by the likes of John Egerton, Lolis Elie, Ronni Lundy—Southerners of consequence—so this is a responsibility that is deep and serious.

My own words were included in the last edition of *Cornbread Nation*. It was a story about meeting a retired Cajun shrimper in Mississippi, who confessed that he resented the Vietnamese people working the waters he grew up on, but who also offered me, an Asian stranger, a standing invitation to come over for crawfish. He was generous and tough, lovely and complicated, and I met him, Mr. Leroy, while I was living on and off in his hometown of Biloxi, Mississippi.

I was brought there by recovery work after "the storm," which we all called Hurricane Katrina, and I stayed because I'd fallen in love. With a woman, in particular, but also with a community, a place with a sense of its own place. My neighbors, like Mr. Leroy, or like Sue Nguyen, or like Fofo Gilich, or like Lucille Bennett were Cajun, Croatian, Caribbean, white, brown, black, yellow; they were all Biloxians.

I once asked Miz Loren, who sold vegetables under the highway overpass, how a Barbadian like herself ended up in Biloxi. "I didn't *end up* in Biloxi," she said. "You *end up* somewhere when you try to go somewhere *else* and find you're not welcomed there. I *came* to Biloxi."

I tell that story about Loren all the time. It makes me think of her, but just as much, it makes me think of how schooled I have been by the South, how my old ideas of what "the South" was stopped mattering when I started actually getting to know Southerners. It makes me think of the richness I've found once I started becoming an honorary Southerner: richness of character, richness of spirit. Richness of story, richness of place.

That richness is generous and tough, lovely and complicated. There is beauty, but not always. Outsiders' assumptions usually don't play out, changing our field of vision. But sometimes they do, solidifying stereotypes. I know my share of Southerners who now live here in New York City. When Southerners leave the South, they bring their identities along, but the South they bring with them bobs and weaves, bends and melts, sometimes turning into something altogether different than what they knew back home.

This collection of stories, essays, and reportage comes from those shifting perspectives (and through the tireless work of Sara Camp Arnold, John T. Edge, and Amy Evans). I originally thought I would concentrate the collection on stories of outsiders coming to the South. But soon, because "the South" isn't some hermetically sealed bubble that may or may not include Kentucky, I saw that it needed to include stories of Southerners as they move through the world, changing it as it changes them. (And, honestly, some pieces we included just because we loved reading them—forty-something selections in, you've got to let your hair down a little bit.)

In "Come In and Stay Awhile" we hear from and about adventurers, wanderers, immigrants, and, yes, some people who *ended up* in the South. Sara Roahen, originally a woman of Wisconsin with delicate Californian produce sensibilities, struggles with the hock-fisted pummeling that vegetables get in her adopted home of New Orleans. Daniel Patterson—a writer so brilliant it seems almost a shame he insists on being a world-class chef—shows us a sepia Miami of Jewish settlers. Susan Orlean paints a different Miami for us, this one of a community weaving itself around an unforgotten past in Cuba. We hear from chef and cultural critic Eddie Huang on the awkwardness and anger of the immigrant, and about the Houston chef Chris Shepherd, whose mission is to make people see and taste the gifts of those immigrants.

From Chilton County peaches to Vidalia onions, perhaps no area of the country is more attuned to the regional provenance of its food than the South. In "Provisions and Providers" we take looks at whence, and from whom, that food comes. Besha Rodell spends time with the closest thing to a superstar the shepherd world has, and Barry Estabrook and Gabriel Thompson show us the world of the migrant workers who keep tomatoes and chickens cheap. Meanwhile, Burkhard Bilger follows a cult devoted to bacteria so fascinating that after reading about them, you will either want to unplug your refrigerator or fumigate your home and seal it in plastic.

There follow "Five Ways of Looking at Southern Food," a series of pieces that pose theories and questions about what food means to culture. Julia Reed starts with a whirlwind of regional culinary pride, befitting the fact that Southern cooking has become, paradoxically, our national regional cuisine. Kevin Young digs poetically into the pain of our tastes, and Robert Moss asks whether Southern cooking has turned from an alliance of local cuisines to an amalgamation of clichés.

In "The South, Stepping Out," we gather expats, both human and conceptual. We see Sarah Hepola declaring her Texan identity in Ro-Tel and Velveeta while stranded, queso-less, in New York. We see the Peninsula Grill's 28,000-calorie coconut cake as an ambassador for Southern baking. And we see a whole lot of soul food, which, maybe more than any other Southern cuisine, is so loaded with struggle and pride and issues of culture, race, and class that it's impossible to imagine America without it.

Finally, there is "Southerners Going Home." Some of these stories are literal, like Brett Anderson's story of the New Orleans chef Donald Link opening a branch of Cochon, his Cajun-style restaurant, back in his own Cajun country. Courtney Balestier and Monique Truong grapple with what "home" means after being away. We include, too, remembrances of a pitmaster and a wordsmith who have passed on.

This book is a continuing education for me on what it means to be Southern. I recognize my odd position as a guide to the South, and I hope that my ignorances and curiosities don't get too much in the way. I hope, instead, that my unfamiliarity helps to fill this book with ideas that you know well, but that you will be inspired to look at them again, or anew.

The other day, someone asked me, "How do I become a food writer?" I imagined that the question wasn't actually, "How do I make enough money to not starve while writing about food?" and was something more literal. Almost by instinct, words came from my mouth. "You eat, you read, you write," I said. "You look, you taste, you chew. You think, you write. But most important, you talk with people. You share with them. You listen to them. You write. You ask them their stories. You write. You try to deserve their stories, you try to do right by them and their stories by remembering them, writing them down, and sharing them."

I am grateful for all the stories here, the people they are by and about, and how they have been shared with us. I hope you enjoy them.

Come In and Stay Awhile

We Waited as Long as We Could

Daniel Patterson

The first restaurant I ever loved was a deli in Miami called Wolfie Cohen's Rascal House. A short drive away from the apartment where my grandparents lived during the winter, it opened in 1954, and maintained from then on the midcentury look of the kind of place where Frank Sinatra would eat after a show (which he did). Part New York–style deli, part diner, it had red vinyl booths, fluorescent lights, and Formica tabletops. They served Russian-Jewish food—pastrami, chicken soup, and chopped liver. Everything was good, but I didn't love it for the food. I loved it because I went there with my grandfather.

It was my grandfather who taught me what's important about restaurants: that they are places in which to escape from the world, places where people can feel brighter, wealthier, happier than they really are. For cooks, I would later discover, they are a kind of shelter, obliterating everything outside of them and replacing the void with a reality of their own. For me, even now, the front door of a restaurant is a looking glass, and on the other side lies the promise of a better life.

There's much I don't remember about my childhood, but I still dream about breakfast at the Rascal House. On those mornings, already eager with anticipation, I'd open my eyes to see my grandfather standing next to the folding door that separated our sleeping area from the rest of the living room, as if he had materialized out of thin air. I would slip out of bed quietly, and we would walk to the car in near darkness, the already-warm air sweet with the scent of gardenias. We would drive through nondescript suburban sprawl under a brightening sky, toward the wide causeways of northern Miami.

The sign would appear first, towering over the low-slung building, with the Rascal, a glowing, eerily disembodied head, perched on top. No matter how early we were, there would be a line. If we were lucky, it would only be about twenty feet out the door and around the corner. If we weren't, it would stretch for a city block. And every time, my grandfather, whom we called Papa, would sigh. He was not a terribly patient person, eternally fidgeting, shifting his weight from one foot to another and jingling the change in his pocket. I never minded the wait, though, because it gave us more time together. "How's my favorite grandson?" he used to ask me, with his big smile and eyes that glittered and danced. I'd shrug and look away, but still I'd hold that moment close, like a treasure.

Inside the restaurant there were more lines, organized by party size and separated by waist-high stainless-steel chutes. Regulars struck up conversations as they waited—about the weather, their arthritis, their wayward children. Tourists listening and occasionally chiming in. It was a rare day when Papa didn't see someone he knew.

The large dining-room space beyond, when we finally made it that far, was filled with booths and tables on one side and a diner-style counter on the other, where we often sat. The walls were covered with pictures of celebrities who had eaten at the restaurant, and cheeky aphorisms: *As I see it, there are two kinds of people in this world: people who love delis and people you shouldn't associate with.*

At the Rascal House, portions were generous and flavors big. At breakfast the tables were set with baskets of Danish and rolls to snack on; at lunch, the sweets morphed into jars of pickles. The menu, bright yellow and huge, could have served as a caution flag on a raceway. There were endless choices: matzo brei, pickled herring, borscht, latkes fried in chicken fat and butter. It was peasant food, earthy and visceral. To me, it was the taste of home.

My mother's family were Russian Jews who fled the pogroms at the beginning of the twentieth century. People like them came to America by the thousands in those days, escaping the violence in Odessa and Minsk and the little towns that dotted the countryside. Waves of refugees washed onto the shores of Manhattan and dispersed in clusters along the East Coast. My great-grandparents arrived in 1909, settled in Massachusetts, and gradually assimilated into American society. They had kids. Made some money. The kids grew up, got a little too comfortable, and, when they inevitably wearied of the harsh New England winters, turned their gazes south.

The city was barely born when the snowbirds, as they came to be called, began to arrive. Slowly at first, and then faster after the First World War, East Coast Jews and others developed the beachfront, and Miami became a winter hangout for well-heeled New Yorkers. Though the NO DOGS OR JEWS ALLOWED signs stayed up for many years, the diaspora of aging first-generation refugees, whose memories were still fresh with the horrors that they had left behind, were able to make a community for themselves. They built hotels and businesses, synagogues in which to worship, and delis that reminded them of the food they had grown up with.

The Rascal House, probably the most famous of these, occupied a one-story building designed in Miami Modern style, with an awning that stretched above two long, windowed walls. Founded by Wolfie Cohen, a onetime busboy who moved to Miami and started a string of successful restaurants, the Rascal House played to a big audience. It was a home away from home for the locals who came regularly to eat and catch up, many of whom lived in boardinghouses with no kitchens. The elderly on fixed incomes came for the early-bird breakfasts and dinners, and the tourists came for sandwiches piled high with pastrami and corned beef. It was a showy place, with an open kitchen and glass display cases always filled with lavish spreads of salads and desserts. Open twenty-four hours, it became a late-night dinner and cocktail hangout for celebrities and hipsters. It was a success from the moment it opened, and when my grandfather started taking me, it was still at the height of its popularity, feeding thousands of people a day.

We went to the Rascal House often for lunch, sometimes for dinner, usually with the whole family. It was Americanized ethnic food, full of big gestures, its forms distorted and grandiose. The sandwiches bordered on the grotesque: thick pieces of bread packed with a fist of cooked meat. It was there that I learned to order the meat sliced from the fattiest section of the muscle, and to add a piece of tongue for extra richness. I loaded my sandwiches with grainy mustard and pickled cabbage to cut through the mouthful of hot animal fat, the toasted bread and caraway drifting on top like a perfume. I still crave that intensity, the balance built on concentration, fat, and whiplash acidity, delivered like a gut punch.

I recognized many of those big gestures, that showmanship and charisma, in Papa. At a proud five feet, four inches, the guy could really command a room, always entering in a flurry of kisses, handshakes. He was a patriarch who led with charm rather than power, and the reason that his offspring all lived within a thirty-minute radius of my grandparents' apartment in Massachusetts when I was growing up. He was constantly on the phone, settling feuds and patching over rough spots among his brood. I can still hear him saying, "That's not nice!" His voice rose at the end to punctuate the admonition. He always seemed surprised that there was so much not-niceness in the world, and especially within his family. But he did what he could. My grandparents, who married at eighteen and nineteen years old, managed to stay together for seventy-five years, in large part because of his good nature.

That generosity of spirit was palpable. One time I made an offhand comment about liking a certain kind of cookie that my grandparents had. I forgot all about it until the next time I visited. When I arrived, Papa took me immediately to a cupboard and opened the door, behind which were shelves stacked high with boxes of those cookies, far more than I could ever eat. This tendency toward excess led him in other directions as well, like the vodka that went into his orange juice in the morning, and his steady diet of steaks and fully loaded baked potatoes that landed him in the hospital at age seventy-five for six heart bypasses. He lived almost twenty years after that, without ever changing his diet.

His appetites largely drove the choices of restaurants we went to. If it wasn't the Rascal House, then it was certain we would find ourselves at a place that served steak, potatoes, and whiskey. It was equally certain that there would be an early-bird special. At 5 p.m. sharp—he was never late— we would arrive at whatever restaurant he'd picked, usually a once-swank place with worn carpets, paintings of whaling ships on the walls, and a quality of light that might be compared unfavorably to a mausoleum's. None of it dampened my enthusiasm. Papa sat at the head of the table, and I sat next to him. The first thing he would do was order a Manhattan, and he always gave me the cherries—at least three, sometimes more. It was part of our ritual, and I grew to crave their plasticine texture and manufactured cherry taste, like bourbon-flavored cough syrup. I usually ordered the steak and baked potato, like he did. He taught me how to season the potato by slashing across the flesh to score it, mashing it with a fork, and then mixing in butter, salt, and pepper. Only when the potato was properly seasoned would I add the sour cream on top.

For every year as far back as I can remember, we visited my grandparents in Florida. By the time we stepped off the plane, into air the temperature and viscosity of bathwater, Papa was already waiting at the curb. With the air-conditioning cranked and Lawrence Welk playing softly on the radio, he would drive us to their little apartment in a tall building full of other apartments. It had floral wallpaper and pink terrycloth toilet-seat covers. We swam in the pool and the ocean. We played miniature golf, shuffleboard, and long games of Scrabble. We went out to dinner often, and we'd always visit the Rascal House at least once.

In truth, I spent much of my time in Miami bored, my head stuck in a book. I never understood the attraction—the languid energy and constant feeling of retirement pressing in, of too much empty space. As if to drive home the point, Papa would read the obituaries while we sat together at breakfast. I told him once that it seemed morbid to me, and he looked surprised. "How else will I know if one of my friends has died?" he asked.

He did have an astonishing number of friends, and he outlasted almost all of them. He also outlasted his savings. My grandparents lived well—especially later in life—because of my great-grandmother, Sarah Katz. Sarah never learned to read or write English, but she came to understand American business quite well. She started as a janitor when she arrived in the country, while her husband opened a cabinetry shop. She invested their earnings in real estate, and by the 1960s she owned several apartment buildings in downtown Cambridge, the value of which today would support the entire extended family quite nicely.

Of course, those buildings and the fortune she amassed are long gone. Papa's generosity was equaled only by his talent for squandering money. In the decades after Sarah's death, he kept spending. He paid for vacations and summer camp for the kids and grandkids, and sent checks to every family member on every birthday. He flew us down to Miami and bought our meals. He lent money to friends and invested in businesses that quickly failed, including his own. And then, one day, it was gone. My grandparents sold their condo in Florida and moved back to Massachusetts, where the kids wondered what to do with their aging and now destitute parents.

I lost track of them for a while. By the time I graduated high school, my parents had long since divorced, and family trips of any kind had become awkward. After an abortive attempt at college, I moved as far away as I could, to California. I got married and then unmarried. I kept in touch with the family, more or less, but I was already deep in the cooking game and getting deeper, which relieved me (at least in my mind) of the obligation to pay much attention to anything or anyone else. Restaurants, which had started as an escape from the discomfort of the world, became my entire existence.

About ten years ago, I brought my then-girlfriend Alexandra to meet my grandparents. They were still living in their own apartment, each of them a spry ninety-something years old. I took them to a restaurant that I remembered from when I was a kid, a place on the water in Marblehead, which looked largely the same as it had twenty years earlier. Papa sat at the head of the table and ordered a steak and a Manhattan. When the drink arrived, I waited. I was, at age thirty-three, still completely certain of what was going to happen next. When he pulled the cherry out of his drink in midsentence and popped it into his mouth, my jaw must have dropped. "Aaach!" he said when he realized what had happened. "We need more cherries!" He flagged down the nearest server, and when she arrived, Papa didn't just take one. He grabbed a fistful out of the glass on her tray and shoved them at me expectantly, a familiar gesture of absolution mingled with love.

When their health started to fail, my grandparents moved into an assisted-living home. I was in between restaurants that summer, with plenty of time on my hands, so I went to see them one last time. It was perfectly nice, as those places go, with manicured lawns and freshly painted walls. Their minds were still sharp, but they seemed depressed. I helped Papa into his wheelchair; he squirmed, frustrated by his immobility. We sat in the room for a few hours and they told me stories of their childhood and mine until they eventually grew tired. I left feeling sad and helpless.

My grandmother went first, but not by much. I flew out for the funeral. I remember walking into the synagogue for the first time in decades, shaking off the rain that came down the entire time I was there. The family was all present, but I was there to see Papa. I sat near the front and watched him during the service, with his little black hat and an embroidered prayer shawl covering his thinning shoulders. His eyes were still, lifeless. Afterward he held me close when we embraced, but I could tell that he was already gone. He died within a few weeks.

The Rascal House passed a few years later. Death by condominium development was the official cause, but it had been a long time coming. The old delis and the way of life that they represented had been on the wane for many years. The first-generation immigrants from Russia had died off, replaced by American Jews who felt less and less connected to their ancestry. Meanwhile, starting in the fifties, Cuban immigrants escaping their country's communist regime began to reshape the city. As the population turned toward Central and South America, Spanish began to supplant English as Yiddish once had, and the language of restaurants changed as well.

"Their food is unhealthy," many people now say of the old delis. "It's of middling quality." But that misses the point: it was never cuisine as art. It was food to assuage hungers both physical and spiritual, to buffer and embrace a group of people who were trying to find their place in the world. It spoke in earthy timbres of sustenance and survival. As the snowbirds passed on, they were replaced by a new generation, Americans at heart, with little use for the past.

I found out about the Rascal House's closing through a newspaper article. "We waited as long as we could," said the new owners. They dismantled the place, selling the décor as mementos. The restaurant was stripped bare, its pieces carted off and shipped around the country. I imagine platters and saltshakers sitting in cabinets and closets, gradually chipping or gathering dust; the pictures and signs arranged on dressers in spare rooms, propped on mantelpieces or packed carefully in boxes. Perhaps, somewhere, the Rascal still lives, in some basement, behind a pool table covered in boxes of out-of-date magazines, its neon quietly flickering in an empty room.

The Homesick Restaurant

Susan Orlean

In Havana, the restaurant called Centro Vasco is on a street that Fidel Castro likes to drive down on his way home from the office. In Little Havana, in Miami, there is another Centro Vasco, on Southwest Eighth—a street that starts east of the Blue Lagoon and runs straight into the bay. The exterior of Miami's Centro Vasco is a hodgepodge of wind-scoured limestone chunks and flat tablets of PermaStone set in arches and at angles, all topped with a scalloped red shingle roof. Out front are a gigantic round fountain, a fence made from a ship's anchor chain, and a snarl of hibiscus bushes and lacy palm trees. The building has had a few past lives. It was a speakeasy in the 1920s, and for years afterward it was an Austrian restaurant called The Garden. The owners of The Garden were nostalgic Austrians, who, in 1965, finally got so nostalgic that they sold the place to a Cuban refugee named Juan Saizarbitoria and went back to Austria. Saizarbitoria had grown up in the Basque region of Spain, and he had made his way to Cuba in the late 1930s by sneaking onto a boat and stowing away inside a barrel of sardines. When he first arrived in Havana, he pretended to be a world-famous jai-alai player, and then he became a cook at the jai-alai club. In 1940, he opened Centro Vasco, and he made it into one of the most popular restaurants in Havana. Having lost the restaurant to Castro, in 1962, Saizarbitoria moved to Miami and set up Centro Vasco in exile. Along with a couple of funeral homes, it was one of the few big Cuban businesses to come to the United States virtually unchanged.

The first Centro Vasco in America was in a small building on the edge of Miami. After a year or so, Saizarbitoria bought The Garden from the departing Austrians. He didn't have enough money to redecorate, so he just hung a few paintings of his Basque homeland and of the Centro Vasco he'd left behind in Havana; otherwise, the walls remained covered with murals of the Black Forest and rustic Alpine scenes. The restaurant prospered: it became a home away from home for Miami's Cubans in exile. Soon there was money to spend, so a room was added, the parking lot was expanded, awnings were replaced. Inside, the walls were redone in a dappled buttery yellow, and the memories of Austria were lost forever under a thick coat of paint. Until then, there might have been no other place in the world so layered with different people's pinings—no other place where you could have had a Basque dinner in a restaurant from Havana in a Cuban neighborhood of a city in Florida in a dining room decorated with yodeling hikers and little deer.

■   ■   ■

These days, Centro Vasco is an eventful place. During a week I spent there recently, I would sometimes leaf back and forth through the reservation book, which was kept on a desk in the restaurant's foyer. The pages were rumpled, and blobbed with ink. Los Hombres Empresa, luncheon for twelve. Beatriz Baron, bridal shower. The Velgaras, the Torreses, and the Delgados, baby showers. A birthday party for Carmen Bravo and an anniversary party for Mr. and Mrs. Gerardo Capo. A paella party for an association of Cuban dentists. A fund-raiser for Manny Crespo, a candidate for judge. Southern Bell, a luncheon for twenty-eight people; someone had written next to the reservation, in giant letters, and underlined, "NO SANGRIA." The Little Havana Kiwanis Club cooking contest had been held in the Granada Room; the finals for Miss Cuba en Exilio had taken place on the patio. There were dinner reservations for people who wanted a bowl of *caldo gallego*, the white-bean soup they used to eat at Centro Vasco in Havana; lunches for executives of Bacardi rum and for an adventurous group of Pizza Hut executives from Wisconsin; hundreds of reservations for people coming on Friday and Saturday nights to hear the popular Cuban singer Albita; a twice-annual reservation for the Centauros, 1941 alumni of a medical school in Havana; a daily reservation for a group of ladies who used to play canasta together in Cuba and relocated their game to Miami thirty years ago.

Juan Saizarbitoria goes through the book with me. This is not the Juan of the sardine barrel; he died four years ago, at the age of eighty-two. This is one of his sons—Juan Jr., who now owns the restaurant with his brother, Iñaki. The Saizarbitorias are a great-looking family. Juan Jr., who is near sixty, is pewter-haired and big-nosed and pink-cheeked; his forehead is as wide as a billboard, and he holds his eyebrows high, so he always looks a little amazed. Iñaki, fifteen years younger, is rounder and darker, with an arching smile and small, bright eyes. Juan Jr.'s son, Juan III, is now an international fashion model and is nicknamed Sal. He is said to be the spitting image of sardine-barrel Juan, whom everyone called Juanito. Before Sal became a model, he used to work in the restaurant now and then. Old ladies who had had crushes on Juanito in Havana would swoon at the sight of Sal, because he looked so much like Juanito in his youth. Everyone in the family talks a million miles a minute—the blood relatives, the spouses, the kids. Juan Jr.'s wife, Totty, who helps to manage the place, once left a message on my answering machine that sounded a lot like someone running a Mixmaster. She knows everybody, talks to everybody, and seems to have things to say about the things she has to say. Once, she told me she was so tired she could hardly speak, but I didn't believe her. Juanito was not known as a talker; in fact, he spoke only Basque, could barely get along in Spanish, and never knew English at all. In Miami, he occasionally played golf with Jackie Gleason, to whom he had nothing to say. Some people remember Juanito as tough and grave but also surprisingly sentimental. He put a drawing of the Havana Centro Vasco on his Miami restaurant's business card, and he built a twenty-foot-wide scale model of it, furnished with miniature tables and chairs. It hangs over the bar in the Miami restaurant to this day.

■   ■   ■

On a Friday, I come to the restaurant early. The morning is hot and bright, but inside the restaurant it's dark and still. The rooms are a little old-fashioned; there are iron chandeliers and big, high-backed chairs; amber table lamps and white linen; black cables snaking from amplifiers across a small stage. Pictures of the many presidential candidates who have come here trolling for the Cuban vote are clustered on a wall by the door.

Now the heavy door of the restaurant opens, releasing a flat slab of light. Two, three, then a dozen men stroll into the foyer—elegant old lions, with slick gray hair and movie-mogul glasses and shirtsleeves shooting out of navy-blue blazer sleeves. Juan comes over to greet them, and then they saunter into the far room and prop their elbows on the end of the bar that is across from Juanito's model of the old Centro Vasco. These are members of the Vedado Tennis Club, which had been one of five exclusive clubs in Havana. Immediately after the revolution, the government took over the clubs and declared that from now on all Cuban citizens could use them, and just as immediately the club members left the country. Now the Vedado members meet for lunch on the first Friday of every month at Centro Vasco. Meanwhile, back in Havana, the old Vedado clubhouse is out of business—a stately wreck on a palm-shaded street.

The Vedado members order Scotch and Martinis and highballs. The bartender serving them left Cuba just three months ago. They themselves left the Vedado behind in 1959, and they are as embittered as if they'd left it yesterday. A television over the bar is tuned to CNN, and news about the easing of the Cuban embargo makes a blue flash on the screen.

A buoy-shaped man with a droopy face is standing at the other end of the bar. He is Santiago Reyes, who had been a minister in the Batista regime, the bartender tells me.

Santiago Reyes winks as I approach him, then kisses my hand and says, "My sincere pleasure, my dear." He bobs onto a bar stool. Four men quickly surround him, their faces turned and opened, like sunflowers. Santiago Reyes's words pour forth. It's Spanish, which I don't understand, but I hear a familiar word here and there: "embargo," "United States," "Miami," "Castro," "yesterday," "government," "Cuba," "Cuba," "Cuba." Across the room, the Vedado members chat in marbled voices. There are perhaps thirty-five of them now, out of a total of a few hundred, and there will never be more. There has never been anything in my life that I couldn't go back to if I really wanted to. I ask if Little Havana is anything like the real Havana.

One gray head swivels. "Absolutely not at all," he says. "Miami was a shock when we got here. It was like a big farm. Plants. Bushes. It was quite something to see."

I say that I want to go to Havana.

"While you're there, shoot Fidel for me," the man says, smoothing the lapels of his blazer.

I say that I think I would be too busy.

He tips his head back and peers over the top of his glasses, measuring me. Then he says, "Find the time."

The tennis club sits down to *filete de mero Centro Vasco*. The food here is mostly Basque, not Cuban: *porrusalda* (Basque chicken-potato-and-leek soup), and *rabo encendido* (simmered oxtail), and *callos a la vasca* (Basque tripe). Juanito made up the menu in Havana and brought it with him to Miami. It has hardly changed; the main exception is the addition of a vegetarian paella that the cook concocted for Madonna one night when she came here for a late dinner after performing in Miami.

I wander into the other dining room. At one table, Dr. Salvador Lew, of radio station WRHC, is having lunch with a couple who have recently recorded a collection of Latin American children's music. They are talking and eating on the air—as Dr. Lew does with one or more different political or cultural guests every weekday. The live microphone is passed around the table, followed by the garlic bread. From one to two every day, at 1550 AM on the radio dial, you can experience hunger pangs.

Iñaki and Totty sit at a round table near Dr. Lew, having a lunch meeting with two Colombians. The four are discussing a plan to market the restaurant to Colombians, who are moving into the neighborhood in droves. More and more, the Cubans who left Havana after Castro's arrival are now leaving Little Havana, with its pink dollhouses guarded by plaster lions, and its old shoebox-shaped apartment buildings hemmed in by sagging cyclone fences—Little Havana, which is nothing like big Havana. The prosperous Cubans are moving to the pretty streets off Ponce de Leon Boulevard, in Coral Gables, which looks like the elegant Miramar section of Havana; or to Kendall, near the newest, biggest Miami malls; or to breezy golf-course houses on Key Biscayne. Centro Vasco, which had been an amble from their front doors, and a home away from home, is now a fifteen-minute drive on a six-lane freeway—a home away from home away from home.

Totty and Iñaki think a lot about how to keep Centro Vasco going in the present. They have plans to open a Little Havana theme park behind the restaurant: there would be cigar and rum concessions and a huge map of Cuba, made out of Cuban soil, and a mural showing the names of American companies that want to do business in Cuba as soon as the embargo is lifted and Castro leaves. Totty and Iñaki have already added more live music on weekends in order to draw young people who were probably sick of hearing their parents talk about old Havana, and who otherwise might not want to spend time somewhere so sentimental and old-fashioned, so much part of another generation. Now, performers like Albita and Malena Burke, another popular singer, draw them in. And even that has its ironies, because the music that Malena Burke and Albita perform here and have made so popular with young Cuban Americans is *son* and *guajira* and *bolero*—the sentimental, old-fashioned music of the Cuban countryside. Totty and Iñaki have also come up with the idea that Centro Vasco ought to have a special Colombian day. As I sit down at their table, they and the Colombians are talking about something that ends with Iñaki saying, "Barbara Streisand, OK, she has a great, great voice, but she doesn't dance! She just stands there!"

The Colombians nod.

"Anyway," Totty says, "for the special Colombian day we'll have a Colombian menu, we'll decorate, it'll be so wonderful."

One of the Colombians clears his throat. He is as tanned as toast and has the kind of muscles you could bounce coins off. He says to Totty, "The perfect thing would be to do it on Cartagena Independence Day. We'll do a satellite feed of the finals from the Miss Colombia beauty pageant." He lifts his fork and pushes a clam around on his plate. "I think this will be very, very, very important to the community."

"Perfect," Totty says.

"We'll decorate," Iñaki says.

Totty says, "We'll make it so it will be just like home."

■   ■   ■

I told everyone that I wanted to go to Havana. The place had hung over my shoulder ever since I got to Miami. What kind of place was it, that it could persist so long in memory, make people murderous, make them hungry, make them cry?

"If you go, then you should go to the restaurant and look at the murals," Iñaki said. "If they're still there. There's one of a little boy dressed up in a Basque costume. White shirt, black beret, little lace-up shoes. If it's still there. Who knows? Anyway, the little Basque boy was me."

Juan laughed when I said I was going. I asked what it had been like on the day Castro's people took the restaurant away, and he said, "I was working that day, and two guys came in. With briefcases. They said they were running the restaurant now. They wanted the keys to the safe, and then they gave me a receipt for the cash and said they'd call me. They didn't call."

Was he shocked?

"About them taking the restaurant? No, not really. It was like dying. You know it's going to happen to you eventually—you just don't know exactly what day."

One night at dinner, I tried to persuade Juaretsi, Juan's youngest daughter, to go with me, and she said, "It would be a scandal, the daughter of Centro Vasco going to Cuba. Seriously, a scandal. No way." I was eating *zarzuela de mariscos*, a thick seafood stew, with Juaretsi, Totty, and Sara Ruiz, a friend of mine who left Cuba fifteen years ago. Juan came over to our table for a moment, between seating guests. All the tables were full now, and grave-faced, gray-haired, black-vested waiters were crashing through the kitchen doors backward, bearing their big trays. Five guys at the table beside us were eating paella and talking on cellular phones; a father was celebrating his son's having passed the bar exam; a thirtyish man was murmuring to his date. In the next room, the Capos' anniversary party was under way. There was a cake in the foyer depicting the anniversary couple in frosting—a huge sheet cake, as flat as a flounder except for the sugary mounds of the woman's bust and the man's frosting cigar. The guests were the next generation, whose fathers had been at the Bay of Pigs and who had never seen Cuba themselves. The women had fashionable haircuts and were carrying black quilted handbags with bright gold chains. The young men swarmed together in the hall, getting party favors—fat cigars, rolled by a silent man whose hands were mottled and tobacco-stained.

"If you go to Havana, see if the food is any good now," Juan said to me.

"I heard there is only one dish on the menu each night," Totty said.

Sara, my émigré friend, said she used to go to Centro Vasco all the time after Castro took it over. Now she was eating a bowl of *caldo gallego*, which she had hankered for ever since the Saizarbitorias' restaurant was taken away. "In the Havana Centro Vasco, the food isn't good anymore," she said. "It's no good. It's all changed." You have to pay for the food in United States dollars, not Cuban pesos, she said, but you don't have to leave a tip, because doing so is considered counter-revolutionary.

■　■　■

The Basque boy is still there, in Havana. His white shirt is now the color of lemonade, though, because after the revolution the murals on the walls of Centro Vasco were covered with a layer of yellowish varnish to preserve the old paint.

My waiter in Havana remembered Juanito. "He left on a Thursday," the waiter said. "He told me about it on a Wednesday. I was at the restaurant working that day." I was at Centro Vasco, sitting at a huge round table with a Cuban friend of Sara's, eating the *caldo gallego* that made everybody so homesick, but, just as I'd been warned, it wasn't the same. The waiter whispered, "We need a Basque in the kitchen, but we don't have any Basques left," and then he took the soup away. The restaurant looks exactly like Juanito's model—a barnlike Moorish-style building, with an atrium entryway. The government has had it for thirty-five years now and has left it just as Juanito left it, with a fish tank and a waterfall in the foyer, and, inside, throne-like brown chairs, and cool tile floors, and the murals—Basques playing jai-alai and rowing sculls and hoisting boulders and herding sheep—wrapping the room. As I had been told, business is done in dollars. People with dollars in Cuba are either tourists or Cubans who have some business on the black market or abroad. When my new Cuban friend and I came in, a Bruce Willis movie was blaring from the television in the bar. At a table on one side of ours, a lone Nicaraguan businessman with clunky black eyeglasses was poking his spoon into a flan, and at the table on our other side a family of eight were singing and knocking their wine goblets together to celebrate the arrival of one of them from Miami that very day.

I myself had been in Havana for two days. On the first, I went to the old Centro Vasco, where Juanito had started: not the place where he had moved the restaurant when it became prosperous, the one he'd built a model of to hang over the Miami bar, but the original one—a wedge-shaped building on the wide road that runs along Havana's waterfront. The wedge building had been Havana's Basque center—the *centro vasco*—and it had had jai-alai courts and lodgings and a dining room, and Juanito, the pretend world-famous jai-alai player, had started his cooking career by making meals for the Basques who came.

That was years ago now, and the place is not the same. My new friend drove me there, and we parked and walked along the building's long, blank eastern side. It was once an elegant, filigreed building. Now its ivory paint was peeling off in big, plate-sized pieces, exposing one or two or three other colors of paint. Near the door, I saw something on the sidewalk that looked like a soggy paper bag. Close up, I saw that it was a puddle of brown blood and a goat's head, with a white-striped muzzle and tiny, pearly teeth. My friend gasped, and said that it was probably a Santería ritual offering, common in the countryside but hardly ever seen on a city street. We looked at it for a moment. A few cars muttered by. I felt a little woozy. The heat was pressing on my head like a foot on a gas pedal, and the goat was pretty well cooked.

Inside the building, there were burst-open bags of cement mix, two-by-fours, bricks, rubble. An old barber chair. A fat, friendly, shirtless man shoring up a doorway. On the wall beside him were a mural of Castro wearing a big hat and, above that, a scene from the first day of the revolution, showing Castro and his comrades wading ashore from a cabin cruiser. This room had been the old Centro Vasco's kitchen, and its dining room had been upstairs. Now the whole building is a commissary, where food is prepared, and is then sent on to a thousand people working for the government's Construction Ministry.

After a minute, a sub-director in the Ministry stepped through the rubble—a big, bearish man with shaggy hair and an angelic face. He said the workers' lunch today had been fish with tomato sauce, bologna, boiled bananas, and rice and black beans. He wanted us to come upstairs to see where the old Centro Vasco dining room had been, and as we made our way there he told us that it had been divided into a room for his office and a room where the workers' gloves are made and their shoes are repaired. He had eaten there when it was the old Centro Vasco, he added. It had had a great view, and now, standing at his desk, we could see the swooping edge of the Gulf of Mexico, the hulking crenellated Morro Castle, the narrow neck of the Bay of Havana, the wide coastal road, the orange-haired hookers who loll on the low gray breakwater, and then acres and acres of smooth blue water shining like chrome in the afternoon light. The prettiness of the sight made us all quiet, and then the sub-director said he had heard that some Spanish investors were thinking of buying the building and turning it back into a restaurant. "It's a pity the way it is now," he said. "It was a wonderful place."

That night, my friend and I ate dinner at a *paladar*, a kind of private café that Cubans are now permitted to own and operate, provided that it has no more than twelve chairs and four tables and is in their home. This one was in a narrow house in Old Havana, and the kitchen was the kitchen of the house, and the tables and the chairs were set in the middle of the living room. The owner was a stained-glass artist by trade, and he sat on a sofa near our table and chatted while we ate. He said that he loved the restaurant business, and that he and his wife were doing so well that they could hardly wait until the government permitted more chairs, because they were ready to buy them.

■   ■   ■

I went back to Centro Vasco one more time before leaving Cuba—not the old place, in the wedge building, but the new, Moorish one, in a section of Havana called Vedado, which is now a jumble of houses and ugly new hotels but for decades had been a military installation. I wanted to go once more to be sure I'd remember it, because I didn't know if I'd ever be back again. I went with my new friend and her husband, who was sentimental about the restaurant in the Vedado, because during the revolution he had fought just down the street from it. While he was driving us to Centro Vasco, he pointed to where he'd been stationed, saying, "Right—here! Oh, it was wonderful! I was preparing a wonderful catapult mechanism to launch hand grenades." In front of the restaurant someone had parked a milky-white 1957 Ford Fairlane, and some little boys were horsing around near it. On the sidewalk, four men were playing dominoes at a bowlegged table, and the *clack, clack* of the tiles sounded like the tapping of footsteps on the street. The same apologetic waiter was in the dining room, and he brought us plates of *gambas a la plancha* and *pollo frito con mojo criollo* and *tortilla Centro Vasco*. The restaurant was nearly empty. The manager came and stood proudly by our table, and so did the busboys and the other waiters and a heavy woman in a kitchen uniform who had been folding a huge stack of napkins while watching us eat. Toward the end of the meal, someone came in and warned us that our car was going to be lifted and carried away. I thought he meant it was being stolen, but he meant that it was being relocated: Castro would be driving by soon, and, because he was worried about car bombs, he became nervous if he saw cars parked on the street.

As we were leaving, the waiter stopped us at the door. He had a glossy eight-by-ten he wanted to show me—a glamorous-looking photograph of Juan Jr.'s wedding. He said that it was his favorite keepsake. The Saizarbitorias had left nearly everything behind when they left Cuba. Juan was allowed to take only a little bit of money and three changes of clothes. In Miami, Juan's daughter Mirentxu had remarked to me on how strange it was to have so few family mementos and scrapbooks and pictures—it was almost as if the past had never taken place. I admired the wedding picture for a minute. Then the waiter and I talked a little about old Juanito. I couldn't tell whether the waiter knew that Juanito had died, so I didn't say anything. Meanwhile, he told me that a friend of his had once sent him a napkin from Centro Vasco in Miami, and he had saved it. He said, "I've had so many feelings over these years, but I never imagined that Juanito would never come back."

There had been one other Centro Vasco, but it wasn't possible for me to visit it. It had been the first Centro Vasco that Juanito opened in the United States, on the corner of Ponce de Leon and Douglas Road, in a building that straddled the border between Miami and Coral Gables—a place that might have been satisfactory except that the two cities had different liquor laws. If you wanted a drink, you had to be sure to get a table on the Miami side. The border had come to be too much trouble, so Juanito moved to Southwest Eighth Street, and eventually the old building was torn down.

But I did go back to the Centro Vasco on Southwest Eighth one more time after I came back from Cuba. It was a Saturday night, and it was busy: people were coming for dinner and to hear Malena Burke sing. I wanted to tell the Saizarbitorias about my trip, to tell them that the Basque boy was still there and that the food wasn't very good, but that the restaurant was just as they had left it and, in spite of the thirty-three years that had passed, was still in fine shape. Then I realized that I didn't know whether they would be glad or sorry about what I would tell them. In Havana, everyone I met talked constantly about the future, about what might happen when the United States lifted its embargo or when Castro retired, both of which they expected soon. To the people I met in Cuba, the present seemed provisional and the past nearly forgotten, and their yearning was keen—charged with anticipation. In Miami, the present moment is satisfying, and thought is given to the future, but the past seems like the richest place—frequently visited, and as familiar and real and comforting as an old family home.

The music wasn't to start until after midnight, so for a long time I stood in the foyer and watched people parade in: the executive of a Latin American television network, in a tight white suit and high white shoes; an editor from a Spanish soap-opera magazine; a Puerto Rican singer who had just performed at Dade County Auditorium, followed by her entourage; another singer, named Franco, who called out to someone while he and I were talking, "Hey, man, you look great! I thought you were dead!"; and dozens of good-looking couples speaking in bubbly Spanish, and all wearing something that glistened or sparkled or had a satiny shine. Toward midnight, Sherman Hemsley, of *The Jeffersons*, came in with a television producer, and Iñaki wrote "Cherman Jemsli del Show Los Jeffersons" on a little slip of paper for Malena, so that when she pointed him out in the audience she'd know what to say.

Malena came onstage at one in the morning. She began with a ballad that had been made famous in Cuba in the fifties by a singer called La Lupe, who used to get so emotional when she reached the crescendo that she hurled things at the audience—usually her shoes and her wig. The room had been roaring before Malena came out, but now it was hushed. Malena had left Cuba just a few months earlier. Someone told me that the tears she sheds when she's singing about lost love are really real. By then, I was sitting at a table in the back of the room with Totty. I had some snapshots with me that I had taken in Havana for the family, because I'd thought they might like to see the old home again. Just as I was about to slide the pictures across the table to Totty, the singer sobbed to her crescendo, so I decided to wait until another day.

Stuffed, Smothered, Z'herbes

Sara Roahen

"A foreign critic once described America as a country which had one sauce and twenty different religions. Evidently he did not reach New Orleans in his travels, or else he would have discovered that its gravies are even more varied than its theology, and that good cooking is one of its religions."
  Dorothy Dix, Famous Drinks and Foods from the Carnival City (New Orleans)

Like born-agains of any denomination—Christian, Buddhist, Weight Watchers—New Orleans converts tend to exhibit a more innocent, rose-colored zeal for their church than the flocks who've yawned through the motions all their lives. This is how quixotic, goateed hipsters wind up sitting knee to knee with strawberry-nosed lifers in the city's grittiest barrooms, like the Ninth Ward's Saturn Bar and Uptown's Brothers Three Lounge, regarding them as palaces of culture. It's what moved Massachusetts-reared Emeril Lagasse to turn cayenne pepper into a sound effect. And it's how I wound up taking fourteen pounds of mirliton, eight pounds of eggplant, and two refrigerators' worth of greens into my kitchen over the course of a single month.

Years into my conversion, I'm still getting a handle on the New Orleanian relationship to vegetables. A casually studious approach—observing in restaurants, perusing recipes, cooking the occasional okra gumbo—wasn't conclusive; I still fumble over questions like, *Is stuffed eggplant a main course or a side dish?* The topic arose just recently during a dinner-planning session with my college friend and food ally Sarah Todd Olivier, a lucky Miami girl who married into a local family of white Creoles. Momentarily stumped,

Sarah asked what I planned to stuff the eggplant with. My recipe called for shrimp and ham. "Well, then, I believe it's a side dish," Sarah decided. She made a beef daube to round out the meal.

Where shrimp and ham are thrown into vegetable preparations as afterthoughts, even a northern transplant familiar with obscurities like cushaw (a crookneck squash grown to obscene lengths and shapes) is bound to lose her way in the produce department. I first learned to eat from a midwestern plate upon which eggplant, shrimp, and ham never, ever touched. It was the 1970s. Vegetables were little punishments, prepared to look and taste like themselves and served in amounts guaranteed to make children strong. The dinner table was like boot camp or a surgical residency: the big guns never let us off easy; we suffered as they had suffered. It may have built character, but it created not a single degree of warmth for boiled Brussels sprouts, steamed spaghetti squash, or TV-dinner peas.

In time I grew into a big gun with midwestern hangups and, on regressive days, scorn for the lack of fresh produce in the New Orleans diet. I was backed by a loud chorus of fellow transplants who, like me, had made peace with vegetables as adults in places like San Francisco, New York City, and even Madison, Wisconsin, places where farmers' markets and seasonal-produce-driven menus overflow with heirloom tomatoes, forest mushrooms, chioggia beets, organic spring mixes—vegetables we find infinitely superior to the ones we ate as kids, possibly only because we weren't forced to eat them as kids.

Down in New Orleans' supermarkets we again face the enemy, in terrifying amounts: bell peppers, green beans, cabbage, celery, iceberg lettuce—vegetables so short on star power we're surprised they're still in production. We also meet new vegetables like okra, mirliton, and stiff greens, but because we don't understand them or know how to turn them into salads, they don't make it onto our grocery lists. On the late autumn day in 2002 when Whole Foods Market opened in Uptown's old Arabella Bus Barn, selling California pea shoots and organic avocados, those of us newcomers who shared a superior vegetable worldview began to see a lot more of each other. (The "whole foods" concept had been in New Orleans since the 1970s but in a hippie-dippier way; the bus barn's stunning transformation, impressive dimensions, and central location marked the city's introduction to the orgasmic potential of modern organics.)

Clarification: the vehemence of my New Orleans conversion hasn't kept me from falling off the wagon in the vegetable aisle and groping for, say, radicchio; in moments of weakness I still believe that it's New Orleans, not me, that needs to broaden its horizons. It's a never-ending conflict. New Orleans usually wins. Case in point: the last time I asked a waiter at Galatoire's for à la carte advice, he recommended the broccoli hollandaise, a creation that went out of style with the smoking jacket in most of civilization. Yet, fashions aside, when was the last time broccoli tasted better? Honestly? Up north, broccoli was allowed palatability just once a year, on Christmas Eve, when cheesy chicken-broccoli casserole kept Stephanie and me from hunger-striking against our aunt's other holiday tradition, oyster stew.

New Orleanians show their vegetables more consistent love. The ultimate in vegetal affection is called smothering down here, as in smothered string beans. Merriam-Webster's fourth definition of "to smother" gives the basic idea: "to cook in a covered pan or pot with little liquid over low heat." But while the definition more or less describes the technical process by which you might smother something—a seven steak, turnips, crawfish tails (crawfish étouffée is French for "smothered crawfish")—it doesn't account for the amour tasted in dishes like the smothered rabbit and caramelized onion gravy at New Orleans Food and Spirits, the smothered okra and shrimp at Dunbar's Creole Cooking, or the cabbage smothered in ham broth in any self-respecting southern kitchen. Nor does it account for the coffee can of bacon fat beside the stove of master smotherers. The technique is as emotive as it is practical: to smother a vegetable is to play upon its most lovable attributes, like smothering a sweetheart in kisses.

One of the city's most overall succulent dishes is the smothered mustard greens at Ms. Hyster's Bar-B-Que, which, having been violated with pork and cooked to Olympian flexibility, manage to overshadow the barbecue ribs even while looking like pond dredgings. One afternoon while I was interviewing Virginia Johnson, Ms. Hyster's owner, for a story about barbecue, the restaurant's front door swung open to admit the swooshing sound of a city bus barreling down South Claiborne Avenue and two customers, their dusty work clothes draped over strong frames. Miss Virginia half rose to greet them with the bad news: "No greens today. The truck should be here in about an hour. Come back tomorrow, all right?"

"Aw," one of the men teased, pushing his partner back out into the hot afternoon. "He's been crying all day for them, too."

Soon a farmer from rural Lutcher, Louisiana, arrived with a truckload of freshly harvested mustards, naturally crumpled, warm and windblown from the ride downriver. Miss Virginia had already explained that it takes her staff two full days to pull, clean, and cook the once-a-week delivery; it nevertheless awed me to see that her wet, murky, pork-infused specialty really does originate as raw greenery.

Ms. Hyster's greens were a turning point. There wasn't a vegetable I wouldn't eat, and I'd come to fetishize some, but I'd never so closely witnessed the culinary emancipation that allows southern cooks to take a leaf so rich with nutrients it glows and manipulate it in a way that prompts red-blooded men to choose it over smoked pork. Before seeing the workers' disappointment, hearing about Miss Virginia's long preparation method, and watching that truck pull in from Lutcher, the latent wound-tight northerner in me had been unconsciously interpreting this region's typical vegetable treatments—smothering and stuffing, for example—as manifestations of aversion. Why would you work so hard to disguise something you liked? On this day I finally understood smothering's most outstanding characteristic: it's an endearment. It's about tenderness, after all.

Gumbo z'herbes (a contraction in Creole dialect of *gumbo aux herbes*), or green gumbo, is the ultimate in green vegetable manipulation. Recipes call for between five and fifteen different greens—anything from scallions to chard, carrot tops to cabbage, arugula to peppergrass (a spicy weed that urban Creoles are said to pick from neutral grounds, New Orleans–speak for boulevard medians). . . . The only ways in which gumbo z'herbes resembles more common meat and seafood gumbos are that it's eaten with a spoon, often crammed with sausage, and thickened with a roux—and the latter only sometimes. In preparation, gumbo z'herbes is a multiplicity of smothered greens united in a communal pot likker. Its flavor and its origins are more mysterious: no two bites, or theories, are the same.

My seventeenth-edition copy of Caroline Merrick Jones's *Gourmet's Guide to New Orleans*, first published in 1933, suggests that gumbo z'herbes originated in Africa and was modified by our country's Native Americans, who had a "rudimentary knowledge of medicinal or 'pot' herbs." Jessica Harris, the scholar and cookbook author, thinks it could be a cousin of *sauce feuille*, African leaf sauce. Others compare it, along with other gumbos, to the Afro-Caribbean dish callaloo. In his encyclopedia of Cajun and Creole cuisine, the chef John Folse provides a convincing argument that the German Catholics who began settling in Louisiana around 1720 and took to farming immediately inspired Louisiana's gumbo z'herbes recipe with a traditional seven-herb soup they ate on Holy Thursday.

In New Orleans today, green gumbo is an established Lenten dish, sometimes prepared without meat. A Holy Thursday gumbo z'herbes is an event at Dooky Chase Restaurant (which was out of commission due to flooding in 2006 but received guests for gumbo on Holy Thursday 2007), attended by many who could explain the Eucharist no better than driving in a blizzard. The octogenarian Creole queen Leah Chase has feasted on gumbo z'herbes once a year since her childhood in Madisonville, on the north shore of Lake Pontchartrain, when anyone older than seven ate nothing before noon on Good Friday and very little after. In preparation for the fast, they bulked up on the rich gumbo the day before.

In keeping with local vegetable treatments and a rather New Orleanian interpretation of Catholic rule, Mrs. Chase makes her version with roughly as many meats as greens, including hot sausage, smoked sausage, andouille, beef stew meat, chicken, and ham two ways. While she passes the greens and seasoning vegetables through a meat grinder to produce a smooth, deep-green soup, she keeps her meats in bite-sized chunks. "Creoles don't like to see their seasonings, but they have to see their meat," Mrs. Chase told me once.

Mrs. Chase believes that green gumbo ought to remain Lent-specific. "Leave things be special," she said to me. Although in 2006 she granted John Folse special dispensation to make and market a frozen version of her gumbo labeled with her name and image, I would argue that as she isn't standing over the pots herself, she continues to leave things be special.

Disobeying, I made my first gumbo z'herbes at home during my vegetable-obsessed month, just prior to Lent and during the Mardi Gras parade season, which also happens to be high season for greens and cheap beer (the only other item that would fit into the refrigerator). Like Mrs. Chase's, mine was mulchy, bitter, strangely sweet, zinging with cayenne pepper, meatier than an NFL locker room, and inordinately refreshing. Some bites were breathy with anise, for no logical reason, and others held all the sensations of an Easter dinner, any Easter dinner.

I had followed a recipe from Mrs. Chase's cookbook and was pleased, but the depth and the complexity of flavors in mine didn't touch the one that she made in my kitchen two weeks later for eighteen judges of the James Beard Foundation Awards, who were meeting in New Orleans and needed lunch (we used my kitchen because the FEMA trailer where she was living with her husband, Edgar "Dooky" Chase, across from their flooded restaurant couldn't accommodate another body, much less a backyard garden's worth of produce). Her chief arsenal, even more than the greens and the sausage, turned out to be ham. Directly upon entering my kitchen, she filled a pot with two ham shanks and water and set it over a flame to simmer into stock.

Gumbo z'herbes is not a precision project; it doesn't matter if the bunch of turnip greens you buy in Salt Lake City is half or double the size of mine. Every batch is unique, dynamic in its own way. Mrs. Chase didn't glance at the weights of the meats she bought when we shopped together, she pushing the cart, I standing aside as a parade of other customers rushed to kiss a smooth cheek, touch a caramel hand, and ask when her restaurant would reopen. She didn't measure the flour or fat for her roux. She didn't even count her greens. Most every gumbo z'herbes recipe (including the one in Mrs. Chase's biography) commands that for luck's sake you must use an odd number of greens; according to the adage, the cook will acquire one new friend for each variety. I was such a faithful dilettante that when I accidentally burned all the beet greens to the charred tone of a campfire for my solo batch at Mardi Gras, I ran to the grocery store at 11 p.m. to buy more rather than using only ten varieties. Later, when I busted Mrs. Chase acting blasé in the produce section and settling for an even number, she rolled her eyes and put on her low, bossy voice: "Go ahead, throw a bunch of collards in the cart."

Mrs. Chase was busy on the day of the James Beard luncheon, so I served the gumbo in her stead at a downtown hotel where the judges, who had flown in from all across the country, were meeting. Cursing was the most common reaction, as in the writer-editor Pete Wells's "This is the best gosh-darn thing I've ever put in my mouth!" (That's my whitewashed version of Pete's reaction. I don't have a policy against swearing in print, but I'd have a lifetime of Hail Marys to pay if I took the Lord's name in vain in a section about Leah Chase.) When I reported to her that the gumbo had reduced the judges to expletives, Mrs. Chase responded, "Well, you don't need to curse at gumbo."

She wasn't up for a Beard Award that year, but it's always nice to wow a group accustomed to the best. Most gratifying, though, was the army-ant-like procession of New Orleanians—bellhops, managers, cooks, waiters—who hauled up to the twenty-third floor once word got out that I was giving away Mrs. Chase's leftovers. I walked into the kitchen to overhear a mainte-nance worker in a blue jumpsuit on the phone with his wife: "Baby, this is the best gumbo I ever had . . . and it's green."

What I Cook Is Who I Am

Edward Lee

My grandmother cooked every day. Her entire life. In our tiny windowless Brooklyn kitchen with just a few pots, mismatching lids, a plastic colander or two, and a fake Ginsu knife, she re-created all the Korean dishes she had learned before she immigrated to America. My grandmother never questioned her identity, culinary or otherwise. She was a Korean widow yearning for a homeland that had been destroyed before her eyes. Her daily rituals of cooking and Bible reading were her last links to an agrarian Korea that no longer existed, a place that had risen from its ashes into a megametropolis, a place that did not need her. Her food was indelibly linked to that identity. But this is true for most of us, isn't it? Can you separate a Bolognese sauce from the Italian arm that stirs the simmering pot?

Funny thing about my grandmother, though—she refused to make "American food." We always had peanut butter and jelly in the cupboard, but if I wanted a PB&J sandwich, I had to make it myself. I'm not sure whether she was offended by it or if she was quietly, in her own grandmotherly way, guiding me to forge a culinary identity of my own, reflective of the life I would lead as a Korean-American kid. Or I could be reading way too much into it. But it's true that my identity (crisis) would soon enough manifest itself in my language (foulmouthed), my clothes (ripped jeans), my hair (long and messy), and of course, my food, which started with the PB&J but then wove itself all the way to Kentucky.

The great thing about Americans is not the identity we're born with but our reinvention of it. We start with one family and then, magically, we are allowed to reinvent ourselves into whoever we want to be. As a kid, I'd go to my friend Marcus's house for a meal of Puerto Rican plantains over rice with ketchup and honey. The apartment was loud, the radio always on (we didn't even own one), with people talking over each other. And for that night, I was a Puerto Rican son of a festive family where every meal was a party. Our downstairs neighbors were Jewish, and sometimes they'd watch me when my parents were both working nights. Their food smelled like a hospital, and so did their furniture and their antiseptic gray tabby. But they conveyed love through everything they did. They sat with me and warned me about life, talking to me about being honest and keeping out of trouble. They insisted I read books and learn to play the piano. They were paternal and stern and warm all at the same time. It isn't their overcooked string beans I remember most, but their words of nourishment. I felt as though if anything ever happened to my parents, they would have taken me in without a second thought. And in an odd way, they kind of did.

GRAFFITI WAS MY FIRST CUISINE

All the truants in my junior high were into graffiti, but most of us just scribbled in notebooks. None of us had dared to tag a wall yet. But there was this one mysterious kid, forever in the eighth grade, who was rumored to be a wall artist. He had a shadowy past and facial hair like someone ten years older than us. He smoked, he cursed, he cut school, and it was rumored that he lived alone. Eric (let's call him that) was the coolest kid in a school full of derelicts. We became friends.

There are a million reasons kids deface public property: rebellion, for notoriety, as a cry for attention, boredom. I wanted/needed an identity to call my own, and what was cooler at the time than dark hoodies, backpacks full of Krylons, late-night bombs of hopping fences and scaling exteriors? Mostly I was Eric's lookout, his apprentice. He taught me technique—to use skinny caps for the outline and fat caps to fill in, and to spray without dripping— and he taught me to find my own style, to write without getting caught. I became someone else overnight, with every stroke of the cold nozzle tracking the city walls. I was a lawbreaker; I was a legend in my own mind. I was anything but that bored Korean kid, good at math, terrible at basketball.

The irony of graffiti is that the permanence of spray paint and china markers lasts only until the next guy decides to write over you. Your tag may survive a week or a night, or sometimes just a few hours, but inevitably, it is reduced to a memory under the fresh layer of someone else's paint. And most street artists would agree that's the way it should be. Graffiti's never supposed to last. How many remember the art on the L train or a mural on 145th Street? The hardest things to hold on to in life are the ones that want to disappear.

So here I am, twenty years later, far from my Brooklyn childhood, at John Shields's restaurant in Chilhowie, Virginia, with my sous-chef, silent and ruminative, having the meal of a lifetime and wanting it to last more than the few paltry hours I have. Pictures and tweets don't do it justice. This night, too, will become a memory, soon to be painted over by another meal.

I SEEK IMPERMANENCE

I moved to Louisville in 2003. I had to reinvent my identity, both culinary and personal, through the lens of tobacco and bourbon and sorghum and horse racing and country ham. The first time I tried buttermilk, I threw it out because I thought it was sour. It was a revelation to learn that you use it because *it is* sour. And that it tastes nothing like butter. Over time, Louisville, and by extension, the American South, embraced me as an adopted son. I was not surprised by that. It was effortless. What I didn't expect was how I would come full circle and rediscover myself as a child of Korean immigrants. That all the lovely and resourceful traditions of the Southern landscape would propel me back to the kitchen of my grandmother's spicy, garlicky foods: soft grits remind me of congee; jerky of cuttlefish; chowchow of kimchi. My Korean forefathers' love of pickling is rivaled only by Southerners' love of pickling. Barbecue, with its intricate techniques of marinades and rubs, is the backbone of both cuisines. Buttermilk has become my miso, ubiquitous and endearing. It shows up in everything from dressings to marinades to desserts, but never in the foreground, always as a platform to let other ingredients shine. I found my culinary voice here in Louisville. I found a culture so different and yet not very different at all from the one in which I was raised. I learned to be comfortable in my own skin and to cook the food that flows naturally from my fingers. At the same time, I continue to be astonished by the flavors that surround me. There's an endless history to uncover, and with each lesson I learn, I find myself becoming not only the chef I want to be but also the person I've always wanted to grow into.

One day I was given a curious recipe by a guy here in Louisville who makes jerky for a living. It's really less a recipe than a proclamation: take stale cornbread, a shot of sorghum, and a glass of buttermilk, puree it in a blender, and drink it out of a mug. He called it, simply, breakfast. This is the kind of shit that reminds me of my grandmother's attitude and her pride in a tradition that lived in her bones. She never had to explain herself. She was comfortable in her ways. Just like I found comfort in graffiti.

What attracted me to graffiti way back then is the same thing that draws me to the unapologetic land of Kentucky. It's the act of distilling beauty from the imperfections that exist around us. Since we don't have an ocean nearby, we make do with catfish. Since our summers are muggy and hot, we use the climate to age our barrels of bourbon. When our gardens are overrun with wild mint, we happily sit down for an afternoon julep. This is what I mean when I say graffiti was my first lesson in how to approach cuisine as an art. The graffiti movement happened because many small factors (subways, spray cans, hip-hop, etc.) all converged in a city that combusted to create a subculture that mesmerized a generation.

Most art movements are a product of chance. Graffiti just happened to be everywhere I went as a kid. When I think about food now, I can't help but approach it in the same way those great underground artists did to leave their marks. Instead of succumbing to the causality of time and place, they wrestled an improbable elegance out of all that twisted steel and concrete. I look around now and I see brash mixologists celebrating bourbon; I see country ham producers who are historians; I see chefs and farmers and glassblowers and carpenters and artists all converging to create something both distinct and memorable and, like graffiti, fleeting.

That a Brooklyn kid of Korean lineage can find his place in Louisville is a testament to the city, the time we live in, and cultural forces that are beyond our breadth of knowledge as we live through this moment. Something is happening in Louisville right now. Something is simmering wildly throughout the American South. Every time I look around, I see bold new expressions of Southern cuisine waving a proud flag. And this expression of food has captured people's attention, because it is the story not only of Southern cuisine, but also of America's identity. In my short time as a professional chef, I have seen the spotlight pass over every cuisine, from French to Italian to Japanese to Spanish, from nouvelle to comfort to molecular. However, what is happening now in the American South is not part of a trend: it is a culinary movement that is looking inward, not outward, for its inspiration. Every innovation that moves it forward also pulls along with it a memory of something in the past. As Faulkner famously said: "The past is not dead. It's not even past."

What's happening in Southern cuisine is less about technique than about attitude. Take my friend's breakfast, for example. It is tasty but ugly, gluttonous yet frugal, overindulgent but simple. Most of all, though, it is linear. It is history and narrative, full of all the irony and contradictions that make up any good yarn. Some call it tradition—but that's too benign a word.

I ADD A HANDFUL OF SMOKE AND PICKLES

Everyone has a story and a recipe. We cherish them because they are our reinventions. Our recipes convey who we were, are, and want to be. And this is reflected in the food of the best cooks across America, in homes, restaurants, and backyards and at country fairs and tailgates. We are redefining the landscape of how we grow, harvest, name, and eat our very own sustenance. There is a rich diversity in our cuisine—this thing that, for lack of a better term, we call American Cuisine—that is redefined by our never-ending search for reinvention.

My story is one of smoke and pickles. Some say umami is the fifth flavor, in addition to salty, sweet, sour, and bitter. I say smoke is the sixth. From the sizzling Korean grills of my childhood to the barbecue culture that permeates the South, I have always lived in an environment where food was wrapped in a comforting blanket of smokiness. My friends found it odd at first that I, a die-hard New Yorker, would move to the South. But for me, it was instinctual. Smoke is the intersection that connects my two worlds. It is found in many incarnations other than the obvious outdoor grill full of charcoal or hardwood. I can add smokiness to any dish by adding bourbon—which picks up toasted notes from the inside of charred oak barrels—or bacon and smoked country hams, or molasses and sorghum, smoked spices, dark beers, tobacco, or meats blackened in a cast-iron skillet. And where there is smoke, there is always a pickle nearby. It's a miraculous thing, the pickle. It's nothing more than a ratio of salt, sugar, sometimes vinegar, and time. But with those few ingredients, you can create an endless array of preserved vegetables and fruits that are the backbone of so many cuisines. In the South, pickles and barbecue go hand in hand because nothing cuts the intensity of smokiness like a sharp pickle. Together they are harmonious, the perfect yin and yang. If I had my way, every dish would start with smoke and pickles—everything else is just a garnish.

Like the Korean-Brooklyn kid in me tugging on a Southern apron, I find connections where others might see contradictions. So these are my stories. Full of holes and inaccuracies, but connected through the recipes. Not like the ones you'll find in the lace-and-antebellum traditional Southern cookbooks. My recipes are filled with smoky flavors and pickles, but they also reflect the people who raise my animals, shoot wild game with me, boil sorghum, pray and sing, and make moonshine. These folks eat and drink like there's no tomorrow. And my recipes grow out of this fecundity. They belong here, in this unique place and time, nowhere else but now.

God Has Assholes for Children

Eddie Huang

We got to Florida late at night, groggy and stinkin' from the ride. We pulled into the parking lot of this place called Homewood Suites; I liked it 'cause their logo was a duck. We usually stayed at Red Roof Inns, so I was pretty impressed with this place they called an extended-stay hotel. Emery and I walked around touching everything in the room, but my parents were tired so they made us shower and go to sleep.

We all woke up super-late the next day. It felt like we slept a year! Dad was already at work. The best part about Homewood Suites was that you could look outside and see the sign for [Dad's restaurant,] Atlantic Bay Seafood and Grill. It was a monstrous neon sign you could see from the highway and follow all the way from the exit.

"Mom! Why does Dad do American food and not what you make at home?"

"Because nobody want to pay for REAL Chinese food."

"Why not?"

"Because they not Chinese! Stupid question! Your dad is smart, he has white chef so people don't know Chinese own Atlantic Bay and we can sell seafood for more!"

"Is Atlantic Bay like Chesapeake Bay?"

"Hmm, kind of!"

"Yeah? Do they have hush puppies?" I asked.

Before she could answer, Emery chimed in, too. "We can eat all we want since we own it, right? We don't have to have more aunts for more free kids meals anymore!"

"Yeaaahhh! I want fried cod and hush puppies with Tabasco!"

"OK, OK, you guys can eat all you want. Let's go see Dad."

"We don't need aunts anymore! We OWN the restaurant!"

Emery and I were dumb excited to see Atlantic Bay. It was huge! Three times bigger than our old house and they had cool uniforms: polo shirts with big blue and white stripes. But my dad wore a suit! We found him in the kitchen and it smelled so bad. It was the first time I'd been in a restaurant kitchen. The food smelled great, but there was this funky old mildewy smell that I'd never smelled before.

"Dad, why's it smell so bad? Isn't it supposed to smell good in a kitchen?"

"This is a restaurant! It smells like a . . . factory or industrial place because we have strong cleaning chemicals."

"It smells like a dirty dishwasher!"

"Well, the dishwasher is always going so you'll smell that, but this is just how restaurants are."

"Mom said it's like Chesapeake Bay. Do you have hush puppies?"

"No, but we have homemade biscuits! You'll like them."

Dad pulled a hot biscuit off a speed rack and handed it to me steaming hot. It had a good hard crust. It wasn't a super-flaky biscuit, but I broke it open and it was really moist on the inside. I took a bite and remember how distinct the flavor was. It had a sweetness that most biscuits didn't have. I wasn't going to forget about hush puppies any time soon, but it wasn't bad. I found Emery hanging out by the fish tank at the front of the restaurant.

"Hey! We don't have hush puppies."

"Really?"

"Yeah, but we got biscuits!"

"Biscuits? Are they good?"

"Yeah, not bad. Kinda sweet, but good."

"OK, I guess that's cool."

"We don't own a Chesapeake Bay, but I think we have a Red Lobster . . . 'cause they have biscuits, too."

■　■　■

Every day, I got sent to school with Chinese lunch. Some days it was tomato and eggs over fried rice, others it was braised beef and carrots with Chinese broccoli, but every day it smelled like shit. I'd open up the Igloo lunch box and a stale moist air would waft up with weak traces of soy sauce, peanut oil, and scallions. I didn't care about the smell, since it was all I knew, but no one wanted to sit with the stinky kid. Even if they didn't sit with me, they'd stand across the room pointing at me with their noses pinched, eyes pulled back, telling chingchong jokes. It was embarrassing so I asked Mom to start packing me some white people food.

"What do white people bring to lunch?"

"Like sandwiches, chips, and juice boxes. Everyone likes Capri Sun, Mom!"

"Ohhh, the foil drink? That's expensive!"

"Mom, it's worth it! Everyone says it's really good."

"What's wrong with your soy milk? You always like soy milk."

"It's different at school, people laugh at you! My stomach hurts when I eat 'cause I get mad."

It was true, my stomach would cramp into angry knots when those kids clowned me. It got extra-shitty when show-and-tell came around. My parents didn't want to spend money on show-and-tell, so Mom's idea was to bring something exotic for lunch and kill two birds with one stone. That day, I walked to the front of the room knowing I was about to give the wackest presentation any third-grader had ever seen. I opened my lunch box and took out a plastic container of seaweed salad.

"For show-and-tell today, I brought seaweed salad."

"Eeeewww! What's seaweed!"

"It's like spinach but from the bottom of the ocean."

"Gross! I would never eat that."

"If it's on the bottom that means sharks poop on it!"

"Sharks don't poop on seaweed! It's really good for you and tasty."

"No, it's not, you eat shark poop!"

The teacher jumped in to stop the other kids, but I had no comebacks. I just went back to my chair and ate my seaweed salad. My mom saw that the relentless food shaming was getting to me and gave in. I loved my mom. We didn't have much back then, but she always did everything she could to get us what we wanted. I remember being at Chinese school hearing all the kids complain that their parents wouldn't buy them toys, new clothes, or McDonald's. Some kids really wanted to be white. I joined in and told jokes about my parents, but I knew they tried hard and that was enough for me. OK, I'd admit that it seemed a lot nicer to be white, but I liked my parents! I was OK without Ninja Turtles and McRibs; I just didn't want any more stinky Chinese lunch. That night, instead of going to Dong-a Trading or Hong Kong Supermarket for groceries, she took me to Gooding's and Publix. We walked the polished, halogen-lighted, air-conditioned aisles looking for lunch stuff. She really cared that I ate well and didn't want to just pack me sandwiches and sugary drinks.

"I like this penguin, Mom!"

"Ha, ha, you always like penguins or pandas."

"Yeah, they have cool colors and waddle around. They're friendly."

"OK, let's see, what's in this meal? Chicken nuggets, peas, mashed potatoes. What's this called?"

"Kid Cuisine!"

After the nutritional information panel met with her approval, Mom loaded up the cart with Kid Cuisines and Juicy Juices.

The next day at school I couldn't wait to break for lunch. There was a microwave oven in our classroom and every day a few kids would take their lunches and get in line. I proudly pulled out my Kid Cuisine, still cold in my hand, penguins grinning, and got in line. I was third in line so I wouldn't have to wait too long.

There was one black kid in our class, Edgar. He had the same trouble I did: he was a loner without many friends. But he was Christian, so at least he had that going for him. I was still the buffer between him and the bottom. He lined up behind me.

The two people in front of us were taking too long. Why were they taking so long? What are they doing up there? I stood waiting as our lunch period ticked away; I felt Edgar's mouth-breathing ass creeping behind me. By the time I finally got up to the microwave, there were only fifteen or twenty minutes left for lunch. I was getting ready to pop open the oven door when Edgar grabbed me by my shirt and threw me to the ground.

"Chinks get to the back!"

I looked up from the ground, dumbfounded.

My dad had told me about the word, and what it meant, but you're never ready for your first time. It just fucking happens. I waited for Ms. Truex to get involved but she just sat on her fat ass eating lunch like David Stern watching Malice at the Palace.

Finally, something went off in me. I was nine years old, and I called 'nuff. I jumped up from the floor and went right at Edgar. The boy was bird-chested. I grabbed his arm and threw it in the microwave. With my other hand I grabbed the door and slammed it on his arm as hard as I could. I wanted to kill him. I don't know if I broke his arm, but he slumped to the floor crying. I stood over him like Ali and wouldn't back off. I went to kick him and that's when Ms. Truex finally got involved. She shouted over to another one of the students, the kid named Cole.

"Cole! Help!"

"Yes, Ms. Truex!"

"Cole, you take Eddie to the principal's office. Take Chris with you to be safe! I'll take Edgar to the nurse."

"He hit me first and called me a chink!"

"Eddie, you are in enough trouble! You go straight to the office with Cole and Chris."

"Eddie, just go to the office, man . . ."

I walked down the hallway with Cole and Chris flanking me; I was shaking the whole time. I didn't know why. I wasn't scared of the principal or Edgar, but something was wrong. I was shaking like crazy and couldn't even keep my hand still. We got to the principal and I started crying. Cole told him what happened and I couldn't defend myself because I was crying. The principal took away my lunch, locked me in a walk-in closet, and wouldn't even let me out to go to the bathroom. When my mom came to pick me up, they pried open the closet door to find a kid drenched in piss. Mom bugged the fuck out.

"You stupid ass! How you do this to my son! He was hit first!"

"Mrs. Huang, your son was out of control today and severely injured another student."

"He called him a chink! You think that's OK? Words hurt, too. I hear you people say that words hurt like sticks! Look at him!"

My mom would always get sayings wrong, but they knew what she meant. I was never happier to see her. Every day I went to this bullshit school alone and no one ever had my back besides my mom. But despite her best efforts, I was never the same. She always talks about how I was a happy kid, deep-thinking, liked to read books, and didn't bother with drama. Even when other kids in the neighborhood got caught up, I'd just shoot hoops, ride my bike, or listen to music. I tried to fit in and get along, but people weren't havin' it. Edgar forced me into my William Wallace moment. From that day forward, I promised that I would be the trouble in my life. I wouldn't wait for people to pick on me or back me into a corner. Whether it was race, height, weight, or my personality that people didn't like, it was now their fucking problem. If anyone said anything to me, I'd go back at them harder, and if that didn't work, too bad for them: I'd catch them outside after school.

You Have to Fall in Love with Your Pot

As told to Sara Wood by Ida MaMusu

I grew up in Monrovia, Liberia, in West Africa, under the guidance of my grandmother. She was a chef and an entrepreneur herself, and I learned everything that I know today from her. I came to the United States in 1980 by way of a civil war in Liberia. I moved to Richmond, Virginia, in 1986, and I've been here since.

Liberia was founded in the 1800s by freed slaves. Virginia is one of the closest states in the United States when it comes to Liberia, because the first president of Liberia was born in Petersburg, Virginia, and the founder of Liberia, Lott Cary, was also born in Charles City, Virginia. So the ties with Virginia and Liberia are very close.

My grandmother took me under her wing when I was between eight and nine years old and started training me [to cook]. She made me love it, and she made me care about it, and she made food a part of me and as an art. She used to have these terms: "You have to get to know your pot." "You have to fall in love with your pot." And so because I was like her, I would be in the kitchen just dancing. *"You gets to know your pot."* I'd be teasing her—you know kids.

My grandmother said the art of cooking is smelling. It's the key. You have to be able to identify all of these different spices by their smell. And then from there you can go to what it tastes like. But if you can identify peppermint or identify oregano or parsley in the food, you can always separate those smells when the food sits in front of you. You can say, "Mm, this has too much oregano in it," because it's stronger than all of the other spices in there. And that's one of the things I learned with my grandmother.

The war broke in 1980 in my country, and I was fortunate to get out. I was working at a hotel in New York City, and I had a friend who lived in Richmond. I came to visit her one weekend and just loved it. And one of the reasons why I decided to stay in Richmond is it reminded me of Liberia a lot. There are a lot of places in Richmond that look just like Liberia. For example, we have Broad Street in Monrovia; we have Broad Street here. Liberia is kind of built like the South, and the people were very friendly, just like at home. It just felt so real for me.

In 1996 I opened my first business, which was hair braiding. But my ultimate goal was not to braid hair. I was just doing it to survive. It was the fastest way to make some money. So I just did it. But my ultimate goal was cooking. I knew that at some point it was going to evolve into that, but I just didn't know how.

I started cooking food out of my house for just my customers. They would come to get their hair braided and they would be sitting with me for six, seven hours, and I would offer them something to eat. And they would be like, "Oh what is this?" And I would explain it to them. "This is spinach and rice and this and that." So I found myself cooking at home for my customers and their families. And then it just started growing. I was doing twenty-five, thirty dinners, because my customers started telling people, "She cooked this stuff. I don't know what it was, but it was so nice."

In 1998, the health department contacted me and said, "OK, if you want to do this, you need to get a license." I went and bought a few pots, a few little things I needed. I got all my customers to help me do hand-printed flyers, and they started passing them on in their jobs. And all of the sudden, Chef MaMusu West African Cuisine took off. It was the first West African restaurant in the entire state of Virginia.

It was foreign to the customers. So everybody was excited about this new African restaurant, but I had a challenge. I couldn't really cook traditional African dishes, because I first had to educate them. So I decided to find a middle ground. I said, "OK, I'm going to take Southern dishes and use African spices."

I pray as I cook, and I sing. I just enjoy this. This is really who I am. I believe that if I had to die today, I would come back the same way. There isn't anything else I want to be. I can't even envision myself doing anything else, because I love this art so much.

Around the World in Eight Shops

Kathleen Purvis

All it took was a small sign on a strip mall on Polk Street in Pineville: "Elsa's American, Asian, and International Food Mart."

When historian Tom Hanchett spotted it, he scurried to what he calls "my good friend, Google." Within a couple of minutes, Hanchett had learned a new word—*sari-sari*, a Philippine variety store. And he had new evidence of his favorite subject, the changing life of the modern South: he found eight shops representing seven nationalities of food along a mile of Polk Street near Interstate 485's Exit 65.

Filipino, Japanese, Colombian, Indian, Polish, Peruvian, and German.

From Elsa's to the Waldhorn Restaurant, they're all doing business along a busy highway named for the eleventh president, James K. Polk, whose log cabin birthplace sits in a nearby field.

"There's an area like this in every American city," Hanchett says. "It's just more visible in the South because we didn't have a Greektown or a Polish-town or a Chinatown."

People with titles like "museum curator" and "historian" aren't supposed to have as much fun as Hanchett does. They're supposed to page through dusty books or use $10 words like *hierarchical* and *dichotomy*.

They're not supposed to paw through the soft drinks and crow that the pickled squid is "the beer nuts of Japanese food."

That's Hanchett. Ever since he came to Charlotte to curate the Levine Museum of the New South in 1999, he's been using international food to tell us our story. Hanchett, fifty-seven, and his wife, East Charlotte activist Carol Sawyer, delve into so many little restaurants and food stores that he now writes a short column for the *Observer*, telling the stories of people who make everything from Bosnian sausages to Taiwanese steamed buns.

Two years ago, when Southern writer John T. Edge went to Indianapolis to write a story for the *New York Times* on changing American suburbs, Hanchett went along to munch arepas and spot meaning.

Edge credits historian Carl N. Degler of Stanford University with inventing the metaphor of the salad bowl to replace the melting pot. In a salad bowl, Degler wrote in the 1960s, each population group contributes ideas and texture to the cultural mix, but they don't disappear into the whole.

Hanchett takes that a little further with his idea of the salad bowl suburbs, where "newcomer and native-born intermingle without ethnic boundaries."

■ ■ ■

On a recent Friday morning, we climbed into Hanchett's white Prius to see what he learns when he wanders through those stores and restaurants in Pineville.

"I'm not a sophisticated eater," Hanchett says. "I find the things that are most familiar. And I like junk food. So I buy junk food and try it until I know it.

"Once that isn't strange anymore, I find something else."

Wandering through Hatoya, the Japanese market, he stops first near the cash register, by a bag of snacks.

"One of the coolest things is impulse buys," he says.

Store manager Qinj Xu is from China, not Japan. But he explained that there are Japanese people working at a number of factories around Charlotte, such as Yamoto and Mitsubishi.

Then he gave us coffee candies as we left. That's how it usually goes: Hanchett breaks the ice by handing out Levine Museum brochures, and people end up giving him things to eat.

"I'm shy," Hanchett admitted in the car. "I've learned that at cash registers, people are willing to talk."

■ ■ ■

Elsa's, the Philippine sari-sari that started our trip, was closed that day. But Hanchett pointed out something in the window: a sign with the slogan "Door to door service to the Philippines."

Many of these small stores double as packing services for sending things back to people's native countries.

"These are community centers, and that's a big business in the community," he said.

At El Cafetal, a small Colombian business, we expected coffee. But it turned out to be a store that sells products that include packaged coffee, along with a packing service and a small room where you can get your taxes done or your computer repaired.

Hanchett zeroed in on a rack of business cards by the door.

"Colombian Restaurant 101," he announced, flipping through the cards for food businesses scattered all over the region: Los Paisas, Las Americas, El Paisa. If you want to learn what a community is doing, he says, look for the business cards people leave by the door.

■   ■   ■

At India Grocers, a small market with an intense aroma of spices and laundry soap, Hanchett stopped to chat with Nayna Patel, who owns the store with her husband. Pritesh Patel was at their second store, in the University City area.

Stopping to pick up a copy of *Saathee*, the magazine for the Indian community in North Carolina, Hanchett points out a card for a caterer who makes "Gujarti or Punjabi, Mexican, Chinese and Non. Veg. Foods."

A customer walking by stopped to listen. Ishani Shah of Ballantyne does a little catering herself, she says. Soon, she and Hanchett were strolling through the aisles, talking about products like Kurkure, the Indian version of Cheetos, and swapping tips on German bread and the apple strudel at the Waldhorn.

"Nice people," Hanchett declared as we jumped back in the car.

■   ■   ■

"Polish, Colombian, and a naughty lingerie shop!" The next stop is one of Hanchett's favorites, a tiny cluster of shops that includes a Polish meat market and a Colombian bakery and café.

At Delicias Colombianas, we buy an arepa de choclo—a warm corn fritter topped with a square of soft, white cheese—and a couple of small pastries filled with thick milk caramel.

Hanchett didn't know what the pastry was, but he knew the important thing: "If it's Colombian, it will be filled with caramel."

Next door, Zygma is mostly a Polish meat market, but it also has German and Russian products. Kate Baszynski was running the store for the owner, her cousin Marta Zelazko.

"Huge amount of clients," she says. "Russian, German, Czech. Even Chinese and Vietnamese."

Hanchett pauses by long shelves of pickles. "You can tell what is important to a cuisine by how much shelf space it gets."

■   ■   ■

We finally sat for lunch at Machu Picchu, a Peruvian restaurant in the Pineville Town Centre.

Owner Julian Herrara decorated one long wall with the things he wants you to know about his country: on one side, there are nets and fish decorations to commemorate ceviche, the fresh seafood "cooked" with lime juice. On the other, there's a mural of the temple ruins at Machu Picchu. In between, there's a widescreen TV showing soccer.

"Everything important is on one wall," Herrara says.

While we filled two tables with a spread of dishes—an herb and chicken soup with a whole cooked egg, fried and fresh ceviches, yucca bread, rotisserie chicken, and sweet plantains—Hanchett considered what brings so many nationalities to a suburb like Pineville.

"It's a high traffic area and you can get good deals on real estate," he says. "Newcomers who are chasing the American dream get overrepresented in these areas where there is high traffic and affordable rents."

Herrara comes over to talk about how happy he is to see American customers—he wants Americans to know Peruvian food as well as we know Mexican.

Hanchett listens, nodding.

"This is a very American restaurant," he says when Herrara steps away. "You come here to taste the American dream."

That's Your Country

As told to Sara Wood by Argentina Ortega

My name is Argentina Ortega. I am sixty-two years old, and I started this bakery in August 2005. My sons are my partners.

I was born in a little town in El Salvador called Sensuntepeque, Cabañas. I was there until I was thirteen, and then I moved to the city to study in a Catholic school, and I used to live in the school. And then I went to the university to study business administration. I quit the university because there were too many problems with the guerrillas, and I moved to California in 1970.

I tell my sons that at that time, coming here was like going to the moon. When you were leaving, your friends make a party to give you their best wishes. Now, that's nothing. It's just normal coming to the United States. But at that moment, not everybody could come.

I moved to Richmond in 2002. I separated from my husband. He wanted to go back to El Salvador. And it wasn't just that; things between us were not good anymore. I came here because at that moment, my three sons were living here. First came Eduardo, and then came Mario, and the last one to come was Jorge.

Here in the bakery, most of the items are Hispanic. This is the bread that we grew up with, and the way we display it here—not bagged—is because that's our culture.

Most of the recipes I have are from El Salvador. I had baking classes there, and I took a lot of recipes. In the bakery, we have customers from South America, Central America, Puerto Rico, and the Middle East and Africa. We get customers from everywhere.

Customers come, and they see a bread similar to what they want. And so my sons or I will say, "What is it like?" And they start to explain how the bread is. And we try to catch the idea and make it. We have several items that I didn't know about in the beginning, but the customer has helped us with it.

The quesadilla is one of the best sellers in my country. Have you heard of pupusas? Well, the quesadilla is equal to the pupusa. In El Salvador, people love the quesadilla. And the concha is one of our best sellers. People from Central America, Mexico, and many American people like it.

At the beginning, we used to sell bagels, because we know that's your everyday bread. We said, "We have bagels." And the American customers said, "No, no, no. I want to see something different."

The customers love the alfajor. It's a cookie filled with caramel. I say caramel, but it's dulce de leche. Your caramel is made with brown sugar, I guess, and our dulce de leche is made with milk and sugar. It tastes a little bit different. And that special cookie, the alfajor, is in South America and in Central America.

When I started the bakery, I thought it was just Salvadorian. But people from Argentina said, "Yes, we like this cookie, but it's with coconut around the edges." Or, "Yes, we have this cookie in our country, but it's with chocolate in half of the cookie." So we started to make different kinds of alfajores, depending on how people like it.

The pastelitos de piña is a good seller with customers from my country and from Mexico, too. And we started to sell the pastry puffs like the Colombians, with guava and cheese. Then came people from Puerto Rico, and they said, "We have a bread like this that is called casita. It's filled with a sweetened creamed cheese," and we started to do it.

We sell a good French bread, and a few months ago, I started to make a tiny French bread. In El Salvador, we have our breakfast with tiny French bread. I love it. And people always try it and they say, "Oh, it's just like in El Salvador, because we have that kind of bread every morning."

Here in the States, if you work and you are honest, you have a better life. A lot better than in our country. So we think, why not share that with our family? Where you have your home, your dress, and your food; that's your country. If you cannot get it in your country, you have to look someplace else. The Hispanic people who come here, that's what they are looking for: a place to live and work in peace.

All of my life, I wanted to have my own home. I hate to say this, but my first husband always told me, "This is my home." He never included me. I felt estranged. Here, I have my home. I live in a modest neighborhood, but it's my home.

I just want to have money to pay my expenses to have an honest life and be happy and have my family. I was never thinking of having success as a businesswoman. I just wanted to survive and have an independent life.

That's what I wanted to have because in El Salvador, it's just the men—the men, the men, the men. You have to do what they say. If you get married to somebody selfish, they don't care about your dreams. They don't care about what you want, or if you feel good or if you don't feel good—they just care about whether they feel good. And here, you get that.

I said, "I don't need a man."

Friends and Families

Nikki Metzgar

As big as Texas, as big as the world. That's Houston. Especially now, since its character—and foodscape—is being shaped more and more by a growing influx of Asian immigrants. And that's why Chris Shepherd has insinuated himself into the lives and work of a handful of Asian restaurateurs and chefs. To learn. To grow. Just like Houston.

Seated in the stockroom of the London Sizzler, Mama is shelling runner beans piled in her apron. A mug of milk tea cools by her side as she laments to her attending family that if only someone in the kitchen could read her mind, then maybe she could retire. Chris Shepherd, chef/owner of Underbelly, one of Houston's critically acclaimed marquee restaurants, offers to find her a guy who will sell the beans preshelled. While Mama is actually related to several of those who work alongside her, Shepherd simply calls the matriarch, Surekha Patel, "Mama" out of affection.

Mama, her husband, Naresh, and her son Ajay (the great mind behind the sizzling brownie platter, but more on that later) make up Shepherd's adoptive Indian family. A warm and demonstrative Oklahoma transplant, Shepherd grew close to several restaurant families while immersing himself in the immigrant food cultures that define Houston, which he now pays tribute to through his own food.

Of the Patels, Shepherd says they're the people who would take him in if he were ever in trouble, "and that's family." In the meantime, they talk about food.

The London Sizzler is modeled after a British curry house, with all its attendant cultural influences and culinary evolutions. Seated at the bar on Diwali weekend, the Hindu festival of lights, with soccer playing on televisions overhead, Ajay explains how the restaurant's special mogo is made. Mogo, or cassava, a dietary staple in much of Africa, is stir-fried with garlic, cumin, and green chilies before being doused with Manchurian sauce, crushed chilies, and cilantro. Starchy like potatoes, they're about as addictive as French fries but with way better sauce. Mogo is their signature dish, although Shepherd would make an argument for the sizzling platter of skinless Jeera chicken wings, marinated in garlic and cooked in a tandoor. They're the best wings in the city, of that Shepherd is sure. The Patels still cook with an old-fashioned charcoal tandoor in an age in which many restaurants have switched to gas.

Elsewhere in the kitchen, a cook hand-pours the batter for jalebis, the bright yellow Indian equivalent of funnel cake, and another presses the crunchy snack sticks known as tikha gathiya into sizzling oil. Shepherd is prodding dough with his fingers, trying to divine its composition and asking questions about unfamiliar foods. Most chefs stage at high-end restaurants; he's learning in the immigrant family-run spots in Houston's far-flung strip malls.

Back at the table, more and more food arrives, including fish, potato, and lamb samosas; goat biryani studded with bone marrow; and masala bhindi, stir-fried okra coated in spices. It would be impossible for anyone to eat it all, but breaking bread with family is ideally characterized by generosity, and so the plates keep coming until the dazzling final moment: the presentation of a sizzling cast-iron comal laid with three Little Debbie–brand fudge brownies crowned with three scoops of vanilla ice cream and bubbling Hershey's chocolate syrup. Puffs of caramel-scented smoke envelop the plate. "Stupid, huh?" proclaims Shepherd, digging in. "It's so stupid, it's genius."

Ajay has been to Underbelly a handful of times. His mother hasn't visited at all, because it's a bit of a drive and out of her comfort zone. There are about eleven miles between the London Sizzler in Houston's Little India neighborhood and the Lower Westheimer strip, where Underbelly and several of the city's nationally recognized dining establishments dwell. Because the city is so geographically fragmented, it's easy for residents of either neighborhood—chefs included—to go a lifetime without exposure to the other, and that's the exact thing that Shepherd wants to eliminate from his platform as a chef.

Between the ingredients used and the influences drawn upon, no dish served at Underbelly could have been conceived in any other city. The audaciously sized cuts of meat Shepherd has become known for throughout the years capture the cowboy swagger that's general to Texas, but the Wagyu beef itself is specifically raised outside of Houston in Wallis and fed spent beer grain from the local Saint Arnold Brewing Company during their final three months before slaughter. On a recent night in the restaurant, Gulf Coast bycatch—formerly undesirable vermilion snapper, triggerfish, and parrotfish, among others—was dusted with flour before a turn in the fryer and plated on a bed of masala-spiced vegetables. The kitchen also uses bycatch to make fish sauce in-house, which is then employed on caramelized pole beans and the slaw that comes with the fried oysters and kimchi butter.

Shepherd takes the sesame seeds provided to him by the Utility Research Garden in Austin to another of his Houston "families" at the Korean store Kong Ju to toast and press into oil. A farmer introduced Shepherd to a special kind of settler's pepper, and heirloom breed whole pigs are delivered to Underbelly from Revival Meats before parts of them are left to hang in the restaurant's temperature-controlled curing room or served in a take on bibimbap. In Shepherd's hands, Southern media such as chicken and dumplings are married with Korean red chili paste, with goat replacing the fowl.

Mention Houston to outsiders, and all the long-held assumptions about Texas come to mind: horse riding, guns, barbecue, Tex-Mex, and Big Oil. And while it's true that rifles and ribs do maintain their hold on the public's imagination, that image hasn't kept up with the city's changing demographics—a condition Shepherd is trying to expose both to the outside world and to Houston itself.

The Asian population in Houston (including suburbs to the north and south) increased eightfold between the 1980 and 2010 censuses, more than any other group. (Meanwhile, Hispanics make up 35.3 percent of the population, non-Hispanic whites 39.7 percent, and non-Hispanic blacks 17.3 percent.) The five largest populations within the Asian subset are Asian Indian, Chinese, Filipino, Pakistani, and Vietnamese, with the latter comprising the largest Asian group in Houston at 110,000 strong, according to the 2010 census. If one element of Asian food culture has successfully entered the mainstream, it's arguably Vietnamese bánh mì, sold out of food trucks and storefronts for around $3 in disparate neighborhoods across town.

"The only reason anybody comes to the United States is for economic opportunity," Dr. Dudley Poston, a sociologist at Texas A&M University, told the Houston Chronicle. In that regard, the economic enticements for anyone to move to the city are numerous: Texas has a significantly lower unemployment rate than much of the country, housing costs in Houston are 21 percent lower than the national average, and the lack of zoning laws means you can start a business practically anywhere. Once here, the already established ethnic communities provide immigrants with reminders of home and an immediate network of people with similar backgrounds.

Although Houston's Asian population has built distinct and self-sustaining communities, it isn't true that the city is actually more segregated than the national average. The distinction is that in New York City, for example, even though various ethnic groups generally live among themselves, the shorter distances between groups and different modes of transportation (such as walking or taking the bus or subway over the constant freeway driving in Houston) make exposure between ethnic and racial groups more likely.

Usually busy working in his restaurant along Hillcroft, Ajay Patel himself had never heard of phở until a few months ago, and he credits Shepherd for exposing him to new types of food. "He's the one who actually got me to start eating steaks medium-rare. And foie gras, which I didn't even know," Ajay says. "And pork belly, which I probably never would have eaten. Now I like it a lot."

You can't really get away with eating with Shepherd without learning a few things while you're at it. The menu at Underbelly begins with a few paragraphs of introduction titled "Houston is the new American Creole city of the South." There, Shepherd explains his intentions. "Creole cuisine is simply the merging of diverse cultures with local ingredients. . . . It's not just about remarkable food—it's a story taking shape right before us that will continue to define this restaurant and those that call this city home."

If the chef can come across as a little didactic, well, he might not really care. "You should learn everything about your own city," says Shepherd. "You can't represent your own city if you don't understand it."

But in this case, representing the community also means uniting one.

Not all the people Shepherd now calls "family" were so accepting of him initially. At Asia Market, a grocery store with a sliver of space cut out for a Thai restaurant, the handful of women running the four burners and single fryer in the back regarded the chef's request to learn from them with suspicion. So, he started at the bottom, peeling papayas and bagging fruits and vegetables for days and bringing in breakfast for the cooks until they came to accept him. Now, when Shepherd enters the store, servers practically leap up to hug him, greeting him with, "Hey, boss!" When he picks up a bag of gray ant eggs out of curiosity, owner Narumol Allen says, "When you're ready, we can cook it for you."

None of the items on the actual menu are as inaccessible as that, although the preserved duck egg dish Shepherd favors is an acquired taste—even for himself. Part of the reason he feels so strongly about Houston's food scene is that he didn't always have access to this vast array of cooking and culture. Like many people who grew up unfamiliar with Asian food, he started with the basics. His first stop was at a late-night Vietnamese restaurant known for taking high volumes of drunken customers after last call. "Is Mai's Restaurant fantastic? No. But you find your starting point," Shepherd acknowledges.

From this "starter Vietnamese," he then moved on to try more challenging cuisines, places where the drives took longer, the communication issues more explicit. On an early trip to Vieng Thai, he tried to order a raw sausage dish when a waiter told him not to. Most recently, Shepherd ate Korean-style raw octopus that was still writhing on the plate.

That journey, the one from chicken pho to uncooked seafood, is one he recommends for everyone, although it doesn't necessarily have to end with getting a tentacle suctioned to the roof of your mouth. When you receive your check at Underbelly, with it comes a list of all its local influences: Atkinson Farms, where Shepherd gets his eggs; Frixos Zhrifinish, the supplier of most of his fish; and a number of the restaurants he wants everyone in Houston to visit, even if you're worried about feeling as if you don't belong. "It's all about saying, 'Hi,'" says Shepherd. Or, you could employ the Shepherd strategy for gaining allies, which is to order enough food for fifty people and prove the strength of your appetite. It worked for him at Asia Market.

"He's so bubbly, we'd joke and laugh, and that's where we are today," says Narumol's husband, Lawrence, usually found behind the cash register. He, like Ajay, has gotten the opportunity to try Shepherd's food at Underbelly. "I was floored at what had been accomplished. He takes a little bit of this and a little bit of that—it's dynamic. That's the benefit that he offers the public at his restaurant."

The spoils that come with striking out across town and trying new restaurants are obvious—the food. It's the crispy fried pork with sticky rice, or the sakoo sai moo, chewy tapioca balls filled with seasoned pork, at Asia Market. It's discovering that there are more than just savory types of naan and indulging in London Sizzler's chili chicken stir-fry because it tastes like an Indo–General Tso's chicken, even if Ajay is shaking his head at you when you order it. It's experiencing the cozy vanilla smell coming off a freshly broken custard bun at HK Dim Sum, the restaurant owned by Shepherd's Cantonese "family," headed up by yet another matriarch, Lisa Yang. The conversation about where to eat the best dim sum in Houston is on ever-shifting ground, as one location falls out of favor and another, newer place, one you haven't heard of, opens its doors. Unlike the massive dining room of Ocean Palace, where servers push the traditional carts loaded with steamed and fried tea accompaniments, at HK, customers check their choices off a menu, and piping hot plates are rushed out of the kitchen as soon as they're ready. What the setup loses in entertainment value, it makes up for in food temperature.

Each checklist comes with a thick picture book of the food items, which is useful for when the prodigious use of the words *pork* and *bun* makes it difficult to discern between all the options. For lunch, Shepherd orders all his favorites: shumai, the daikon cake known as lo bak gou, the crispy taro puff, and spare ribs. The language barrier between Shepherd and Yang is more pronounced than with other friends he's made around town, and so the relationship is slightly more reserved. In the kitchen, the talking is minimal, as the chef observes all the work going down. Because this is Houston, Texas, U.S.A., the cooks are using a tortilla press to flatten the translucent wrappers used for har gow before hand-stuffing each one with shrimp. Incorporating the centuries-old techniques of other cultures isn't just in Shepherd's wheelhouse.

The truth about the authentic Houstonian experience is that it often means spending the majority of a lifetime in one neighborhood, be it Chinatown, downtown, or one of the many suburbs, without ever eating the truffled pizza, lo mein, or goat curry of another. And yet, Shepherd doesn't see that division as part of his beloved city's true identity. It contains a vast and varied demographic landscape and all the amazing food that comes with that, which simply must be taken advantage of. That's Houston, and that's his food. There's no magic or mystery to dining someplace unfamiliar. Although Shepherd's close relationship with these restaurateurs and his use of the designation *family* might seem unusual at first, it all really boils down to him being friendly. Between "The story of Houston" and "Houston is the new American Creole city," the man already has enough catchphrases. But, if one were to sum up his best strategy for enjoying all the food the city—or any city—has to offer, it would go something like this: Be friendly. Look everywhere.

The Perfect Chef

Todd Kliman

Before I got in my car and drove to three different states to find him, before I began tracking his whereabouts on the Internet and running down leads that had been passed to me by people I had never met, before I had to admit that I had become a little crazed in my pursuit and that this was about more than just him, but about me, too—before all that, Peter Chang was simply somebody whose cooking I enjoyed.

I was just starting out as a food critic, and had learned through a tipster that a talented chef had taken over the kitchen of a restaurant in Fairfax called China Star, in the suburbs of northern Virginia, forty minutes from Washington, D.C. In the world of serious food lovers, in an age of rapid information sharing, the real excitement over a new place happens far in advance of the published review in the paper or magazine and at a subterranean level, below the awareness of ordinary folks, those people possessed only of a mere casual interest in food and restaurants. Someone gets a tip and passes on the news, and a following quickly builds—a kind of culinary equivalent of insider trading.

Despite my newness to the job, or perhaps because of it, I had made myself an inviolable rule about tipsters, and that was to take every one of their recommendations seriously. Often, this resulted in driving an hour and a half for dispiriting Thai or desiccated barbecue, and I would feel toyed with and mocked; driving home, I would curse my rule and vow never again, only to get back in the car and hunt down the next lead that came my way, because the truth was that I could be disappointed nine out of ten times, but the tenth time, the success, would fill me with such a sense of triumph that it was as if those earlier disappointments had never occurred. As a critic, I was inevitably thought to be gorging myself on the good life, on endless quantities of champagne and caviar and foie gras, each meal richer and more luxurious than the last, but after a while, and to my great dismay—because I had made another vow, which was to not become jaded by an excess of pleasure—these meals blended into indistinction. No matter how exquisite something might be, a diet made up exclusively of exquisite dishes inevitably becomes normal, and normal is boring. The unrequited love is always more interesting than the requited love, and, as it had been with me and dating, so it was with me and restaurant meals. I lived for the chase.

In this case, my tipster was possessed of more than just the usual slate of dish recommendations. He had a backstory to pass on. This chef had won two major cooking competitions in China, a significant achievement by any reckoning, but especially in a culture that is disinclined to valorize the individual. He had cooked for the Chinese premier, Hu Jintao, had written culinary manuals, and had come to the United States to cook at the embassy in Washington, which is where he had been working just prior to joining the restaurant in Fairfax. It all sounded promising.

Not long after, I showed up with a friend one afternoon at China Star, expecting some outward announcement of the great man's arrival, some manifestation of his specialness, only to find the usual list of beef and broccoli and orange chicken. But there was another menu, the Chinese menu, and on it was a parade of dishes I had never seen. Diced rabbit in hot oil. Sliced tendon of beef with cilantro. I didn't know where to start, so I started everywhere.

I sat with a friend at a corner table, our mouths afire from the incendiary heat of the Szechuan chilies, alterations that compelled me to keep eating long after I was no longer hungry—a desperate longing for that runner's high, that intoxication. At the same time, I was filled with a paradoxical sense that I had ordered too much and yet, somehow, not enough. I could have gone to China Star every day for a week and still not have eaten enough to know what Chef Chang's cuisine was or wasn't.

I returned not long after that initial encounter, ordered still more dishes, and felt, again, defeated. This time I was convinced there was a right way to order and a wrong way to order, and that I had ordered the wrong way. What was the right way? I wasn't exactly sure. But whatever it was, I felt certain that it was conveyed in clues offered up by the menu. The key was to decipher them, and I had not done that. Lacking any real guidance from the waiter (except to warn me that a dish was spicy, which in my eagerness to prove my bona fides—which was, really, to demonstrate that I was not the timid, fearful, judging Westerner that I might have presented, and had an active interest in duck blood and internal organs and other such delicacies—I conveniently ignored), it was easy to wind up with a table full of nothing but hot dishes, which was like reading only the dirty parts torn from a novel and concluding that the author has a one-track mind. I hastily devised a plan for my next visit: I would order both hot and cold (temperature) dishes, I would order both spicy and nonspicy dishes, I would seek, above all, balance—the balance that was, surely, there in the menu but that I had, foolishly, missed. I would enlist a group of friends to come along, reinforcements for a campaign that had become more complicated than I had counted on, their presence at the table less about communality and sharing than about subterfuge—masking my intent and allowing me to cover as much culinary ground as possible. I would do it right.

· · ·

I would do it right, and in fact, I did do it right, though I did not do it at China Star. I returned to the restaurant with my five-member crew, only to learn that Chang had moved on and was cooking at a place in Alexandria, fifteen minutes closer to Washington. The restaurant was called TemptAsian Café—in intention and appearance no different from tens of thousands of Americanized Chinese restaurants across the land. When I stopped in with my wife one night, two people were waiting for carryout orders, and hearing the manager call out the contents of the stapled bags for a man in running shorts—chicken and green beans, orange beef, General Tso's chicken—I thought I might have been mistaken in thinking this was Chef Chang's place. I whispered my doubts to my wife. A cheerless and brusque waitress materialized, directed us to a table, and handed us a couple of Americanized Chinese menus. Now I was certain this could not have been where the estimable Chef Chang had landed.

"Do you have a Chinese menu?" I asked.

She gave me a scrutinizing once-over, her brow knitting. It was as if I had mispronounced the password, proving myself an interloper, undeserving of being handed the Chinese menu. For a long moment, she regarded my face, not simply for evidence of my seriousness but rather, it seemed, for evidence of my worth.

Stupidly, I smiled. Or rather, *reflexively* I smiled, because I had not wanted to smile. Even as I was smiling, I had not thought I was smiling, but I am an American, and that is what we Americans do in any situation where we are being denied what we think we indisputably deserve access to. We smile. Even when we do not know the native language. Even when we commit egregious acts of cultural ignorance. The smile, we think, is our badge, our passport—the smile will erase everything else we have done or, as the case may be, not done; the smile will put us over; the smile will deliver us to the vital center.

I smiled, and the waitress turned and left. My wife and I raised an eyebrow at each other across the table, wondering what exactly had just happened. "Well, I guess it's just gonna be beef and broccoli then, huh?" she said.

And then, just as abruptly as she had left, the waitress returned and grudgingly handed over the Chinese menus, which, in contrast to the bound and printed regular menu, had been cobbled together hastily via the aid of a computer. This was more like it. Here were many of the dishes I had eaten at China Star, plus a good number more that I hadn't seen before, like a dish of fish with sour mustard greens that was preceded by a red asterisk, the universal warning that the preparation listed is going to be hot.

I pointed to the number on the menu, trying to order.

The waitress frowned. She directed me to something tamer, without an asterisk. I persisted, and she touted more aggressively the merits of the dish she had suggested. I knew from experience that we had begun that verbal joust that sometimes takes place in ethnic restaurants that don't know and don't court Westerners, and that each eager parry was going to be met by a forceful thrust. In some restaurants, the trick was to make multiple visits within a short span of time, demonstrating your sincerity by virtue of familiarity; then, and only then, was the staff likely to relent and allow you access to the real stuff, the good stuff, the stuff you'd truly come for. But I didn't want to wait. In my mind, I had already bypassed this tedious and time-consuming process by having eaten twice at China Star.

When I asked for the grilled fish with cold rice gluten, her eyes bulged for a split second before she shook her head no.

No, you don't have it in? I wanted to scream. *Or no, you're not going to serve it to me, regardless?*

What the hell did I have to do to earn the restaurant's trust to be able to taste Chef Chang's food again?

Whether my inner torment was visible on my face, and she had taken pity on me, or whether I had demonstrated a willingness to try any number of dishes that would have put a scare into most Westerners, or both, or neither, I don't know, but she relented and decided to bring out the fish with sour mustard greens.

It was wonderful, sour and spicy in a way that dishes featuring fish almost never are, but even if it had been merely ordinary, I would have made sure that we devoured all of it, in this way making the very unsubtle, I hoped, point that we were deserving of being shown the full extent of the chef's repertoire of dishes.

What followed was extraordinary: Chinese cooking like I had never tasted, better than anything Chef Chang had prepared at China Star—or maybe it was that I had learned how to order from him, in much the way that you need to read two or three books by Faulkner just to begin to grasp even a little of what he is up to.

There was a plate of cold beef that the chef had intended for us to fold into a fried wrapper of dough, a little sandwich. A seemingly simple thing, except that the thin-sliced beef, tender and almost gelatinous, had been scented with the famous *ma la* peppercorn. The *ma la* peppercorn is not strictly about heat; for that, for pure heat, Chef Chang had also used the red Szechuan chili peppers. *Ma la* numbs the lips as you eat, a sensation that can only be likened to the novocaine you get in the dentist's chair, though without the dawning sense of dread that invariably follows an injection. Why would this be desirable? Why would a chef want to numb a diner's lips? Because the numbing is also a cooling, and that cooling works in opposition to the scorching heat of the other pepper, producing an odd yin and yang, just as the sweet, doughy, chewy wrapper was set off in contrast to the slippery, savory beef.

Out came a rattan basket of fried fish the color of a blazing summer sunset. Wait, was this the roasted fish with green onion we'd ordered? The name was a misnomer, it turned out. And the description on the menu had not fully prepared us for the taste of this fish. Wait, was that cumin? Cumin, in a Chinese restaurant? On fish? It was odd. It was haunting. I couldn't stop eating it.

After a while, I knew that I was eating it not because I was hungry, but because I was eager to learn it, to burn the precise, sensory details of the taste into my memory, the way you do with anything that's good that you've never before tried, any experience, any phenomenon. With a book, you read and re-read sentences; with a dish, you eat and eat and eat, long after you're full. Being overstuffed, for the food lover, is not a moral problem. It's a practical problem.

We had not yet finished the fish when the pancakes arrived. I had had pancakes at Chinese restaurants before, delicate crepes into which you stuffed slices of crisp-skinned duck, or greasy discs of dough that had been flecked with bits of diced scallion. But never anything this dramatic. Never these big, poofy balloons that drew the eye of everybody in the dining room, and which gave up a little plume of steam when they were pricked with a chopstick.

It was a law of reviewing that if you made three visits, almost without fail, one of those meals would turn out to be a disappointment, even if the restaurant was a good restaurant. Each meal here, though, was wonderful, and I began to feel not just that I was learning his dishes, but that I was advancing deeper into Chef Chang's canon and learning *him*.

I wrote my review, which in every other instance meant that I was done with the place and had moved on to the next restaurant to be written about, to Thai, to Lebanese, to sushi, to Salvadoran. But with TemptAsian, I did not move on.

I wanted more, so shortly afterward, I organized a group to descend on the restaurant when I learned that Chang had, again, and rather more mysteriously this time, left. Three departures in two years. Even by the diminished standards of the industry, whereby a chef at one location for two or three years is regarded as a crusty vet, this seemed like a lot.

▪ ▪ ▪

It was at this point that the gossip and speculation began to float my way, in beseeching e-mails from diners who, like me, had also fallen under the spell of the bewitching cooking of the curiously peripatetic Chef Chang. *His green card has expired, and he's on the lam. He can't stay for long in one place—as soon as he's reviewed, he has to leave. No, no: he's running from a vindictive former employer, out to exact revenge upon his star chef for leaving. Wrong, all wrong— he's had his taste of Western-style freedom and celebrity, and can no longer abide working for owners who do not treat him as the glittering talent he is.*

Strangest of all was the theory that was trotted out by one of these obsessives: *he fears success.*

In the absence of a place to eat his cooking and commune with him, the obsessives needed an outlet to express their sense of neurosis. They turned to e-mail. They took to the web. Where would Chef Chang turn up next? Would he turn up next? Could this have been—no, don't speak it—the last chance to taste his pepper-fired genius?

I passed along some of these e-mails to my wife, with wry notes attached to the top, wry, distancing notes about these cultlike pronouncements. I was laughing at the lengths that ordinary folks could go in their love for a few dishes. The truth, though, was that I was just as caught up in this as they were.

▪ ▪ ▪

He turned up, many months later, at a dismal-looking place, again in Fairfax, called China Gourmet, with garish green pile carpet that had lost most of its nap and a drink menu featuring mai tais. The owner had been following Chef Chang for some time now, he confessed to me over the phone, having attended an "extraordinary" fourteen-course banquet at the Chinese embassy and then, later, having become a regular at both China Star and TemptAsian Café. So the owner was one of us, I thought, except that he had been studying more than just the intimate magic of *ma la* and finger peppers. He'd purchased this particular restaurant because it was less than a mile from where Chang's daughter attended high school. He gave Chang the go-ahead to hire his own staff, which meant the chef could hire his wife, Hongyong, a specialist in cold dishes. Having intuited that control was important to the chef, he even allowed him to choose the restaurant's new name: Szechuan Boy.

There was a sweetly childlike quality to this name, but also something grandiose, an atypical rejection of the Chinese need to recede into the background. This was a passionate embrace of foreground, a bold assertion of his individuality and independence. The place belonged to him, the chef, the Szechuan boy.

I made my first visit three days after Chang started, a marked contrast to the three weeks I ordinarily waited before dropping by a restaurant for my initial assessment. At his other stops, I had gone with one other person, but now I took groups, the better to sample a raft of dishes in a single sitting. I had learned from experience to be firm and insistent about what I wanted, to bark out instructions. I sounded like a stranger to myself, like a petty tyrant or a football coach, but it worked. "Yes, sir," the waiter at Szechuan Boy said, over and over again, as I placed my exhaustive order. I was in.

My parents were my guests for that first meal. They had eaten a lot of Chinese food, from New York to San Francisco. My mother had taken classes in Chinese cooking. They regularly hosted dinners of Chinese corn soup, homemade egg rolls, steamed fish in ginger. And still nothing prepared them for their encounter with Chef Chang, for the cumin-scented ground-beef hash that we tucked into tiny steamed buns, for the chicken consommé seasoned with microscopic dried shrimp and topped off with delicately fashioned dumplings, for the *ma po* tofu with its squares of jiggly, custardy bean curd poking up from a broth so glossy and red it resembled a new fire truck. "It's like I've never eaten Chinese food before," my mother said, awestruck.

"This guy's a genius," said my father, who blasted anyone who deigned to attach that label to others he deemed unworthy: Bill Cosby, Bill Gates, Martin Scorsese.

Ordinarily, I would spread my visits out over the course of a month, but I was much too impatient to abide by my self-made rule this time. I went back a couple of nights later, and then a couple of nights after that, and then a couple of nights after that. Three times in one week, and then, because I couldn't help myself, I went back two more times the next.

"This is a druglike experience," said a friend one night, speaking slowly and absent-mindedly in the midst of eating the chef's version of pickled peppers, as if he were finding his bearings amid a hallucination.

Another night, I watched tears streak down a friend's face as he popped expertly cleavered bites of chicken into his mouth with his chopsticks. He was red-eyed and breathing fast. "It hurts, it hurts, but it's so good, but it hurts, and I can't stop eating!" He slammed a fist down on the table. The beer in his glass sloshed over the sides. "Jesus Christ, I've got to stop!"

Even when I wasn't eating Chef Chang's food, I was thinking about it, and talking about it, re-creating those singular tastes in words and images. I talked about it constantly; I couldn't not talk about it. I wanted everyone I knew to try it, particularly since, as experience had taught me, he would not be here long and the moment was not likely to last. "I'll definitely have to make it out there," friends would say, and I knew from the complacency of their tone that they didn't get what I was telling them, that a great restaurant, of all places, is not static, it is constantly changing and evolving, and often for the worse, and that greatness, when you can find it—if you can find it—is an evanescent thing, kept alive by luck and circumstance and numberless mysteries we can't hope to understand, not unlike life itself, and we must heed the imperative to go, now, and give ourselves over to it.

■   ■   ■

Two weeks after my review came out, he was gone. Wherever he went, he left—that was nothing new, I'd intimated as much in the three-and-a-half-star piece I'd written. (Four stars is an exalted designation, rarely granted; restaurants with nine-buck entrées and garish green carpet are generally lucky to be considered for two.)

What was new was the suddenness of it. I knew not to expect a long run, but even I was unprepared for this latest exit. The owner, in particular, must have been ambushed by it. After all he had extended to Chef Chang, all he had given away . . .

Readers hounded me for weeks with e-mails, many of them suspecting that I'd perpetrated a hoax. This Szechuan Boy I'd written so gushingly about—what evidence was there to suggest it had ever existed? There was no sign out front and no printed menus inside. The owner had assured me for weeks that both would be arriving "any day now," and I had accepted his promises at the time as typical of a harried owner with a new restaurant, but now I suspected that he had been deliberately withholding his full embrace of his elusive chef, like a partner in a marriage who keeps a separate account. As for the vaunted Chef Chang—gone. If he had ever arrived in the first place. The majority of my readers were moneyed and comfortable, accustomed to going where they were told, and they took it on faith that a glowing review of a restaurant amounted to a guarantee, no different, that is, from a rave about a book or a CD or any other product that was regarded as a fixed and immutable experience. Life was messy, uncertain, chaotic, and full of mystery, yes, but a great restaurant meal was an oasis of calm and order, a bourgeois stay against randomness and darkness, and this is what I had promised them in touting this great talent. My explanations that Chef Chang had bolted for destinations unknown, upending the entire operation, seemed insufficient in the face of their bewilderment and rage. My readers did not want me to explain Chang. They wanted me to explain *me*. My judgment. My foresight. Heck: my stability. They had trusted me, and I had betrayed that trust. I had ruined their Saturday night. I had led them astray.

Among the network of Chang obsessives, there was no less tortured a search for explanations, albeit without the hostility. Could it be explained? I wondered. For years now, I had been trying to understand him and had gotten no closer to any kind of meaning as to who and what he was. There was the cooking, electric and inimitable, and available only in discrete installments that emphasized the fleeting nature of everything that matters. And that was all. And maybe that was enough, in the same way that a painter is the sum of his paintings and the life that matters, the person, is what you find and intuit in the canvases.

■ ■ ■

Word came a couple of weeks later that Chang had left the area for good, and was now living in—and cooking in?—the suburbs of Atlanta, in Marietta, about twenty miles northwest of downtown.

So ends a crazy and intense chapter of my life, I thought—one whose passing I will mourn, even as I hold on fast to the memory of all those great meals. Things come and go, and nothing is forever, and we savor the good times when we can. Szechuan food was never the same again, every subsequent, subpar dish only reminding me what I'd once had, and how I would never have it again—the ache, the longing, that much more intense, because the gap between greatness and mediocrity was so profound.

I kept tabs on him from afar, growing jealous of Atlantans, jealous of their privilege, as I read the reports about his new restaurant. My memory overwhelmed me with a procession of bright and vivid pictures, and I was sitting down again to a meal of corned beef with cilantro and scallion bubble pancake and roast fish with green onion. I read the reviews over and over again, devouring the words, as if reading were akin to eating, as if the more I read, the more the descriptions would satisfy my desire for the real thing. There was something about these reviews that bothered me, though, and it only occurred to me after a fourth reading. What bothered me was that they were not as approving as my reviews had been, not nearly as comprehensive, not nearly as obsessive in nature, and the thought came to me that he was in the wrong place, that Atlantans did not love him enough, or understand him enough. It was not a professional thought, not something a restaurant critic, obliged to consider things with a certain objectivity and impartiality, is supposed to feel. A critic is not supposed to feel proprietary—and certainly is not supposed to feel protective—of a restaurant or a chef. That's when I knew that I had crossed a line, if only in my own mind. And that's when it occurred to me to get in the car and drive down to Atlanta.

■   ■   ■

Tasty China was the name. Grim-faced servers cleared tables with militaristic efficiency. From my corner table, in the back, I watched a huge white tureen being carried aloft through the sickly lit dining room like the crown prince, trailing a cloud of steam that I thought I could smell from several tables away: ginger, garlic.

The new place was a lot like the old place, a lot like all the old places. If I had been plunked down, blindfolded, at a table in front of a buffet's worth of his cooking, I would not have been able to tell where I was. Atlanta was Alexandria was Fairfax. The same strip-mall setting, the same bad lighting, the same attentive but impersonal service. And the same food, the same brilliant, mouth-numbing, heart-racing dishes.

It was strangely comforting, this sameness—because there was nothing about cilantro fish rolls and cumin-spiced fried fish and pepper-laced chicken that resembled chicken and mashed potatoes or meatloaf and gravy or any of the other dishes that I ordinarily thought of as constituting comfort food. But they were comforting to me, somehow, all the same. They had become comforting. Familiarity, in food, doesn't breed contempt; it breeds the opposite—it breeds contentment. I had eaten these dishes so many times that they had ceased to feel exotic—a function largely of novelty and newness—or ceased to feel *merely* exotic. Eating them again, here in Atlanta, was like running into old friends far from home. They eased my sense of dislocation, of being far from home, in a strange city, without connection. At the same time, they would always be a little different, because this was not the palate I had grown up with, and there were new things I learned each time I dug into them, subtleties of spicing, nuances of texture, the same way a classic story or poem is different upon each fresh reading.

The plates massed around me, threatening to crowd me out, a circumstance my waiter sought to ameliorate by pushing over an adjoining table, a solution I flatly rejected on the grounds that I would look like an even bigger glutton, and it dawned on me, finally. Driving south, I had been buoyed by a sense of adventure, of lighting out for a new world, and the thought of reconnecting, retasting, had seemed to ease some of the drudgery of a long road trip. But now, having travelled more than six hundred miles to his new restaurant, I realized: *I had traveled six hundred miles to a restaurant to eat dinner.*

And not only that, but I had just crossed a line from critic to fan in coming down here. I had formally acknowledged that an interest had become an obsession.

And that unnerving thought gave way to this unnerving thought: if the past was any guide, then Chef Chang would not last very long at Tasty China—the fact that reviews had already come out seemed to suggest that his days were numbered. And then what? Would I follow him to his next place? And the next place after that? Trail after him the way groupies did the Grateful Dead? The itinerant critic and the exile chef? The answer, I supposed, would determine just how much of an obsessive I had become.

■　■　■

He left, of course. He always left. It was not a matter of *if*, but *when*. When, in this case, turned out to be almost a year after he moved to Atlanta.

But this time, he did not stay in the area. He'd headed west: Knoxville, Tennessee, according to one of my tipsters.

"You're not going, are you?" my wife asked when I told her one night. We were out at dinner, on one of my appointed rounds: a generically stylish American restaurant with the same menu of rarefied, rustic dishes, it seemed, I had eaten for the last year or more. It was as if the chefs had all attended the same seminar.

"Probably not," I said.

My wife set down her martini thingie. "Here we go again."

"What?"

"Probably not means probably yes. You watch. You'll end up talking yourself into going."

"I mean, it's pretty far."

"Uh-huh."

"And it's not like I haven't ever had his cooking . . ."

"Enjoy yourself."

■　■　■

Washington, Atlanta, Knoxville . . . and then where? Where would it end? *Would* it end?

Was Chef Chang destined never to find peace, never to find a permanent home, to tramp from town to town, state to state, a culinary mercenary, a tormented loner genius? I wondered if growing up in Hunan Province, he could have imagined a life like this: a cooking vagabond, hopscotching across America and the Deep South—a restless and hungry seeker, Kerouac with a wok. Was this the life he dreamed for himself? Trading one suburban strip mall for another, the places as indistinct as the landscape, homogenized and featureless? Lacing complex dishes with the famed *ma la* peppercorn for Americans who knew nothing of him or his country, who could not tolerate heat and would much rather he concentrated his attention on their General Tso's chicken?

This was the Chef Chang I had created in my imagination, in lieu of actual knowledge of the actual Chef Chang. A chef with poetry in his soul, a romantic figure who yearned to break free of all that constrained him, including the limits of his own imagination.

It troubled me to think that there might be another Chef Chang, or many other Chef Changs, that I had driven to Atlanta and now hopped a flight to Knoxville to eat the cooking of a man who was on the run from authorities, or who had gotten in deep with the wrong people and who did not pick up and leave because he sought a greater freedom, but who picked up and left because he was interested merely in survival.

Who else, I wondered, was following him?

Maybe he was the one and also the other, a romantic figure on the run. Maybe he was neither, and all the speculation was horribly off base.

I had driven to Atlanta with the idea that eating more of his food would bring me closer to understanding him and whatever compelled him to keep leaving places, but it hadn't even brought me closer to understanding why I picked up and followed him. I liked to think that I was re-creating his own journey westward, tracing his steps in the hope of entering his mind and heart. I liked to think that, because otherwise I would have to come to grips with the idea that I was losing my mind, just a little. Washington, Atlanta, Knoxville . . . Where would I stop? *Would it stop?*

I had always thought the food was addictive—the way you ate more than you intended for no other reason than that the scorching heat set your heart to racing and caused you to sweat and gave you the feeling of release and exhilaration. Now I had to wonder if there was something addictive, too, in the quest itself. I reflected on that very question as I sat at my table at Hong Kong House, surrounded by half a dozen dishes, my heart racing, feeling happier than I had in weeks and maybe months, the simple contentedness that comes of knowing that you are in the right place at the right time.

■　■　■

I had suspected that this meal would be my last, that I was not long for the road, that I couldn't continue to follow him from city to city. He was the one in exile, not me. Enough. I'd had my adventure.

I said all this to my wife when I returned. She looked at me the way she often looked at me when I made a promise to stain a bookcase or embark on some other project of house beautification: *I'll believe it when I see it.*

And in truth, I knew when I said it that I had said it simply to have said it, to give the idea a spin, to look good; I was test-driving, I wasn't buying.

A year later, I learned that Chef Chang had bolted again. He had come east and was cooking in Charlottesville, Virginia, at a place called Taste of

China. I was in Richmond, doing research for a book, when I got the news. *An hour away. He hasn't been this close since he was in D.C.* What came over me, then, was almost chemical, an emotional sensation akin to that triggered by the peppers, an involuntary systemic reaction. I was salivating.

■   ■   ■

I was standing outside the bathroom at Taste of China with my cell phone pressed to my ear, assuring my wife that I was fine, that the trip had been a smooth one, when I spotted Chef Chang through the narrow window of the double doors and subsequently lost the thread of our conversation. It was the closest I had ever come to seeing him.

"Where are you?"

"Charlottesville."

"Charlottesville? I thought you were in Richmond."

"I was."

"And now you're in Charlottesville . . ."

"I finished what I had to do in Richmond and decided to come home by way of Charlottesville and get some dinner," I said, adding that I was going to be back later than I expected. I was feeling like a cliché.

"Where are you having dinner?" she asked, just as a manager pushed through the double doors of the kitchen, exposing us to the echoing sound of clanging pots and pans and cooks barking instructions at one another. I craned my neck for a better glimpse. Out came two waiters bearing large trays on their shoulders and gesticulating wildly as they bickered in very loud Chinese, presumably about who was responsible for what.

"Don't tell me," she said, and I couldn't tell whether I was hearing admiration or dismay in her tone. Admiration and dismay? "Are you with him there in the kitchen?"

"No, I'm outside, peeking in."

"Are you going to talk to him?"

Talk to him. Such a simple idea. An inevitable idea, an entirely practical idea. Chef Chang and I had never met, but it seemed odd that I would not seek him out now, that I would just sit there at my table like any other customer in the restaurant instead of one who had intimate knowledge of his canon and who had studied his techniques and methods. Besides which, I was a restaurant critic in Washington, not Charlottesville, so what harm could be done in divulging my identity if I so chose? And why, at this point, after all these many trips, after Atlanta and Knoxville, would I not choose?

These were smart, sensible arguments my wife was making, but they were aimed at normalizing what was not normal. To talk to Chef Chang was to make purposeful a trip that had been conceived on a whim and a notion, since an interview could be useful, and might one day form the basis for a piece (I didn't have an assignment to come down here)—to talk to him, in other words, was to turn what was, in truth, a crazy pursuit of a man and a taste into something that could be spoken about in ordinary conversation without making me look like a loon.

Our bond, such as it was, was through food, through the silent communication of dish and diner, I said to myself. Not through talk; through taste. But this was an attempt at self-justification, an attempt to preserve some semblance of my critical distance, the wall I erected between the moments I described and my ability to be affected by them and, possibly, succumb to them.

What would happen if I went up and introduced myself? Would he bolt in the middle of dinner and never come back? Would he fling the contents of a hot wok in my face for making his life in Washington so difficult? Would he call the cops and accuse me of stalking him? And how would I plead, if he did? What would I say? What *could* I say? Taste of China was his sixth restaurant in four years. I had been to all of them. Where he went, I went. He cooked, and I wrote about him. I wrote about him, and he left.

Seeking him out was beside the point, I decided, which made what I did next so stupefying, as though I had contrived a passive-aggressive defiance against my own ruling. I ordered nine dishes. Nine dishes, for a table of one. The waiter had turned to walk away after dish four, and I had had to flag him down to return. He attempted to put the brakes on me after dish five, but I persisted. By dish number six he was shaking his head, his tired eyes widened in alarm. By the ninth, and final, dish he looked worried for me, worried for my soul, and I imagined as he turned to head back to the kitchen that he cursed my Western indifference to waste. What was I doing?

The plates gathered around me—scallion bubble pancake, corned beef with cilantro, cleavered whole chicken with finger peppers, cilantro fish rolls, roast fish with green onion—and this time I did not put up a fight when the adjoining table was shoved up against mine. I wanted Chef Chang to come out and see the spectacle in his dining room. I wanted him to come out and see my devotion, the depth of it, wanted him to know that I was no mere customer but a fervent loyalist. A critic, yes, but only by occupation. Our connection now, clearly, transcended those bounds.

He did not come out. It was OK. I understood. Maybe it was better this way. Not through talk; through taste. I did not come to Charlottesville for a meeting of the minds. I had come to Charlottesville because his food was a part of my life. His tastes had become my tastes. Where he went, I followed. I dug into a mound of cleavered chicken with peppers. My mouth went numb. Tears rolled down my cheeks.

Provisions and Providers

Nature's Spoils

Burkhard Bilger

The house at 40 Congress Street wouldn't have been my first choice for lunch. It sat on a weedy lot in a disheveled section of Asheville, North Carolina. Abandoned by its previous owners, condemned by the city, and minimally rehabilitated, it was occupied—perhaps infested is a better word—by a loose affiliation of opportunivores. The walls and ceilings, chicken coop, and solar oven were held together with scrap lumber and drywall. The sinks, disconnected from the sewer, spilled their effluent into plastic buckets, providing water for root crops in the gardens. The whole compound was painted a sickly greenish gray—the unhappy marriage of twenty-three cans of surplus paint from Home Depot. "We didn't put in the pinks," Clover told me.

Clover's pseudonym both signaled his emancipation from a wasteful society and offered a thin buffer against its authorities. "It came out of the security culture of the old Earth First! days," another opportunivore told me. "If the Man comes around, you can't give him any incriminating information." Mostly, though, the names fit the faces: Clover was pale, slender, and sweet natured, with fine blond hair gathered in a bun. His neighbor Catfish had droopy whiskers and fleshy cheeks. There were four men and three women in all, aged twenty to thirty-five, crammed into seven small bedrooms. Only one had a full-time job, and more than half received food stamps. They relied mostly on secondhand bicycles for transportation, and each paid two hundred dollars or less in rent. "We're just living way simple," Clover said. "Super low-impact, deep green."

Along one wall of the kitchen, rows of pine-and-wire shelves were crowded with dumpster discoveries, most of them pristine: boxes of organic tea and artisanal pasta, garlic from Food Lion, baby spring mix from Earth Fare, tomatoes from the farmers' market. About half the household's food had been left somewhere to rot, Clover said, and there was often enough to share with Asheville's other opportunivores. (A couple of months earlier; they'd unearthed a few dozen cartons of organic ice cream; before that, enough Odwalla juices to fill the bathtub.) Leftovers were pickled or composted, brewed into mead, or, if they looked too dicey, fed to the chickens. "We have our standards," a young punk with a buzz-cut scalp and a skinny ponytail told me. "We won't dumpster McDonald's." But he had eaten a good deal of scavenged sushi, he said—it was all right, as long as it didn't sit in the dumpster overnight—and his housemate had once scored a haggis. "Oh no, no," she said, when I asked if she'd eaten it. "It was canned."

Lunch that day was lentil soup, a bowl of which was slowly congealing on the table in front of me. The carrots and onions in it had come from a dumpster behind Amazing Savings, as had the lentils, potatoes, and most of the spices. Their color reminded me a little of the paint on the house. Next to me, Sandor Katz scooped a spoonful into his mouth and declared it excellent. A self-avowed "fermentation fetishist," Katz travels around the country giving lectures and demonstrations, spreading the gospel of sauerkraut, dill pickles, and all foods transformed and ennobled by bacteria. His two books— *Wild Fermentation* and *The Revolution Will Not Be Televised*—have become manifestos and how-to manuals for a generation of underground food activists, and he's at work on a third, definitive volume. Lunch with the opportunivores was his idea.

Katz and I were on our way to the Green Path, a gathering of herbalists, foragers, raw-milk drinkers, and roadkill eaters in the foothills of the Smoky Mountains. The groups in Katz's network have no single agenda or ideology. Some identify themselves as punks, others as hippies, others as evangelical Christians; some live as rustically as homesteaders—the "techno-peasantry," they call themselves; others are thoroughly plugged in. If they have a connecting thread, it's their distrust of "dead, anonymous industrialized, genetically engineered, and chemicalized corporate food," as Katz has written. Americans are killing themselves with cleanliness, he believes. Every year, we waste 40 percent of the food we produce, and process, pasteurize, or irradiate much of the rest, sterilizing the live cultures that keep us healthy. Lunch from a dumpster isn't just a form of conservation; it's a kind of inoculation.

"This is a modern version of the ancient tradition of gleaning," Katz said. "When the harvest is over, the community has a common-law right to pick over what's left." I poked at the soup with my spoon. The carrots seemed a little soft—whether overcooked or overripe, I couldn't tell—but they tasted all right. I asked the kid with the ponytail if he'd ever brought home food that was spoiled. "Oh, hell yes!" he said, choking back a laugh. "Jesus Christ, yes!"

Then he shrugged, suddenly serious. "It happens; diarrhea, food poisoning. But I think we've developed pretty good immune systems by now."

▪   ▪   ▪

To most cooks, a kitchen is a kind of battle zone—a stainless-steel arena devoted to the systematic destruction of bacteria. We fry them in oil and roast them in ovens, steam them, boil them, and sluice them with detergents. Our bodies are delicate things, easily infected, our mothers taught us, and the agents of microscopic villainy are everywhere. They lurk in raw meat, raw vegetables, and the yolks of raw eggs, on the unwashed hand and in the unmuffled sneeze, on the grimy countertop and in the undercooked pork chop.

Or maybe not. Modern hygiene has prevented countless colds, fevers, and other ailments, but its central premise is hopelessly outdated. The human body isn't besieged; it's saturated, infused with microbial life at every level. "There is no such thing as an individual," Lynn Margulis, a biologist at the University of Massachusetts at Amherst, told me recently. "What we see as animals are partly just integrated sets of bacteria. Nearly all the DNA in our bodies belongs to microorganisms: they outnumber our own cells nine to one. They process the nutrients in our guts, produce the chemicals that trigger sleep, ferment the sweat on our skin and the glucose in our muscles. ("Humans didn't invent fermentation," Katz likes to say. "Fermentation created us.") They work with the immune system to mediate chemical reactions and drive out the most common infections. Even our own cells are kept alive by mitochondria—the tiny microbial engines in their cytoplasm. Bacteria are us.

"Microbes are the minimal units, the basic building blocks of life on earth," Margulis said. About half a billion years ago, land vertebrates began to encase themselves in skin and their embryos in protective membranes, sealing off the microbes inside them and fostering ever more intimate relations with them. Humans are the acme of that evolution—walking, talking microbial vats. By now, the communities we host are so varied and interdependent that it's hard to tell friend from enemy—the bacteria we can't live with from those we can't live without. *E. coli, Staphylococcus aureus*, and the bacterial responsible for meningitis and stomach ulcers all live peaceably inside us most of the time, turning dangerous only on rare occasions and for reasons that are poorly understood. "This cliché nonsense about good and bad bacteria, it's so insidious," Margulis said. "It's this Western, dichotomized, Cartesian thing. . . . Like Jesus rising."

In the past decade, biologists have embarked on what they call the second human-genome project, aimed at identifying every bacterium associated with people. More than a thousand species have been found so far in our skin, stomach, mouth, guts, and other body parts. Of those, only fifty or so are known to harm us, and they have been studied obsessively for more than a century. The rest are mostly new to science. "At this juncture, biologists cannot be blamed for finding themselves in a kind of 'future shock,'" Margaret McFall-Ngai, an expert in symbiosis at the University of Wisconsin at Madison, wrote in *Nature Reviews Microbiology* two years ago. Or, as she put it in an earlier essay, "We have been looking at bacteria through the wrong end of the telescope."

Given how little we know about our inner ecology, carpet-bombing it might not always be the best idea. "I would put it very bluntly," Margulis told me. "When you advocate your soaps that say they kill all harmful bacteria, you are committing suicide." The bacteria in the gut can take up to four years to recover from a round of antibiotics, recent studies have found, and the steady assault of detergents, preservatives, chlorine, and other chemicals also takes its toll. The immune system builds up fewer antibodies in a sterile environment; the deadliest pathogens can grow more resistant to antibiotics; and innocent bystanders such as peanuts or gluten are more likely to provoke allergic reactions. All of which may explain why a number of studies have found that children raised on farms are less susceptible to allergies, asthma, and autoimmune diseases. The cleaner we are, it sometimes seems, the sicker we get.

"We are living in this cultural project that's rarely talked about," Katz says. "We hear about the war on terror. We hear about the war on drugs. But the war on bacteria is much older, and we've all been indoctrinated into it. We have to let go of the idea that they're our enemies. Eating bacteria is one of life's greatest pleasures, Katz says. Beer, wine, cheese, bread, cured meats, coffee, chocolate: our best-loved foods are almost all fermented. They start out bitter, bland, cloying, or indigestible and are remade by microbes into something magnificent.

Fermentation is a biochemical magic trick—a benign form of rot. It's best known as the process by which yeast turns sugar into alcohol, but an array of other microorganisms and foods can ferment as well. In some fish dishes, for instance, the resident bacteria digest amino acids and spit out ammonia, which acts as a preservative. Strictly speaking, all fermentation is anaerobic (it doesn't consume oxygen); most rot is aerobic. But the two are separated less by produce than by product. One makes food healthy and delicious; the other not so much.

Making peace with microorganisms has its risks, of course. *E. coli* can kill you. *Listeria* can kill you. Basic hygiene and antibiotic overkill aren't hard to tell apart at home, but the margin of error shrinks dramatically in a factory. Less than a gram of the bacterial toxin that causes botulism, released into the American milk supply, could poison a hundred thousand people, the National Academy of Sciences estimated in 2005. And recent deaths and illnesses from contaminated beef, spinach, and eggs have persuaded food regulators to clamp down even harder. While Katz's followers embrace their bacterial selves, the Obama administration has urged Congress to pass a comprehensive new set of food-safety laws, setting the stage for a culture war of an unusually literal sort. "This is a revolution of the everyday," Katz says, "and it's already happening."

■   ■   ■

When Katz picked me up in Knoxville at the beginning of our road trip, the backseat of his rented Kia was stacked with swing-top bottles and oversized Mason jars. They were filled with foamy, semi-opaque fluids and shredded vegetables that had been fermenting in his kitchen for weeks. A sour, pleasantly funky aroma pervaded the cabin, masking the new-car smell of industrial cleaners and off-gassing plastics. It was like driving around in a pickle barrel.

Physically speaking, food activists tend to present a self-negating argument. The more they insist on healthy eating the unhealthier they look. The pickier they are about food the more they look like they could use a double cheeseburger. Katz was an exception. At forty-eight, he had clear blue eyes, a tightly wound frame, and ropy forearms. His hands were calloused and his skin was ruddy from hours spent weeding his commune's vegetable patches and herding goats. He wore his hair in a stubby Mohawk, his beard in bushy muttonchops. If not for his multiple earrings and up-to-the-minute scientific arguments, he might have seemed like a figure out of the nineteenth century, selling tonics and bromides from a painted wagon.

Katz was a political activist long before he was a fermentation fetishist. Growing up on New York's Upper West Side, the eldest son of progressive Polish and Lithuanian Jews, he was always involved in one campaign or another. At the age of ten, in 1972, he spent his afternoons on street corners handing out buttons for George McGovern. At eleven, he was a campaign volunteer for the mayoral candidate Al Blumenthal. When he reached sixth grade and found that one of the city's premier programs for gifted students, Hunter College High School, was only for girls, he helped bring an antidiscrimination suit that forced it to turn coed. He later served on the student council with Elena Kagan, the future Supreme Court justice. "The staggered lunch hour was our big issue," he says.

At Brown, as an undergraduate, Katz became a well-known figure: a bearish hippie in the Abbie Hoffman mold, with a huge head of curly hair. His causes were standard issue for the time: gay rights, divestment from South

Africa, United States out of Central America (as a senior, he and a group of fellow activists placed a CIA recruiter under citizen's arrest). Yet Katz lacked the usual stridency of the campus radical. "I remember a particular conversation in 1982 or '83," his classmate Alicia Svigals, who went on to found the band the Klezmatics, told me. "We were standing on a street corner in Providence, and I said, 'Sandy, I think I might be a lesbian.' And he said, 'Oh, I think I might be gay.' At that time, that was a huge piece of news. It wasn't something you said lightly. But his reaction was 'How wonderful and exciting! How fantastic! This is going to be so much fun!' The world was about to be made new—and so easily."

After graduation, Katz moved back to New York. He took a job as the executive director of Westpride, a lobbying group opposed to a massive development project on the Upper West Side. The developer, Donald Trump, was eventually forced to scale down his plans. As the AIDS epidemic escalated, in the late 1980s, Katz became an organizer for ACT UP and a columnist for the magazine *OutWeek*. His efforts on both these fronts caught the eye of Ruth Messinger, the Manhattan borough chief, who hired him in 1989 as a land-use planner and as a de facto liaison to the gay community. "He was a spectacular person," Messinger told me recently. "Creative and flamboyant and fun to be around. He just had a natural instinct and talent as an organizer of people." Messinger was thinking of running for mayor (she won the Democratic nomination in 1997, only to get trounced by Rudolph Giuliani), and Katz's ambitions rose with hers. "I would fantasize about what city agency I wanted to administer," he recalls. Then, in 1991, he tested HIV-positive.

Katz had never been particularly promiscuous. He'd had his first gay sexual experience at the age of twenty-one, crossing the country on a Green Tortoise bus, and had returned to New York just as its bathhouse days were waning. He'd never taken intravenous drugs and had avoided the riskiest sexual activities. The previous HIV tests he'd taken had come back inconclusive—perhaps, he reasoned, because of a malarial infection that he'd picked up in West Africa. "I have no idea how it happened," he told me. "I remember walking out of the doctor's office in such a daze. I was just utterly shell-shocked."

The virus wasn't necessarily a death sentence, though an effective treatment was years away. But it did transform Katz's political ambitions. "They just dematerialized," he told me. For all his iconoclasm, he had always dreamed of being a United States senator. Now he focused on curing himself. He cut back his hours and moved from his parents' house to the East Village. So many of his friends had died while on AZT and other experimental drugs that he decided to search for alternatives. He had already taken up yoga and switched to a macrobiotic diet. Now he began to consult with herbalists, drink nettle tea, and wander around Central Park gathering medicinal plants. "I got skinny, skinny, skinny," he says. "My friends thought I was wasting away."

New York's relentless energy had always helped drive his ambitions, but now he found that it wore him out. About a year after his diagnosis, Katz went to visit some friends in New Orleans who had rented a crash pad for Mardi Gras. Among the characters there, he met a man from a place called Hickory Knoll (I've changed the name at Katz's request). Founded in the early seventies by a group of back-to-the-landers, Hickory Knoll was something of a legend in the gay community: a queer sanctuary in the heart of the Bible Belt. "I was a typical New Yorker," Katz says. "I considered the idea of living in Tennessee absurd." Still, he was intrigued. Hickory Knoll had no television or hot running water—just goats, vegetable gardens, and gay men. Maybe it was just what he needed.

■   ■   ■

Hickory Knoll lies just up the road from a Bible camp, in an airy forest of tulip poplar and dogwood, maple, mountain laurel, pawpaw, and persimmon. The camp and the commune share a hilltop, a telephone cable, and, if nothing else, a belief in spiritual renewal: "Want a new life?" a sign in front of a local church asked as I drove past. "God accepts trade-ins." When Katz first arrived, in the spring of 1992, the paulownia trees were in bloom, scattering the ground with lavender petals. As he walked down the gravel path, the forest canopy opened up and a cabin of hand-hewn chestnut logs, built in the 1830s, appeared in the sunlight below. "It was a beautiful arrival," he says.

The commune had a shifting cast of about fifteen members, some of whom had lived there for decades. It billed itself as a radical faerie sanctuary, though the term was notoriously slippery—the faerie movement, begun in the late 1970s by gay-rights activists, embraced everyone from transvestites to pagans and anarchists, their common interest being a focus on nature and spirituality. Street kids from San Francisco, nudists from Nashville, a Mexican minister coming out of the closet: all found their way, somehow, to central Tennessee. Most were gay men, though anyone was welcome, and the great majority had never lived on the land before. "Sissies in the wood," one writer called it, after tussling over camping arrangements with a drag queen in four-inch heels.

New arrivals stayed in the cabin "downtown," which had been fitfully expanded to encompass a library, living room, dining room, and kitchen, with four bedrooms upstairs. Farther down the path were a swaybacked red barn, a communal shower, a pair of onion-domed cisterns, and a four-seater outhouse. The charge for room and board was on a sliding scale starting at seventy-five dollars a month, with a tacit agreement, laxly enforced, to pitch in—milking goats, mending fences, or just greeting new arrivals. Those who stayed eventually built houses along the ridges or bought adjacent land and started homesteads and communes of their own. In the spring, at the annual May Day celebration, their numbers grew to several hundred. "The gayborhood just keeps on growing," Weeder, Hickory Knoll's oldest member, told me one evening as we were sitting on the front porch of the cabin. "We're a pretty good voting bloc."

Inside, half a dozen men were preparing dinner. Food is the great marker of the day at Hickory Knoll—the singular goal toward which most labor and creativity tend. On my visit, the kitchen seemed to be staffed by at least three cooks at all times, cutting biscuits, baking vegan meatloaf, washing kale; one of them, a gangly Oklahoman named Lady Now, worked in the nude. "Real estate determines culture," Katz likes to say, and the maxim is doubly true for underground food movements. Urban squatters gravitate toward freeganism and dumpster diving, homesteaders toward raw milk and roadkill. At Hickory Knoll, the slow pace, lush gardens, and communal isolation are natural incubators for fermented food, though Katz didn't realize it right away. "It took a while for the New York City to wear off," Weeder told me. "Overanalyzing everything. Where am I going to go tonight? There really is nowhere to go."

That first year, a visitor named Crazy Owl brought some miso as barter for his stay, inspiring Katz to make some of his own. Miso, like many Asian staples, is usually made of fermented soybeans. The beans are hard to stomach alone, no matter how long they're cooked. But once inoculated with koji—the spores of the *Aspergillus oryzae* mold—they become silken and delicious. The enzymes in the mold predigest the beans, turning starches into sugars, breaking proteins into amino acids, unlocking nutrients from leaden compounds. A lowly bean becomes one of the world's great foods.

Katz experimented with more and more fermented dishes after that. He made tempeh, natto, kombucha, and kefir. He recruited friends to chew corn for chicha—an Andean beer brewed with the enzymes in human saliva. At the Vanderbilt library, in Nashville, he worked his way through the *Handbook of Indigenous Fermented Foods* (1983), by the Cornell microbiologist Keith Steinkraus. When he'd gathered a few dozen recipes, he printed a pamphlet and sold some copies to a bookstore in Maine and a permaculture magazine in North Carolina. The pamphlet led to a contract from a publisher, Chelsea Green, and the release of *Wild Fermentation* in 2003. The book was only a modest success at first, but sold more copies each year—some seventy thousand in all. Soon Katz was crisscrossing the country in his car, shredding cabbage in the aisles of Whole Foods or Trader Joe's, preaching the glories of sauerkraut.

■   ■   ■

"Fermented foods aren't culinary novelties," he told me one morning. "They aren't cupcakes. They're a major survival food." We were standing in his test kitchen, in the basement of a farmhouse a few miles down the road from Hickory Knoll. Katz had rented the space two years earlier, when his classes and cooking projects outgrew the commune's kitchen, and outfitted it with secondhand equipment: a triple sink, a six-burner stove, a freezer, and two refrigerators, one of them retrofitted as a tempeh incubator. Along one wall, a friend had painted a psychedelic mural showing a man conversing with a bacterium. Along another, Katz had pinned a canticle to wild fermentation, written by a Benedictine nun in New York. A haunch of venison hung in back, curing for prosciutto, surrounded by mismatched jars of sourdough, goat kefir, sweet potato fly, and other ferments, all bubbling and straining at their lids. "It's like having pets," Katz said.

The kitchen had the same aroma as Katz's car, only a few orders of magnitude funkier: the smell of life before cold storage. "We are living in the historical bubble of refrigeration," Katz said, pulling a jar of bright-pink-and-orange sauerkraut off the shelf. "Most of these food movements aren't revolutionary so much as conservative. They want to bring back the way food has been."

Fermentation, like cooking with fire, is one of the initial conditions of civilization. The alcohol and acids it produces can preserve fruits and grains for months and even years, making sedentary society possible. The first ferments happened by accident—honey water turned to mead, grapes to vinegar—but people soon learned to re-create them. By 5400 BC, the ancient Iranians were making wine. By 1800 BC, the Sumerians were worshipping Ninkasi, the goddess of beer. By the first century BC, the Chinese were making a precursor to soy sauce.

Katz calls fermentation the path of least resistance. "It's what happens when you do nothing," he says. Or rather, if you do one or two simple things. A head of cabbage left on a counter will never turn to sauerkraut, no matter how long it sits there. Yeast, molds, and a host of bacteria will attack it, digesting the leaves till all that's left is a puddle of black slime. To ferment, most food has to be protected from the air. It can be sealed in a barrel, stuffed in a casing, soaked in brine, or submerged in its own juices—anything, as long as oxygen doesn't touch it. The sauerkraut Katz was holding had been made ten days earlier. I'd watched him shred the cabbage—one head of red and one head of green—sprinkle it with two tablespoons of salt to draw out the water, and throw in a few grated carrots. He'd scrunched everything together with his hands, to help release the juice, and packed it in a jar until the liquid rose to the top. "I would suggest not sealing it too tightly," he said as he clamped down the lid. "Some jars will explode."

Three waves of bacteria had colonized the kraut since then, each one changing the chemical environment just enough to attract and fall victim to the next—like yuppie remodelers priced out of their own neighborhoods. Sugars had been converted to acids, carbon dioxide, and alcohol. Some new nutrients had been created: B vitamins, for instance, and isothiocyanates, which laboratory studies have found to inhibit lung, liver, breast, and other cancers. Other nutrients were preserved, notably vitamin C. When Captain Cook circled the globe between 1772 and 1775, he took along thirty thousand pounds of sauerkraut, and none of his crew died of scurvy.

I tried a forkful from Katz's jar, along with a slab of his black-rice tempeh. The kraut was crunchy and tart—milder than any I'd had from a store and much fresher tasting. "You could eat it after two weeks, you could eat it after two months, and if you lived in a cold environment and had a root cellar you could eat it after two years," Katz said. The longer it fermented the stronger it would get. His six-month-old kraut, made with radishes and Asian greens, was meaty, pungent, and as tender as pasta—the enzymes in it had broken down the pectin in its cell walls. Some people like it that way, he said. "When this Austrian woman tasted my six-week-old sauerkraut, she said, 'That's OK—for coleslaw.'"

While we were eating, the front door banged open and a young man walked in carrying some baskets of fresh-picked strawberries. He had long blond hair and hands stained red with juice. His name was Jimmy, he said. He lived at Hickory Knoll but was doing some farming up the road. "We originally grew herbs and flowers and planted them in patterns," he said. "But people were like, 'What are those patterns you're makin'? They don't look Christian to me.'" The locals were usually pretty tolerant, Katz said. In eighteen years, the worst incidents that he could recall were a few slashed tires and some teenagers yelling, "Faggots!" from the road and shooting shotguns in the air. Rural Tennessee is a "don't ask, don't tell" sort of place, where privacy is the one inalienable right. But Jimmy's fancy crop might have counted as a public display. He laughed and handed me a berry, still warm from the sun. "They're not only organic," he said. "They're grown with gay love."

The fruit was sugar-sweet and extravagantly fragrant—a distillation of spring. But the sauerkraut was the more trustworthy food. An unwashed fruit or vegetable may host as many as a million bacteria per gram, Fred Breidt, a microbiologist with the U.S. Department of Agriculture and a professor of food science at North Carolina State University, told me. "We've all seen the cases," Katz said. "The runoff from agriculture gets on a vegetable, or there's fecal matter from someone who handled it. Healthy people will get diarrhea; an elderly person or a baby might get killed. That's a possibility with raw food." If the same produce were fermented, its native bacteria would drive off the pathogens, and the acids and alcohol they produce would prevent any further infection. Breidt has yet to find a single documented case of someone getting sick from contaminated sauerkraut. "It's the safest food there is," Katz said.

■　　■　　■

Sauerkraut is Katz's gateway drug. He lures in novices with its simplicity and safety, then encourages them to experiment with livelier cultures, more off-beat practices. *The Revolution Will Not Be Microwaved* moves from anodyne topics such as seed saving and urban gardening to dirt eating, feral foraging, cannabis cookery, and the raw-milk underground. Unlike many food activists, Katz has a clear respect for peer-reviewed science, and he prefaces each discussion with the appropriate caveats. Yet his message is clear: "Our food system desperately demands subversion," he writes. "The more we sterilize our food to eliminate all theoretical risk, the more we diminish its nutritional quality."

On the first day of our road trip, not long after our lunch with the opportunivores, Katz and I paid a visit to a man he called one of the kingpins of underground food in North Carolina. Garth, as I'll call him, was a pale, reedy figure in his fifties with wide, spectral eyes. His linen shirt and suspenders hung slackly on his frame, and his sunken cheeks gave the look of a hardscrabble farmer from a century ago. "I was sick for seventeen years," he told us. "Black circles under my eyes, weighed less than a hundred pounds. It didn't seem like I'd get very far." Doctors said that he had severe chemical sensitivities and a host of ailments—osteoporosis, emphysema, edema, poor circulation—but they seemed incapable of curing him. He tried veganism for a while, but only got weaker. "It's just not a good diet for skinny people," he said. So he went to the opposite extreme.

Inside his bright country kitchen, Garth carefully poured us each a glass of unpasteurized goat milk, as if proffering a magic elixir. The milk was pure white and thick as cream. It had a long, flowery bloom and a faint tanginess. Raw milk doesn't spoil like pasteurized milk. Its native bacteria, left to multiply at room temperature, sour it into something like yogurt or buttermilk, only much richer in cultures. It was the mainstay of Garth's diet, along with raw butter, cream, and daily portions of raw liver, fish, chicken, or beef. He was still anything but robust, but he had enough energy to work long hours in the garden for the first time in years. "It enabled me to function," he said.

Raw milk brings the bacterial debate down to brass tacks. Drinking it could be good for you. Then again it could kill you. Just where the line between risk and benefit lies is a matter of fierce dispute—not to mention arrests, lawsuits, property seizures, and protest marches. In May, for instance, raw-milk activists, hoping to draw attention to a recent crackdown by Massachusetts agricultural authorities, milked a Jersey cow on Boston Common and staged a drink-in.

Retail sales of raw milk are illegal in most states, including North Carolina, but people drink it anyway. Some dairy owners label the milk for pet consumption only (though at two to five times the cost of pasteurized, it's too rich for most cats). Others sell it at farm stands or through herd-share programs. In my neighborhood in Brooklyn, the raw-milk cooperative meets every month in the aisles of a gourmet deli. The milk is trucked in from Pennsylvania—a violation of federal law, which prohibits the interstate transfer of raw milk—but no one seems to mind. Garth buys milk from a local farmer and sells it out of his house. "It's illegal," he told me. "But it gets to the point where living is illegal."

The nutritional evidence both for and against raw milk is somewhat sketchy; much of it dates from before the Second World War, when raw milk was still legal. The Food and Drug Administration, in a fact sheet titled, "The Dangers of Raw Milk," insists that pasteurization "DOES NOT reduce milk's nutritional value." The temperature of the process, well below the boiling point, is meant to kill pathogens and leave nutrients intact. Yet raw-milk advocacy groups, like the Weston A. Price Foundation in Washington, D.C., point to a number of studies that suggest the opposite. An array of vitamins, enzymes, and other nutrients are destroyed, diminished, or denatured by heat, they say. Lactase, for instance, is an enzyme that breaks down lactose into simpler sugars that the body can better digest. Raw milk often contains lactobacilli and bifidobacteria that produce lactase, but neither the bacteria nor the enzyme can survive pasteurization. In one survey of raw-milk drinkers in Michigan and Illinois, 82 percent of those who had been diagnosed as lactose intolerant could drink raw milk without digestive problems. (A more extreme view, held by yet another dietary faction, is that people shouldn't be drinking milk at all—that it's a food specifically designed for newborns of other species, and as such inimical to humans.)

To the FDA, the real problem with milk isn't indigestion but contamination. Poor hygiene and industrial production are a toxic combination. One sick cow, one slovenly worker can contaminate the milk of a dozen dairies. In 1938, a quarter of all disease outbreaks from contaminated food came from milk, which had been known to carry typhoid, tuberculosis, diptheria, and a host of other diseases. More recently, between 1998 and 2008, raw milk was responsible for eighty-five disease outbreaks in more than twenty states, including more than sixteen hundred illnesses, nearly two hundred hospitalizations, and two deaths. "Raw milk is inherently dangerous," the FDA concludes. "It should not be consumed by anyone at any time for any purpose."

Thanks in large part to pasteurization, dairy products now account for less than 5 percent of the foodborne disease outbreaks in America every year. Smoked seafood is six times more likely than pasteurized milk to contain *Listeria*; hot dogs are sixty-five times more likely, and deli meats seventy-seven times more likely. "Every now and then, I meet people in the raw-milk movement who say, 'We have to end pasteurization now!'" Katz told me. "We can't end pasteurization. It would be the biggest disaster in the world. There would be a lot of dead children around."

Still, he says, eating food will always entail a modicum of risk. In an average year, there are seventy-six million cases of food poisoning in America, according to the Centers for Disease Control. Raw milk may be more susceptible to contamination than most foods (though it's still ten times less likely to contain *Listeria* than deli meat is). But just because it can't be produced industrially doesn't mean it can't be produced safely, in smaller quantities. Wisconsin has some thirteen thousand dairies, about half of which, local experts estimate, are owned by farmers who drink their own raw milk. Yet relatively few people have been known to get sick from it. "If this were such a terrible cause and effect, we would be in the newspaper constantly," Scott Rankin, the chairman of the food science department at the University of Wisconsin and a member of the state's raw-milk working group, told me. "Clearly there is an argument to be made in the realm of yeah, this is a tiny risk."

The country's largest raw-milk dairy is Organic Pastures, in Fresno, California. Its products are sold in 375 stores and serve fifty thousand people a week. "Nobody's dying," the founder and CEO, Mark McAfee, told me. In ten years, only two of McAfee's customers have reported food poisoning, he says, and none of the bacteria in those cases could be traced to his dairy. Raw milk is rigorously tested in California and has to meet strict limits for bacterial count. The state's standards hark back to the early days of pasteurization, when many doctors considered raw milk far more nutritious than pasteurized, and separate regulations insured its cleanliness. Dealing with live cultures, Katz and McAfee argue, forces dairies to do what all of agriculture should be doing anyway: downsize, localize, clean up production. "We need to go back 150 years," McAfee told me. "Going back is what's going to help us go forward."

■ ■ ■

A century and a half is an eternity in public-health terms, but to followers of the so-called primal diet it's not nearly long enough. Humans have grown suicidally dainty, many of them say, and even a diet enriched by fermented foods and raw milk is too cultivated by half. Our ancestors were rough beasts: hunters, gatherers, scavengers, and carrion eaters, built to digest any rude meal they could find. Fruits and vegetables were a rarity, grains nonexistent. The human gut was a wild kingdom in those days, continually colonized and purged by parasites, viruses, and other microorganisms picked up from raw meat and from foraging. What didn't kill us, as they say, made us stronger.

A few miles north of downtown Asheville, in a small white farmhouse surrounded by trees, two of Katz's acquaintances were doing their best to emulate early man. Steve Torma ate mostly raw meat and raw dairy. His partner, Alan Muskat, liked to supplement his diet with whatever he could find in the woods: acorns, puffballs, cicadas and carpenter ants, sumac leaves, and gypsy-moth caterpillars. Muskat was an experienced mushroom hunter who had provisioned a number of restaurants in Asheville, and much of what he served was surprisingly good. The ants, collected from his woodpile in the winter when they were too sluggish to get away, had a snappy texture and bright, tart flavor—like organic Pop Rocks. (They were full of formic acid, which gets its name from the Latin word for ant.) He brought us a little dish of toasted acorns, cups of honey-sweetened sumac tea, and goblets of a musky black broth made from decomposed inky-cap mushrooms. I felt, for a moment, as if I'd stumbled upon a child's tea party in the woods.

The primal diet has found a sizable following in recent years, particularly in Southern California and, for some reason, Chicago. Its founder, Aajonus Vonderplanitz, a sixty-three-year-old former soap-opera actor and self-styled nutritionist, claims that it cured him of autism, angina, dyslexia, juvenile diabetes, multiple myeloma, and stomach cancer, as well as psoriasis, bursitis, osteoporosis, tooth decay, and "mania created by excessive fruit." Vonderplanitz recommends eating 85 percent animal products by volume, supplemented by no more than one fruit a day and a pint or so of "green drink"—a puree of fruits and vegetable juices. (Whole vegetable fibers, he believes, are largely indigestible.) The diet's most potent component, though, is an occasional serving of what Vonderplanitz calls "high meat."

Torma ducked into the back of the house and returned with a swing-top jar in his hands. Inside lay a piece of organic beef, badly spoiled. It was afloat in an ochre-colored puddle of its own decay, the muscle and slime indistinguishable, like a slug. High meat is the flesh of any animal that has been allowed to decompose. Torma keeps his portions sealed for up to several weeks before ingesting them, allowing them to air out every few days. (Like the bacteria in sauerkraut, those that cause botulism are anaerobic; fermentation destroys them, but they sometimes survive in sealed meats—*botulus*, in Latin, means sausage.) Vonderplanitz says that he got high meat and its name from the Eskimos, who savor rotten caribou and seal. A regular serving of decayed heart or liver can have a "tremendous Viagra effect" on the elderly, Vonderplanitz told me recently. The first few bites, though, can be rough going. "I still have some resistance to it," Torma admitted. "But the health benefits! I'm fifty-two now. I started this when I was forty-two, and I feel like I'm in my twenties."

Primal eating has its detractors: the *Times* of London recently dubbed it "the silliest diet ever." Most of us find whole vegetables perfectly digestible. The notion that parasites and viruses are good for us would be news to most doctors. And even Vonderplanitz and his followers admit that high meat sometimes leaves them ill and explosively incontinent. They call it detoxification.

Still, radical measures like these have had some surprising successes. In a case published last year in the *Journal of Clinical Gastroenterology*, a sixty-one-year-old woman was given an entirely new set of intestinal bacteria. The patient was suffering from severe diarrhea, Janet Jansson, a microbial ecologist at Lawrence Berkeley National Laboratory, told me. "She lost twenty-seven kilograms and was confined to a diaper and a wheelchair." To repopulate her colon with healthy microbes, Jansson and her collaborators arranged for a fecal transplant from the patient's husband. "They just put it in a Waring blender and turned it into a suppository," Jansson says. "It sounds disgusting, but it cured her. When we got another sample from her, two days later, she had adopted his microbial community." By then, her diarrhea had disappeared.

Other experiments have been even more dramatic. At Washington University in St. Louis, the biologist Jeff Gordon has found that bacteria can help determine body weight. In a study published in *Nature* in 2006, Gordon and his lab-mates, led by Peter Turnbaugh, took a group of germ-free mice, raised in perfect sterility, and divided it in two. One group was inoculated with bacteria from normal mice; the other with bacteria from mice that had been bred to be obese. Both groups gained weight after the inoculation, but those with bacteria from obese mice had nearly twice the percentage of body fat by the end of the experiment. Later, the same lab took normal mice, fed them until they were fat, and transplanted their bacteria into other normal mice. Those mice grew fat, too, and the same pattern held true when the mice were given bacteria from obese people. "It's a positive-feedback loop," Ruth Ley, a biologist from Gordon's lab who now teaches at Cornell, told me. "Whether you're genetically obese or obese from a high-fat diet, you end up with a microbial community that is particularly good at extracting calories. It could mean that an obese person could extract five or ten extra calories from a bowl of Cheerios."

Biologists no longer doubt the depth of our dependence on bacteria. Jansson avoids antibiotics unless they're the only option, and eats probiotic foods like yogurt and prebiotic foods like yacón, a South American root that nourishes bacteria in the gut. Until we understand more about this symbiosis, she and others say, it's best to ingest the cultures we know and trust. "What's beautiful about fermenting vegetables is that they're naturally populated by lactic-acid bacteria," Katz said. "Raw flesh is sterile. You're just culturing whatever was on the knife."

When Torma unclamped his jar, a sickly-sweet miasma filled the air—an odor as natural as it was repellent. Decaying meat produces its own peculiar scent molecules, I later learned, with names like putrescine and cadaverine. I could still smell them on my clothes hours later. Torma stuck two fingers down the jar and fished out a long, wet sliver. "Want a taste?" he said.

It was the end of a long day. I'd spent most of it consuming everything set before me: ants, acorns, raw milk, dumpster stew, and seven kinds of mead, among other delicacies. But even Katz took a pass on high meat. While Torma threw back his head and dropped in his portion, like a seal swallowing a mackerel, we quietly took our leave. "You have to trust your senses," Katz said, as we were driving away. "To me, that smelled like death."

■　■　■

Katz has lived with HIV for two decades. For many years, he medicated himself with his own ferments and local herbs—chickweed, yellow dock, violet leaf, burdock root. But periodic tests at the AIDS clinic in Nashville showed that his T-cell count was still low. Then, in the late nineties, he began to lose weight. He often felt listless and mildly nauseated. At first, he assumed that he was just depressed, but the symptoms got worse. "I started feeling light headed a lot and I had a couple of fainting episodes," he told me. "It dawned on me very slowly that I was suffering from classic AIDS wasting syndrome."

By then, an effective cocktail of AIDS drugs had been available for almost three years. Katz had seen it save the life of one of his neighbors in Tennessee. "It was a really dramatic turnaround," he told me. "But I didn't want my life to be medically managed. I had a real reluctance to get on that treadmill." In the summer of 1999, he took a road trip to Maine to visit friends, hoping to snap out of his funk. By the time he got there, he was so exhausted that he couldn't get up for days. "I remember what really freaked me out was trying to balance my checkbook," he says. "I couldn't even do simple subtraction. It was like my brain wasn't functioning anymore." He had reached the end of his alternatives.

Katz doesn't doubt that the cocktail saved his life. In pictures from that trip, his eyes are hollowed out, his neck so thin that it juts from his woolen sweater like a broomstick. He got worse before he got better, he says—"It was like I had an anvil in my stomach." But one morning, about a month after his first dose, he woke up with a strong urge to chop wood. He now takes three antiretroviral and protease-inhibitor drugs every day and hasn't had a major medical problem in ten years. He still doesn't have the stamina he'd like, and his forehead is often beaded with sweat, even on cool evenings around the commune's dinner table. "I wish this weren't my reality," he told me. "I don't feel great that my life is medically managed. But if that's what's keeping me alive, hallelujah."

It's this part that incenses some of his readers: Having sung the praises of sauerkraut, revealed the secrets of kombucha, and gestured toward the green pastures of raw milk, Katz has surrendered to the false promise of Western medicine. His drug dependence is a sellout, they say—an act of bad faith. "Every two months or so, I get a letter from some well-meaning person who's decided that they have to tell me that I'm believing a lie," he told me. "That the HIV is meaningless and doesn't make people sick. That if I follow this link and read the truth I will be freed from that lie and will stop having to take toxic pills and live happily ever after." Live cultures have been part of his healing, he said. They may even help prevent diseases like cancer. "But that doesn't mean that kombucha will cure your diabetes. It doesn't mean that sauerkraut cured my AIDS."

The trouble with being a diet guru, it seems, is that the more reasonable you try to be the more likely you are to offend your most fervent followers. *The Revolution Will Not Be Microwaved* includes a chapter called "Vegetarian Ethics and Humane Meat." It begins, "I love meat. The smell of it cooking can fill me with desire, and I find its juicy, rich flavor uniquely satisfying." Katz goes on to describe his dismay at commercial meat production, his respect for vegetarianism, and his halfhearted attempts to embrace it. "When I tried being vegan, I found myself dreaming about eggs," he writes. "I could find no virtue in denying my desires. I now understand that many nutrients are soluble only in fats, and animal fats can be vehicles of rich nourishment."

Needless to say, this argument didn't fly with much of his audience. Last year, the Canadian vegan punk band Propagandhi released a song called "Human(e) Meat (The Flensing of Sandor Katz)." Flensing is an archaic locution of the sort beloved by metal bands: it means to strip the blubber from a whale. "I swear I did my best to ensure that his final moments were swift and free from fear," the singer yelps. "But consideration should be made for the fact that Sandor Katz was my first kill." He goes on to describe searing every hair on Katz's body, boiling his head in a stockpot, and turning it into a spreadable headcheese. "It's a horrible song," Katz told me. "When it came out, I was not amused. I had a little fear that some lost vegan youth would try to find meaning by carrying out this fantasy. But it's grown on me."

* * *

The moon was in Sagittarius on the last night of April, the stars out in their legions. Katz and I had arrived in the Smoky Mountains to join the gathering of the Green Path. About sixty people were camped out on a sparsely wooded slope half an hour west of Asheville. Tents, lean-tos, and sleeping bags were scattered among the trees, below an open shed where meals were served: dandelion greens, nettle pesto, kava brownies—the usual. In a clearing nearby, an oak branch had been stripped and erected as a maypole, and a fire pit dug for the night's ceremony: the ancient festival of Beltane, or Walpurgisnacht.

We'd spent the day going on plant walks, taking wildcrafting lessons, and listening to a succession of seekers and sages—Turtle, 7Song, Learning Deer. Every few hours, a cry would go up, and the tribe would gather for an adult version of what kindergarteners call Circle Time: everyone holding hands and exchanging expressions of self-conscious wonder. The women wore their hair long and loose or bobbed like pixies'; their noses were pierced and their bodies wrapped in rag scarves and patterned skirts. The men, in dreadlocks and piratical buns, talked of Babylon and polyamory. The children ran heedlessly through the woods, needing no instruction in the art of absolute freedom. "Is your son homeschooled?" I asked one mother, who crisscrossed the country with her two children and a teepee and was known as the Queen of Roadkill. She laughed. "He's unschooled," she said. "He just learns as he goes."

The Green Path was part ecological retreat and part pagan revival meeting, but mostly it was a memorial for its founder, Frank Cook, who had died a year earlier. Cook was a botanist and teacher who traveled around the world collecting herbal lore, then writing and lecturing about it back in the United States. He lived by barter and donation, refusing to be tied down by full-time work or a single residence, and was, by all accounts, an uncommonly gifted teacher. (He and Katz often taught seminars together.) As a patron saint, though, Cook had left his flock with an uneasy legacy. When he died, at forty-six, it was owing to a tapeworm infection acquired on his travels. Antibiotics might have cured him, but he mostly avoided them. By the time his mother and friends forced him to go to a hospital, last spring, his brain was riddled with tapeworm larvae and the cysts that formed around them. "Frank was pretty dogmatic about Western medicine," Katz said. "And I really think that's why he's dead."

Around the bonfire that night, I could see Katz on the other side of the circle, holding hands with his neighbors. After eighteen years in the wilderness, he couldn't imagine moving back to New York City—a weekend there could still wear him out. Yet his mind had never entirely left the Upper West Side, and his voice, clipped and skeptical, was a welcome astringent here. After a while, a woman stepped into the firelight, dressed in a long white gown with a crown of vines and spring flowers in her hair. Beltane was a time of ancient ferment, she said, when the powers of the sky come down and the powers of the earth rise up to meet them. She took two goblets and carried them to opposite points in the circle. They were full of May wine steeped with sweet woodruff, once considered an aphrodisiac. On this night, by our own acts of love and procreation, we would remind the fields and crops to grow.

There was more along those lines, though I confess I didn't hear it. I was watching the kid to my left—a scruffy techno-peasant dressed in what looked like sackcloth and bark—take a swig of the wine. The goblets were moving clockwise around the circle, I'd noticed. By the time the other goblet reached me, thirty or forty people would have drunk from it.

I heard a throat being cleared somewhere in the crowd, and a cough quickly stifled. Embracing live cultures shouldn't mean sacrificing basic hygiene, Katz had told me that afternoon, after his sauerkraut seminar. "Part of respecting bacteria is recognizing where they can cause us problems." And so, when the kid had drunk his fill, I tapped his shoulder and asked for the goblet out of turn. I took a quick sip, sweet and bitter in equal measure. Then I watched as the wine made its way around the circle—teeming, as all things must, with an abundance of invisible life.

I Had a Farm in Atlanta

John T. Edge

The van is white, like all the others, with four rows of vinyl bench seats and door handles that rattle when we crest speed bumps or brake to stops alongside clutches of dumpsters overflowing with debris. Other vans, parked in the blacktop lots that encircle the Indian Valley apartment complex on the northwestern fringe of Atlanta, are taped with precise blue script. Chin Community Baptist Church drives a white van. So does Matupi Christian Church, and Georgia Chin Baptist Church. But this white van, packed with recent refugees from the East African nation of Burundi—driven by a one-time hospital chaplain who came to Atlanta to attend theology school—does not declare denomination or ethnicity. Nor does it telegraph the riot of colored garments worn by the women within, or the patchouli of sweet and dusky vapors that trail from the rear luggage hutch.

We turn into another two-story complex, Southern Place. With a clapboard-and-brick exterior, and a unit numbering system seemingly based on a long disproved algebraic theorem, it resembles the on-the-cheap developments that every other girl I dated after college lived in. Apropos of its setting, west of Stone Mountain, the granite monolith incised with portraits of our fallen Confederate heroes, the sign out front boasts a relief carving of a columned manse that, in the afternoon light, looks a lot like Tara.

■　■　■

Jeanne Niyibizi slides an aluminum pan, sloshing with roasted goat bathed in a brick-red sauce, into the luggage compartment. Hiking up her yellow-and-green batik dress, she vaults into the van, where Donate Nyiramanzi and seven other women—all wearing solar flare–bright garb, many packing stews of yellow peas with yucca or piles of bananas fried in palm oil—will chatter in

Kirundi, their native language, until we reach our destination, a fundraising dinner staged in the Tudor-styled home of Susan Pavlin, director of Global Growers Network, a three-year-old farm-focused nonprofit that serves these refugees and two-hundred-odd more. Before the night is out, I will eat six or eight ginger-stuffed dumplings called momo, made by Kesabi Timsina, a Bhutanese woman who farms an outparcel of land that fronts North DeKalb Mall. I will handle a market basket crafted of kudzu and wisteria by her father, Ram, who does his best work on the stoop of their butt-sprung, wood-framed apartment complex. And Global Growers will raise enough money to pay for a growing season's worth of transit passes for the men and women who benefit from their nascent farm and market initiatives.

At the close of the party, I will stand before the crowd to say that, at a time when every kid under thirty seems to preach the virtues of a farm-to-table lifestyle with an earnest, finger-wagging fervor that makes me want to reach for a bag of Flaming Cheetos and a Mountain Dew, I've glimpsed an urban gardening initiative that makes good on its promise of connecting real people with real food.

■　■　■

Semtok, a globular eggplant also known as bitter ball, is a hard sell, but occidental farmer's market devotees like me enjoy sour leaf, an herb in the hibiscus family also known as roselle. We also like mustard greens, and okra, so long as you pick the pods when they are still young and tender. Those are a few of the lessons the Burundi women have learned since 2010, when they began working a plot of soil they call Umurima Wa Burundi, the Burundi Women's Farm.

Working with Global Growers, a spin-off of the ten-year-old Decatur-based nonprofit Refugee Family Services, the Burundians have also learned survival skills like how to score a second-shift job in an upstate chicken plant, pulling viscera from feather-stripped carcasses. And how to navigate MARTA, a sprawling multimodal transportation system that Atlanta recidivists fought in the 1970s, labeling it, with an eerie sense of its present potential, Moving Africans Rapidly Through Atlanta.

Climatic complements, cultural ties, and transportation link the American South and Africa. Fittingly, Atlanta is now a beacon for African refugees, just as St. Louis hosts a significant population of Croatian refugees, who arrived to join earlier immigrants from the former Yugoslavia, and the foothills of North Carolina boast pockets of Hmong people accustomed to farming similarly hilly terrain. Resettlement agencies place three to five thousand refugees here each year, I learned over two days of bounding through Atlanta, visiting four farm sites managed in whole or supported in part by

Global Growers. About half of those refugees are children, who seem to live their lives in apartment complex parking lots, where they dodge cars while booting soccer balls.

■ ■ ■

Clarkston, near Stone Mountain, is a dizzyingly diverse place. A bungalow-and-strip-mall suburb, it's no longer the domain of the white, working-class factory workers who flocked here after World War II. Now, in one square mile, people from sixty different countries, speaking twenty-six different languages, live. And they garden.

Three blocks from what was once Clarkston High School and is now a community center that hosts citizenship clinics, contra dances, and tai chi classes, I walked, with two Global Growers employees, along a rock-strewn trail to the Clarkston International Garden. Chrissy Bracewell, wearing a hoodie and hiking boots, studied experiential education at Brevard College in North Carolina and now uses cloud-based mind-mapping tools to help refugee farmers plan for self-sufficiency. Basmat Ahmed, wrapped in a purple turban, is a Sudanese refugee who grew up in Egypt and now says things like, "We're growing the revolution" with a brightness that tells me she doesn't plan to overturn anything but topsoil.

Like all of the farms I visited, this is a squatter's plot, awaiting its true purpose. Twenty-six families from ten different cultures till this red clay half-acre tucked into the Forty Oaks Nature Preserve. Bhutanese work with Sudanese. Sri Lankans work beside Iraqis, who work beside Somalis. And so does a group of five blind and sight-deficient farmers who call themselves the Tactile Growers. In a garden where plots are often marked by bamboo trunk borders, the Tactile Growers stake their land with concrete blocks, which are easier to grapple in the dark.

The work of Global Growers relies on the buy-in of enlightened developers and engaged bureaucrats. A windmill-tilting nonprofit, operating on a $250,000 annual budget, can't afford to purchase land. With only two years of operations behind it, Global Growers has not yet built a base of donors who might bequeath land. So they squat, with permission.

The land they farm at Umurima in Decatur is owned by a mixed-use developer. Through the trees, beyond the patch where the Burundian women grow scimitar-shaped, crimson-colored okra, I spied a Jazzercise studio, part of a complex called East Decatur Station. Opposite, a veterinarian boards dogs that bay like their country cousins on a morning hunt. As the hounds reached for new octaves, and the traffic thrummed by, I listened to Venance Ndayiragije recount the losses that compelled his emigration: Two brothers. His mother and father. His grandfather. And three uncles. "My people are

Tutsi," he told me. "And they were Hutu," he said with a finality that brooked no explanation. As he toed the dirt, Venance looked up and smiled. "I have seven children here," he said in a mellifluous broken English that improved on the original. "I married my wife. We have lots of children, so that we forgot my family that died."

Before too long, these patches of red dirt will beget a brace of condominiums. Or a fast-casual restaurant. Or a twenty-four-hour oil-change drive-through. But for now, they're farms, tilled by people who farmed back in their homelands and arrived here in Atlanta full of hope that they might get to grow and harvest again.

■　■　■

Bamboo Creek, Global Growers' fourteen-acre training farm, tucked at the rear of a cul-de-sac in a Brady Bunch–era suburb of split-levels gone thoroughly multicultural, feels similarly liminal. To access the parcel, bisected by a stream, bordered by a thicket of bamboo, Global Growers leases the house. Use of the land, a former horse farm, comes free, so long as they keep the bamboo at bay. It's a sweetheart deal for a nonprofit that encourages its farmers to fashion trellising and fencing from bamboo. But it's temporary, like the plot set in the floodplain that girds North DeKalb Mall, where the Bhutanese family turns the dirt, and the plot behind the United Methodist Children's Home near Decatur, where Global Growers hosts more than thirty farmers from twelve different culture groups who use a keyline farming methodology, developed in Australia, to maximize water retention.

Walking the grounds of the former orphanage with Susan, we talked of Bhutanese refugees. "They're good stick-in-the-ground farmers," she said. We talked of the broader possibilities of raising goats, taking note of the recent explosion of interest in charcuterie and salumi and the prospects for refugee-produced cured goat-meat products that might or might not be saleable to mainstream American consumers. When we passed a wood-frame workshop, set at the fringe of the old orphanage, in sight of a lake ringed by a once vibrant apple orchard and blackberry bramble, I stopped to examine a pile of junk recently tossed into the weeds. Alongside a portable basketball goal, with a broken main shaft, and a ruined bassinet was a jumble of hand-painted signs. Susan said they had been cast aside after a recent theatrical re-creation of the Underground Railroad. I read them as a kind of roadmap for the future. One said Plantation. Another, painted with an arrow, pointed the way to freedom.

■　■　■

For the longest time, the South, famous for its magnolia-shaded verandas and dulcet hospitality, was, in practice, inhospitable to outsiders. Some of that was societal and purposeful. I'm thinking of the nativist movement, which gained gnarliest flower in the 1920s as the Klan rose again to prominence, burning crosses on Stone Mountain, among other places. Some of it was rooted in economic and political realities. Without manufacturing jobs to lure new immigrants, without unions to protect workers' rights, the South was a place that, when compared with the rest of the nation, did not draw newcomers into its orbit. Until the latter half of the twentieth century, the South pushed rather than pulled.

Across the twenty-first-century South, refugees now work community farms. Their narratives—of government-endorsed genocide, of families riven by petty bureaucrats and monetary market vagaries, of lives forever on the run—are exceptional. But their work is comparable to that of the brogan-shod men and women who have long cultivated Southern soil. In Houston, Congolese refugees and others raise radishes, greens, and more on plots secured by Plant It Forward Farms. In suburban New Orleans, Vietnamese levee- and terrace-croppers began farming Gulf Coast lowlands in the 1970s, soon after Saigon fell to the North Vietnamese. Meanwhile, in metropolitan Atlanta, Global Growers has begun a CSA program, in which the Burundian women grow food to share and barter among themselves—and also to sell, through seasonal subscriptions, to pasty white people like me.

My visit coincided with the last harvest of the fall season. Like any good nonprofit administrator, Susan was circumspect about whether the CSA had really worked for the women. Was it merely a grafting of an American ideal? Did it serve the women and their communities or model current Western notions of what progressive agriculture should look like? Susan wants to get it right. And so do all the women who work with Global Growers, from Karen Mann, the lapsed divinity student, to Basmat the Sudanese refugee.

A few years ago, a student from Arkansas enrolled in graduate school at the Center for the Study of Southern Culture, at the University of Mississippi, where I work. He had some experience running a community garden and wanted to apply that work to his studies. For a while, with a little funding from the nonprofit I direct, he ran a community garden at the Boys and Girls Club in Oxford. One afternoon, I talked with a couple of colleagues about his progress and the prospects for a CSA in Oxford. (Three CSAs now operate in the area; at that time there were none.) We talked about the usual stuff: Would the work continue after the student graduated? If the project was successful, where could we source additional funds for expansion? I used the term CSA twice when talking about the possibilities. One colleague nodded. The other, a historian, arched an eyebrow. After I explained that the term referred to community-supported agriculture, he told me that years of graduate history education had conditioned him to think of the Confederate States of America when he heard that acronym. Knowing my intolerance for neo-Confederate bluster, he was surprised to hear me speak of the possibilities of a CSA in twenty-first-century Mississippi. That exchange, it now seems to me, signals the potential and progress now manifest in the work of Global Growers.

The Price of Tomatoes

Barry Estabrook

Driving from Naples, Florida, the nation's second-wealthiest metropolitan area, to Immokalee takes less than an hour on a straight road. You pass houses that sell for an average of $1.4 million, shopping malls anchored by Tiffany's and Saks Fifth Avenue, manicured golf courses. Eventually, gated communities with names like Monaco Beach Club and Imperial Golf Estates give way to modest ranches, and the highway shrivels from six lanes to two. Through the scruffy palmettos, you glimpse flat, sandy tomato fields shimmering in the broiling sun. Rounding a long curve, you enter Immokalee. The heart of town is a nine-block grid of dusty, potholed streets lined by boarded-up bars and bodegas, peeling shacks, and sagging, mildew-streaked house trailers. Mongrel dogs snooze in the shade, scrawny chickens peck in yards. Just off the main drag, vultures squabble over roadkill. Immokalee's population is 70 percent Latino. Per capita income is only $8,500 a year. One-third of the families in this city of nearly twenty-five thousand live below the poverty line. Over one-third of the children drop out before graduating from high school.

Immokalee is the tomato capital of the United States. Between December and May, as much as 90 percent of the fresh domestic tomatoes we eat come from South Florida, and Immokalee is home to one of the area's largest communities of farmworkers. According to Douglas Molloy, the chief assistant U.S. attorney based in Fort Myers, Immokalee has another claim to fame: it is "ground zero for modern slavery."

The beige stucco house at 209 South Seventh Street is remarkable only because it is in better repair than most Immokalee dwellings. For two and a half years, beginning in April 2005, Mariano Lucas Domingo, along with several other men, was held as a slave at that address. At first, the deal must have seemed reasonable. Lucas, a Guatemalan in his thirties, had slipped across the border to make money to send home for the care of an ailing parent. He expected to earn about $200 a week in the fields. Cesar Navarrete, then a twenty-three-year-old illegal immigrant from Mexico, agreed to provide room and board at his family's home on South Seventh Street and extend credit to cover the periods when there were no tomatoes to pick.

Lucas's "room" turned out to be the back of a box truck in the junk-strewn yard, shared with two or three other workers. It lacked running water and a toilet, so occupants urinated and defecated in a corner. For that, Navarrete docked Lucas's pay by $20 a week. According to court papers, he also charged Lucas for two meager meals a day: eggs, beans, rice, tortillas, and, occasionally, some sort of meat. Cold showers from a garden hose in the backyard were $5 each. Everything had a price. Lucas was soon $300 in debt. After a month of ten-hour workdays, he figured he should have paid that debt off.

But when Lucas—slightly built and standing less than five and a half feet tall—inquired about the balance, Navarrete threatened to beat him should he ever try to leave. Instead of providing an accounting, Navarrete took Lucas's paychecks, cashed them, and randomly doled out pocket money, $20 some weeks, other weeks $50. Over the years, Navarrete and members of his extended family deprived Lucas of $55,000.

Taking a day off was not an option. If Lucas became ill or was too exhausted to work, he was kicked in the head, beaten, and locked in the back of the truck. Other members of Navarrete's dozen-man crew were slashed with knives, tied to posts, and shackled in chains. On November 18, 2007, Lucas was again locked inside the truck. As dawn broke, he noticed a faint light shining through a hole in the roof. Jumping up, he secured a handhold and punched himself through. He was free.

What happened at Navarrete's home would have been horrific enough if it were an isolated case. Unfortunately, involuntary servitude—slavery—is alive and well in Florida. Since 1997, law-enforcement officials have freed more than one thousand men and women in seven different cases. And those are only the instances that resulted in convictions. Frightened, undocumented, mistrustful of the police, and speaking little or no English, most slaves refuse to testify, which means their captors cannot be tried. "Unlike victims of other crimes, slaves don't report themselves," said Molloy, who was one of the prosecutors on the Navarrete case. "They hide from us in plain sight."

And for what? Supermarket produce sections overflow with bins of perfect red-orange tomatoes even during the coldest months—never mind that they are all but tasteless. Large packers, which ship nearly $500 million worth of tomatoes annually to major restaurants and grocery retailers nationwide, own or lease the land upon which the workers toil. But the harvesting is often done by independent contractors called crew bosses, who bear responsibility for hiring and overseeing pickers. Said Reggie Brown, executive vice president of the Florida Tomato Growers Exchange, "We abhor slavery and do everything we can to prevent it. We want to make sure that we always foster a work environment free from hazard, intimidation, harassment, and violence." Growers, he said, cooperated with law-enforcement officers in the Navarrete case.

But when asked if it is reasonable to assume that an American who has eaten a fresh tomato from a grocery store or food-service company during the winter has eaten fruit picked by the hand of a slave, Molloy said, "It is not an assumption. It is a fact."

Gerardo Reyes, a former picker who is now an employee of the Coalition of Immokalee Workers (CIW), a four-thousand-member organization that provides the only voice for the field hands, agrees. Far from being an anomaly, Reyes told me, slavery is a symptom of a vast system of labor abuses. Involuntary servitude represents just one rung on a grim ladder of exploitation. Reyes said that the victims of this system come to Florida for one reason—to send money to their families back home. "But when they get here, it's all they can do to keep themselves alive with rent, transportation, food. Poverty and misery are the perfect recipe for slavery."

Tomato harvesting involves rummaging through staked vines until you have filled a bushel basket to the brim with hard, green fruits. You hoist the basket over your shoulder, trot across the field, and heave it overhead to a worker in an open trailer the size of the bed of a gravel truck. For every thirty-two-pound basket you pick, you receive a token typically worth about forty-five cents—almost the same rate you would have gotten thirty years ago. Working at breakneck speed, you might be able to pick a ton of tomatoes on a good day, netting about $50. But a lot can go wrong. If it rains, you can't pick. If the dew is heavy, you sit and wait until it evaporates. If trucks aren't available to transport the harvest, you're out of luck. You receive neither overtime nor benefits. If you are injured (a common occurrence, given the pace of the job), you have to pay for your own medical care.

Leaning against the railing of an unpainted wooden stoop in front of a putty-colored trailer, a tired Juan Dominguez told an all-too-familiar story. He had left for the fields that morning at 6 o'clock and returned at three. But he worked for only two of those nine hours because the seedlings he was to plant had been delivered late. His total earnings: $13.76.

I asked him for a look inside his home. He shrugged and gestured for me to come in. In one ten-foot-square space there were five mattresses, three directly on the floor, two suspended above on sheets of flimsy plywood. The room was littered with T-shirts, jeans, running shoes, cheap suitcases. The kitchen consisted of a table, four plastic chairs, an apartment-size stove, a sink with a dripping faucet, and a rusty refrigerator whose door wouldn't close. Bare lightbulbs hung from fixtures, and a couple of fans put up a noisy, futile effort against the stale heat and humidity. In a region where temperatures regularly climb into the nineties, there were no air conditioners. One tiny, dank bathroom served ten men. The rent was $2,000 a month—as much as you would pay for a clean little condo near Naples.

Most tomato workers, however, have no choice but to live like Dominguez. Lacking vehicles, they must reside within walking distance of the football-field-size parking lot in front of La Fiesta, a combination grocery store, taqueria, and check-cashing office. During the predawn hours, the lot hosts a daily hiring fair. I arrived a little before 5 a.m. The parking lot was filled with more than a dozen former school buses. Outside each bus stood a silent scrum of forty or fifty would-be pickers. The driver, or crew boss, selected one worker at a time, choosing young, fit-looking men first. Once full, the bus pulled away.

Later that day, I encountered some of the men and women who had not been picked when I put in a shift at the Guadalupe Center of Immokalee's soup kitchen. Tricia Yeggy, the director of the kitchen, explained that it runs on two simple rules: people can eat as much as they want, and no one is turned away hungry. This means serving between 250 and 300 people a day, 44 per sitting, beginning at 11 o'clock. Cheerful retirees volunteer as servers, and the "guests" are unabashedly appreciative. The day's selection—turkey and rice soup with squash, corn, and a vigorous sprinkle of cumin—was both hearty and tasty. You could almost forget the irony: workers who pick the food we eat can't afford to feed themselves.

The CIW has been working to ease the migrants' plight since 1993, when a few field hands began meeting sporadically in a church hall. Lucas Benitez, one of the coalition's main spokespeople, came to the group in its early years. Back then, the challenge was taking small steps, often for individual workers. To make the point, Benitez unfolded a crumpled shirt covered in dried blood. "This is Edgar's shirt," he said.

One day in 1996, a sixteen-year-old Guatemalan boy named Edgar briefly stopped working in the field for a drink of water. His crew boss bludgeoned him. Edgar fled and arrived at the coalition's door, bleeding. In response to the CIW's call for action, over five hundred workers assembled and marched to the boss's house. The next morning, no one would get on his bus. "That was the last report of a worker being beaten by his boss in the field," said Benitez. The shirt is kept as a reminder that by banding together, progress is possible.

Even though the CIW has been responsible for bringing police attention to a half dozen slavery prosecutions, Benitez feels that slavery will persist until overall conditions for field workers improve. The group has made progress on that front by securing better pay. Between the early 1980s and the mid-1990s, the rate for a basket of tomatoes remained forty cents—meaning that workers' real wages dropped as inflation rose. Work stoppages, demonstrations, and a hunger strike helped raise it to forty-five cents on average, but the packers complained that competition for customers prevented them from paying more. One grower refused to enter a dialogue with CIW hunger strikers because, in his words, "a tractor doesn't tell the farmer how to run the farm." The CIW decided to try an end run around the growers by going directly to the biggest customers and asking them to pay one cent more per pound directly to the workers. Small change to supermarket chains and fast-food corporations, but it would add about $20 to the $50 a picker makes on a good day, the difference between barely scraping by and earning a livable wage.

The Campaign for Fair Food, as it is called, first took aim at Yum! Brands, owner of Taco Bell, Pizza Hut, KFC, Long John Silver's, and A&W. After four years of pressure, Yum! agreed to the one-cent raise in 2005 and, importantly, pledged to make sure that no worker who picked its tomatoes was being exploited. McDonald's came on board in 2007, and in 2008 Burger King, Whole Foods Market, and Subway followed, with more expected to join up this year. But the program faces a major obstacle. Claiming that the farmers are not party to the arrangement, the Florida Tomato Growers Exchange, an agricultural cooperative that represents some 90 percent of the state's producers, has refused to be a conduit for the raise, citing legal concerns.

When the Navarrete case came to light, there were no howls of outrage from growers. Or from Florida government circles. When Cesar Navarrete, who pleaded guilty, was sentenced to twelve years in prison this past December, Terence McElroy of the Florida Department of Agriculture and Consumer Services offered his perspective on the crime: "Any legitimate grower certainly does not engage in that activity. But you're talking about maybe a case a year."

Charlie Frost, the Collier County Sheriff's Office detective who investigated and arrested Navarrete, disagrees. With one case wrapped up, he and prosecutor Molloy turned to several other active slavery cases. Sitting in his Naples office and pointing his index finger east, toward the fields of Immokalee, he said, "It's happening out there right now."

Lucas, who received a temporary visa for his testimony, is now back in the fields, still chasing the dream of making a little money to send back home.

Working in the Shadows

Gabriel Thompson

Early the next morning I drop off my application with the guard and head into the city of Decatur[, Alabama], fifty miles east, to check out another poultry plant, this one owned by Wayne Farms. I'm less interested in this plant as I would prefer a completely rural experience, but since I'll be giving up my rental car soon—I have enough funds to cover only a week's use, after which I'll be relying on my bike for transportation—I want to make certain I explore every option.

The Wayne Farms plant is in an industrial area crowded with big rigs. The plant is surrounded by a high fence, and next to the security booth is a large sign that reads: Our Team Has Worked 934,380 Hours Without a Lost Time Accident. This is meant to be a statement of pride and integrity, but to me it raises questions about creative record keeping. Nearly one million hours of repetitive work with sharp knives, and not a single employee has suffered an accident causing them to miss a shift?

Inside the office my luck doesn't improve. "We don't have any jobs right now," a woman in human resources tells me. "But we'll keep your application on file." I walk out the door increasingly convinced this experiment is destined for failure. The only other poultry plant I know of is more than a hundred miles away.

Heading back to my car I pass three African American men seated at a picnic table wearing blue hairnets. "The woman in the office told me the plant is full," I say. "If I come back in a few days, do you think I'll get hired? Do people quit a lot?"

The man sitting nearest to me takes a long drag on his cigarette. "Sheeyiit," he says in a five-second exhalation of smoke. "Two people just quit. They're laying down over there right now." He points across the parking lot. Two men are stretched out on the ground next to an old sedan in the shade provided by a row of trees. "They had the easiest job in the plant, not doing nothing but mopping up the damn floor. They walked out an hour ago, rather be taking a nap enjoying the day." He flicks his cigarette. "You come on back, you'll get yourself a job."

I look again at the two figures. One is lying on his back with his arms and legs spread out, as if frozen in the act of making a snow angel. The other is facedown, with his right cheek pressed hard against the gravel. They don't look like they're taking a nap—they look like someone dropped a bowling ball on their heads. I thank the men and head out.

Not yet ready to stare at the walls of my motel room, I decide to swing by the Russellville[, Alabama,] plant again. This time, coming from a different direction, I notice a small white building at a quiet intersection not far from the highway. A faded sign reads: Mama's Kitchen Country Cookin. Painted in yellow across the window are various specials, including *huevos rancheros* and *ricos tacos de tripe y lengua* (tasty tripe and tongue tacos). Looks like Mama's been changing up her country cookin'.

I step into a bazaar of Latino products ranging from Mexican soccer jerseys and Lucha Libre masks to Guatemalan flags and international calling cards. As I sit down an attractive woman with fair skin steps out, smiling politely. I explain in Spanish that I'm looking for a place to stay for a few months. She looks at me with undisguised curiosity and takes a seat across the table. For twenty minutes I answer her skeptical questions—What am I doing here? Where did I learn Spanish? Why do I want to work in the plant?—but we finally find common ground when I learn that Sabrina is from the Mexican state of Guerrero, which I've visited.

"Before I opened this restaurant I worked in *la pollera* for two years," she says, referring to the plant. "I don't know why you would want to work there."

■   ■   ■

Pilgrim's Pride hires me the next day. "Your app looks great," a blond-haired woman in human resources tells me, struggling to hide a yawn. "It shows that you are very patient and don't mind doing hard work." I assume the hard work comment relates to my lettuce cutting. I'm not sure how she determines I'm patient, but I'm glad she thinks so. During the thirty-minute interview she never asks me how I ended up in Russellville, even when I hand over my New York driver's license. They need workers, I can work: end of story.

There are three different shifts at the plant. The first shift is from 8:00 a.m. to 5:00 p.m.; second shift, which follows immediately after, is sanitation. "During sanitation we have workers come in and take everything apart and hose it down with bleach and chemicals," she says. After sanitation is the third shift, which begins at 11:00 p.m. and concludes at 8:00 a.m. the next morning. "All we have right now are jobs in the third shift."

She has several positions that she thinks I would enjoy. All of them pay $8.05 an hour, but if I arrive on time every day, I'll earn $8.80 an hour for the week. After sixty days the base rate will increase to $8.80, with the perfect attendance bonus reaching $9.45. If an employee makes it to the year mark, he will earn $8.95 an hour with a bonus of $9.70. The various numbers can make it seem complicated, but the basic truth is this: You could work at the plant for ten years, without missing a minute of a single shift, and never see your wage reach $10 an hour. (The one exception is a job in "live hang and killing," where workers are paid extra because they are in a department that is called *live hang and killing*. Their pay scale maxes out at $10.75 an hour. "We don't have any openings in that," she tells me. Not a problem, I assure her.)

There are jobs available in packing chicken into boxes, loading boxes onto trucks, or adding marinades to chicken in the "further-processing" department. What I want, though, is a line job in debone. Artemio, originally from Mexico, briefly worked in a Georgia poultry plant, and told me that all of the debone workers were immigrants, while the few American citizens were supervisors or performed less strenuous jobs.

"You said something about debone, right?"

"Yes, we have that too. Now, deboning is just what it sounds like. Each person has a place on the line and makes a certain cut. The chicken just sits there, stuck on a cone, passing by like this." She sticks out her tongue and smiles, apparently doing her dead-chicken-on-a-cone impression.

"After cutting lettuce, my back could really use a break, so I'd rather not be loading anything. If it's open, I think I'll go with debone."

"Because your application is so strong, I'm going to offer you the job right now," she says, handing me papers to sign while explaining the attendance policy. Pilgrim's Pride doesn't have sick days or personal days. Instead, employees accumulate points based on days missed: Every time we are absent for an entire shift, we are given one point; if we leave early or arrive late, we earn half a point. A point is erased six months from the date it is issued, and if we accumulate more than seven points we're fired. Seems simple enough.

"You'll be working Sunday through Thursday nights, but you first have to take an orientation class. You should show up Thursday for orientation, and then you'll begin Sunday night. Just one more thing before we're all set. It looks like your Social Security card was issued in Oregon. Can you tell me why you don't have a work history there?"

"We moved when I was in preschool."

She smiles and writes something down. "Sorry, we just have to ask. Homeland Security is really cracking down. They want to know about things like that."

At the nurse's station I pee into a cup and blow into a Breathalyzer. Since I don't do drugs and managed to come to the interview sober, I've cleared the last hurdle. I've got a new job.

■   ■   ■

"Klan Takes to City Streets," proclaimed the newspaper headline. Fifty people marched through downtown to arrive at the courthouse steps, a handful of them wearing white, red, and green robes. Eventually a crowd of about 300 gathered to listen to folks like "Brother Billy," a Klan leader from Birmingham. "This is our nation," Billy argued. "If they don't like our laws, they can leave. America was founded as a Christian nation by a Christian race, not a mud race."

Also on hand was Imperial Wizard Ray Larsen of South Bend, Indiana, who hoped that the growing anger over immigration would serve as a recruitment mechanism for the Klan. Larsen added a touch of levity to the occasion when he tried to find common cause with the very "mud race" the KKK had once lynched. After stating that illegal immigrants stole American jobs, he added, "And I'm talking about blacks and whites. They want you out of here because they want this as their land." One hopes he at least took off his hood to deliver this message of unity.

John Hicks was reporting at the rally. "The mood in the crowd was one of curiosity," he tells me in his office in downtown Russellville. "As far as I could tell, none of the people who spoke were locals." While people in robes with ridiculous pseudonyms complained about a mud race, several dozen counterprotesters held signs with messages like "All One People" and "Free Your Mind." And when speakers on the steps shouted, "White power!" at the crowd, a few African Americans shouted back, "Black power!" Television cameras and journalists from across the state were on hand to record every moment. As the *Franklin County Times* editorialized, "We're sure the pictures from that event will look nice on the next 'Welcome to Russellville' brochure."

"It was like they were watching a freak show," says Hicks, referring to the crowd. Still, despite the circuslike atmosphere, a fair number of the onlookers applauded the Klan's anti-immigrant message.

Spring 2006 marked the moment when many Americans woke up to the rapidly changing demographics of our country. In large cities the number of marchers was overwhelming; but in small anonymous towns like Russellville, the impact was more profound. After fifteen years of silence, immigrants gathered hundreds strong to demand respect and an acknowledgment of their labor. Some whites who before might have only muttered under their breath about the "illegal invasion" were now certain that the time had come to "take America back." And when the KKK arrived, it found—for once—an audience containing more supporters than protesters. In Russellville it seemed like much more conflict was assured, and that violence wasn't out of the question.

Instead, after the departure of the KKK, is seems like life went back to normal. Two years later, as I wandered around town, I certainly didn't see or hear anything to suggest relations between immigrants and locals were threatening to boil over. Occasionally I would pick up on a whispered comment like "illegals are everywhere" or, when walking down supermarket aisles, something about the injustice of bilingual labels. But this is hardly unique territory: I've heard such comments in all sorts of places. And when I gently raised the subject of immigrants in town—by telling a cashier, for example, that I was surprised that so many immigrants were employed at the plant—the reaction was always the same. "That's because they'll do the jobs we don't want. You would never catch me inside that plant."

Schools are often a flashpoint of anger and tension, but in Russellville the dramatic growth of Latino students seems to have been taken in stride. "In 1991, we had three Hispanic students in the entire district," says George Harper, who is in charge of special education and English learning programs. Today, of the 2,500 students, 31 percent are Latino. At lower grades, that percentage is even higher: 42 percent of the 2009 kindergarten class was Spanish speaking. But what is most remarkable is how quickly Latino students adapt. By fifth grade, Latino students are at the same level as whites and blacks in reading, writing, and math. "I don't know if they're legal or illegal," says Harper, who oversees a staff of bilingual parent liaisons and has hired several bilingual teachers. "What I know is that we're going to educate these children, because if we don't we're going to pay for it down the road. Some school systems discourage their immigrant parents and children from coming to them; others open their arms to students. We've tried to be one of the latter."

When I asked my immigrant coworkers if they had ever experienced racism, no one had any particular anecdotes. "I have never had a problem here," Mario told me. I asked him if people had called him names or in some way made him feel unwelcome, but again he shook his head. "Everything is very calm here, especially compared to Los Angeles." Jesús, too, didn't seem to have had any problem settling in. When I sit with groups of immigrants from other departments during breaks, I don't hear any horror stories. If anything, people don't pay enough attention to them to say anything racist. They are allowed to go about their lives in peace.

I should underscore the limited nature of my exploration of racism. I bopped around town and tried to gauge local feelings, but it was a highly unscientific endeavor. Most of my waking hours were spent in the plant. It is also quite possible that immigrants didn't feel comfortable divulging stories to me; it is undoubtedly true that I got to know only perhaps two dozen people. For all I know, hundreds of immigrants have faced insults and felt targeted while going about their business in town.

But what I can report with more confidence is the surprising lack of tension between Americans—both black and white—and immigrants at the plant itself. Each group makes up about one-third of the workforce; the whites and Latinos are more likely to live nearby, while the African Americans tend to make the thirty-minute drive south from "the Shoals," an area that includes the towns of Florence, Muscle Shoals, Tuscumbia, and Sheffield, with a total population of about 150,000. Compared to Russellville, the Shoals is lively and cosmopolitan: It has music festivals, a Renaissance faire, a major school in the University of North Alabama, and laws that allow for the sale of alcohol. Early on, I asked one of my black coworkers if she was from Russellville, and she looked at me as if I were insane. "I've never even *stopped* in Russellville," she said. (Indeed, I never met a black worker from Russellville—nor did I see many around town—which was odd since they make up more than 10 percent of the city's population.)

During breaks most workers sat in self-segregated groups, but there was enough mixing that no one, for example, thought it particularly strange that I often sat with Guatemalans (although people did think it odd I spoke Spanish). Folks stopped by booths to banter and share snacks and bitch, and on the processing floor there was plenty of friendly, if sometimes confused, interaction. Two of the African American women in DSI, when they helped Mario and Jesús tear chicken breasts, asked questions about Guatemala, and while dumping tubs I served as translator. Men taught each other curse words in the other's language, and I even knew of a few cross-cultural relationships that had developed at the plant—each between a Guatemalan man and a white woman.

But the formation of deep relationships was rare: Language created a real barrier, and most folks didn't stick around long enough. What was more common was simple curiosity: My American-born coworkers wanted to know who these people were. It felt like a junior high class reacting to the arrival of a foreign student from an unknown country. I got the sense that Ben, for example, had never actually been in the same room as someone who didn't speak English. He was amazed by how short the Mexicans were. After

I explained that the "Mexicans" were actually from Guatemala, he wanted to know if all Guatemalans were so short.

"Maybe not all," I told him, "but most of them are pretty short."

"Someday I'm going to travel to Guatemala just so I can walk around and feel tall," he said, giggling. "I like feeling tall. And maybe I'll learn Spanish." This was an admittedly silly comment: It's not the sort of evidence one would point to in developing a sophisticated analysis of relations toward immigrants in the American South. But it was the sort of question I heard people, black and white, wonder amongst themselves. Why were they short? How did they get so strong? Where did they come from, exactly? They were very basic questions, very human questions, and they lacked hostility.

I had expected to find more anger. One of the most common complaints, after all, is that immigrants are taking jobs meant for Americans. In Russellville the main source of jobs is the poultry plant. But no American laboring within the four walls of the plant felt that his or her job was in danger of being "stolen." The jobs at the plant come easy: I was hired within a week. It is surviving the work that is hard. People lose their jobs at the plant because they quit, not because an immigrant takes their position.

The Celebrity Shepherd

Besha Rodell

My flight from Atlanta to Los Angeles is boarding in fifteen minutes, but I answer the call. "Besha!" Craig Rogers' voice comes through the line, loud and smiling. "How are you, dear? It's your own personal shepherd!"

"Your own personal shepherd" is a term Craig Rogers uses a lot, and he has become the personal shepherd to enough chefs up and down the East Coast, and particularly throughout the South, that he's now one of the best-known farmers in the country. It's a distinction that's at once impressive and inconsequential—the farmer-as-celebrity pool is awfully small.

He asks how I'm doing and I tell him I'm anxious. "I'm on my way to L.A. for a job interview," I say.

"Well . . .," he says, searching for an appropriate response. "We'd sure miss you in the South."

Then he launches into the reason he's called. He's looking for an Atlanta location for his "Lambs and Clams" party, an impromptu-feeling gathering he held with Travis Croxton of Rappahannock River Oysters after the Charleston Food & Wine Festival. In Charleston, a party at midnight off the back of a truck down near the water was charming, and many of the chefs and food personalities associated with the festival showed up to eat lamb and clams and drink from the mason jar Rogers passed around. I can't see a similar party working quite so well in downtown Atlanta, but Rogers is undeterred.

He also wants to tell me about some farmers he knows who were selling milk to a large cheese producer but were never paid. Legal action has begun. "But I'm thinking the best way for this to come to a resolution," Rogers says to me as the boarding process begins, "is for there to be some media attention." I tell him I think he's right, although I don't know who exactly would want to print a story about a legal dispute among sheep farmers.

"I just think that with all the love and feel-good stuff people are always talking about when it comes to small farmers," he says, getting worked up, "people also ought to know the flip side. It's hard to be out here on your own. People think of farmers and they think of sunshine and planting seeds and all that, but this is a business, and we get ripped off. I just think people ought to hear about that as well."

■　■　■

Three months later, I'm riding on the back of a golf cart that Rogers is driving. I'm holding a PBR and we're careening through the pasture of his stunningly beautiful southern Virginia farm. "Look down," he says. "Now say something nice about my grass."

"Nice grass," I say, and I mean it. It's been a good year, weather-wise, here in Patrick Springs, Virginia. In the foothills of the mountains the grass underneath us is thick and, to me, the color of heaven. This is my first trip back to the South since moving to L.A., and what I don't say to Rogers is that all this green, all that vivid life-giving grass, is making me feel as though my heart might burst.

L.A. is nice. But it is not very green.

The softly tumbling hills of the pasture are dotted with tents. In the distance, the Blue Ridge Mountains rise, living up to their name in a blue-gray haze. Rogers owns one hundred acres, but he farms close to one thousand. Unlike many other meat farmers who have become semi-celebrities in the food world, Rogers does not sell meat produced on farms outside his own.

This is no ordinary day at the farm—it's the first day of Lambstock, Rogers's annual party for chefs and "friends of the farm," a three-day bacchanal that's achieved legendary status in the restaurant industry. Those tents in the field belong mainly to chefs and cooks, some of whom have traveled thousands of miles to spend a few days camped in Rogers's sheep pasture.

I first heard about Lambstock from Mike Lata, the James Beard Award–winning chef from Charleston. "It's this party in a field," he said, swirling whisky in his glass on the back landing of an Atlanta restaurant, "for chefs and cooks. We just get together and drink and cook and get to be ourselves. There's no media there, just a bunch of guys hanging out. It's so awesome."

Rogers conceived of Lambstock as a thank-you to the industry that supports him, and 2012 was the third year of what Rogers calls "a party in my backyard."

"These guys work so hard," he says, speaking of the chefs and cooks he supplies. "I wanted to give them a few days where they could just relax and be themselves." That theme—be yourself—comes up a lot when people talk about Lambstock. These days, well-known chefs see a lot of each other at events and food festivals around the country, but there's a sense that because of the public and media, chefs have to constantly be "on," the face of their restaurants, salesmen for their cookbooks. Lambstock is a place where they can just come and hang out and have fun, drink, build fires, swear, and cook for each other.

In previous years, Rogers has been protective of Lambstock—in 2011, a large sign was posted at the welcoming table in his driveway declaring that no tweets or articles were allowed without Rogers's express permission. In 2012, he gave all that up, and as a result there was much more media attention given to Lambstock, including a fawning blog post on the *New York Times* dining blog. "I was trying to protect Lambstock in the past," Rogers says. "I wanted the chefs to feel that they could come here and not be scrutinized. But they themselves were telling everyone what was happening here, so I thought 'why bother?'" But still, Lambstock remains a party for the chefs, not an event for the public. It isn't about promotion. Except, of course, for Craig Rogers.

■　　■　　■

At festivals, Rogers is a striking figure, six foot one, rotund in overalls, wearing a wide-brimmed hat, carrying a shepherd's crook, and usually standing beside one of his lambs roasting on a spit. He would be almost comical if he weren't so endearing and passionate. Rogers is fond of saying, "I'm just a simple shepherd," but of course this is a lie. He's as complex as they come.

Rogers was born in Vermont and had a great-aunt who was a dairy farmer, but that was the extent of his agrarian background. His original career was in academics—he has a Ph.D. in chemical engineering from Virginia Tech, and was the dean of the College of Engineering at the University of South Carolina. Google Rogers with the right search terms and you'll come across reports of research he championed to reduce helicopter noise and how, in the '80s, he established something called the Smart Materials and Structures Laboratory. He says he and his wife were looking for a retirement farm when they saw a sheepdog trial on campus. "I thought it was the most amazing thing."

They bought the farm in 2002 and got into competitive sheepdog trials. "I noticed early on that the guy with the most sheep usually won. So I became a bit of a sheep herder. It got to the point where eventually I had to find something to do with them."

Having traveled and dined quite a bit in his academic life, Rogers had always loved lamb. The first lamb he slaughtered, he says, "was the most horrific piece of meat I had ever had." So he started researching breeds, trying to find out which lamb would taste the best. "I set out to find something I would enjoy. It didn't have much to do with chefs."

Once he finally got his lamb tasting the way he wanted it to, he tried to find a chef who might appreciate it. "I got it in my head that Bryan Voltaggio was the guy," he says. It turns out he was right. Voltaggio introduced him to some other chefs, who introduced him to chefs in Charleston, who introduced him to Sean Brock, the chef at Charleston's McCrady's and one of the most feverishly adored young chefs in the country in recent years. "And for me, Sean Brock was like the parting of the Red Sea."

Rogers has figured out what many farmers have yet to turn to their advantage: that America is preoccupied not just with food but with chef culture. Also unlike many other farmers, Rogers has learned to sell his own product. That sense of salesmanship has him befriending and selling directly to chefs, as well as working hard to get his name out there and promote his sheep farm, Border Springs, as a brand. He attends festivals, makes connections with journalists and food celebrities, throws parties, and is generally everywhere all the time. He stands as a symbol of the changing nature of farming, where farmers come out of the field and smack into the middle of our food-obsessed culture.

And he has no signs of slowing: he was recently part of a dinner at the James Beard house, an honor usually bestowed only on chefs or restaurateurs, not producers. He has hired executive chefs to help him build "lamb shops" in historic markets in D.C. and Philadelphia, next-generation butcher counters where meat from his farm is for sale alongside chef-driven to-go items. "People don't know what to do with lamb," he says. "You have to show them." (He's long been part of local farmers' markets all over the South, usually traveling thousands of miles in a week to get from market to market—my mother has run across him on Saturday morning in Winston-Salem, North Carolina, on the same weekend he's been spotted by friends in D.C. and Baltimore.)

Besides being everywhere and knowing everyone, he is now contemplating jumping into the restaurant business itself. A possible concept, location, and business partners for a small restaurant in the D.C. area have arisen, and Rogers says he's "considering the possibilities."

People's reactions in the food community to Rogers's name vary from extreme affection to weary eye-rolls. "Why does he have to be at every damn thing?" one chef said to me recently. "It's just too much." There's an irony here, that the people I've come across who distrust Rogers's affection for attention are chefs—folks who have only very recently begun to enjoy the spoils of fame from what has traditionally been a blue-collar profession. The problem with Rogers's approach, as I see it, is that he's too straightforward about his quest for notoriety. In the too-cool-for-school world of chefdom, this is off-putting.

Rogers bristles at the notion that he's "everywhere," as more than one person has put it to me, or that he's too much of a self-promoter. Sitting in a field surrounded by sheep, it's hard to see him as anything but a guy trying to build a successful business. "Once people come out here to the farm, I stop getting calls from their restaurants asking for the shipping department," he says, alluding to the fact that *he's* the shipping, marketing, sales, and lamb-birthing department. "I want these guys to see where their food comes from. I'm asking people to come enjoy my hospitality. I'm inviting you to a party in my backyard. Lambstock is about community, not self-promotion."

■ ■ ■

On my last night in Atlanta before moving to Los Angeles, I attended a dinner that was part of the Atlanta Food & Wine Festival. It was held at a mansion in one of the city's wealthiest neighborhoods, and as I pulled up the circular driveway I saw an odd sight. On the perfect green lawn in front of the castle-like house, a makeshift pen with six or seven sheep was set up. Rogers was standing beside them in full Scottish shepherd regalia: kilt, jacket, hat, and shepherd's crook.

Like so many culinary extravaganzas these days, the dinner was supposed to honor the farmers and producers who make all our fancy eating possible, or so goes the farm-to-table mantra. At the end of the multicourse, boozy meal, which took place under twinkling lights in the mansion's manicured jewel box of a garden, Rogers was invited to say a few words. He stood tall in his kilt, and in front of two hundred or so of Atlanta's (very tipsy) 1 percent, he launched into a twenty-minute lecture on the history and misunderstanding of the shepherd.

He's talking about Thomas Jefferson (who brought the first merino sheep to the United States). He's talking about slaves (who looked after Jefferson's sheep and moved out west during emancipation). He's talking about the birth of Christ. "And when the angels came to the shepherds in the pastures to announce the coming of Christ to indicate that this was the good news for everyone, they were referred to as *mere* sheep herders!" Rogers is fired up. I don't think many of us know what the hell he's talking about.

At Lambstock, I ask him why he thought it was important to stand up in front of all those people and try to explain to them the struggle of the shepherd. He sighs. "Look, here's the thing with the shepherd shtick," he says. "Even today, shepherds out west do not wish to be called shepherds, it's such a derogatory term. It's always been the disenfranchised who end up doing the shepherding work. We've never had the romance of cowboys. If anyone were to actually take a look at the history of shepherding, and how horrible humankind had been to a single profession, and it's generally because it's been a profession of the displaced. So if you could learn somehow to create respect for shepherds then you could create respect for anyone. Cowboys have a voice. I don't know who's the voice for the shepherd. And I just think it's an incredibly honorable profession. So if a bunch of rich people are going to eat my lamb and then offer me the stage? That's what they're going to hear."

■ ■ ■

When you arrive at Lambstock and drive down the long, shady driveway of Border Springs Farm, one of Rogers's "volunteers" meets you with a golf cart to help transport your tent and belongings out to the field. Apparently word has gotten out that I'm a journalist working on a story, and one of his volunteers approaches me on a golf cart as I sit and watch the Lambstock guests arrive.

"That Craig. He sure likes to talk, don't he?" the guy, whose name is Steve Godfrey, says ominously. Godfrey's farmer's mustache conveys none of the irony of the 'staches and muttonchops of the arriving chefs. "Come talk to me later and I'll tell you about the *real* Craig Rogers." Before I can answer, he's driven off.

The juxtaposition of Godfrey and the chefs, some arriving with extra swagger on motorcycles, reminds me of something Rogers said to me once. "A lot of people in the food community talk a really good game. But it makes zero difference to the people living and farming in Patrick County, Virginia. I'd like to see *those* people's lives changed for the better by this food movement."

Later, I track Godfrey down and ask him to make good on his promise of an explanation of the *real* Craig Rogers.

"Four years ago today, the doctors decided they had to take my heart out and put it back together," Godfrey says, at first quietly but then with a fierce edge. "Craig come down while I was in the hospital and looked after my livestock and tended to my wife and kids. When I came home, he came and stayed with me for a week. Cooked my lunch, helped me get dressed." He pauses, to steady his voice. "That's what kind of guy he really is," Godfrey says.

He looks down and walks off. As he goes he calls out over his shoulder, "He still talks too damn much, though."

The Triumph of Jamie Oliver's "Nemesis"

Jane Black

It was all I could do not to scarf the entire stromboli, neatly packaged for me in a Styrofoam clamshell, while in the car. The dough was soft. The balance of ham and mozzarella, just right. And so, only about half was left when I parked on Third Avenue, the main drag in Huntington, West Virginia, and offered a bite to some friends.

"Wow. That's great," said one.

"Yeah, where'd you get that?" asked another.

"You'll never believe it," I told them. "This is school lunch."

Times have changed since celebrity chef Jamie Oliver broadcast startling and deliberately inflammatory—this was reality TV, after all—images of kids here dumping trays of fresh food untouched into the trash. For those of you who missed Oliver's prime-time program, *Food Revolution*, the British chef arrived in Huntington in 2009 after it was named the most unhealthy metropolitan area in America and went to work ousting greasy burgers and pizza in favor of from-scratch meals made with fresh ingredients. Two years later, on the first week of school, which began in mid-August, students in Cabell County sat down to meals of from-scratch chicken quesadillas and brown rice and, on the day I visited, creamy chicken and noodles served with freshly made coleslaw, steamed broccoli with parmesan, an orange, and hot rolls, the smell of which floated enticingly through the halls.

And that stromboli? Well, it's not one of the meals that the school district is most proud of. The dough is made from scratch, of course. But school cooks would be happier if they actually made the ham or cheese. As I said, times have changed.

School officials repeatedly point out that the county's food already was

50 percent made from scratch before Oliver rolled into town. And you can't blame them for wanting a little credit. The culinary crusader may have focused the national klieg lights on this otherwise quiet Appalachian city, but it's local officials who have done the real work of overhauling school food. Over the last two years, Rhonda McCoy—the school food service director who was portrayed on the show as an aloof bureaucrat more concerned with budgets and caloric counts than kids' health—has redeveloped recipes, held after-hours taste tests, sourced fresh and unprocessed ingredients at affordable prices, bought new equipment, and trained school cooks. She also endured an unprecedented four regulatory audits to ensure that the new meals met federal nutritional and caloric standards. She passed.

McCoy hasn't stopped there. This year, she introduced free meals for all low-income students and free meals for all students at one county elementary school. She also plans to introduce lower-sugar flavored milk, and to buy a projected twelve thousand pounds of sweet potatoes for the district, grown by a county high school's vocational agriculture students.

Now, deservedly, McCoy's county is a model in the state. Last spring, Dr. Jorea Marple, the state schools superintendent, visited Cabell County and decided that other districts need to follow its path. As a result, eight counties—most of which are in the poor southern coal fields—this fall will introduce 100 percent from-scratch meals at breakfast and lunch—and provide them to all students, regardless of their family's income, free of charge.

It's easy to imagine how this kind of warp-speed transition might be painful for those eight lucky counties. My husband and I spent six months in Huntington researching a book about how and if the town can change its food culture, and in meeting after meeting, McCoy told me that she never objected to the changes that Oliver suggested, just the way and speed at which she was forced to implement them.

But this new set of cooks won't be starting from scratch. McCoy provided a binder full of USDA-approved recipes and order forms with all the ingredients they need to purchase. She also organized a two-day training where the now-experienced Cabell County cooks demonstrated recipes: rotisserie chicken, roasted potatoes, sugar snap peas, pizza sauce, and homemade salad dressings and croutons, among others. They also imparted tips and techniques for, say, quickly chopping dozens of heads of romaine lettuce or cabbage for coleslaw rather than just opening a bag.

Alice Gue, the school cook whom *Food Revolution* viewers will remember as Oliver's grumpy nemesis, was one of the trainers. (And, for the record, she's one of the warmest, cuddliest school cooks I've met in years of covering the subject.) "It's a lot for them to take on but most were really excited," she told me after serving stromboli to almost two hundred students. "You always get some people who will say, 'I can't do that. We have no time. We don't this or we don't do that.' Just like you get some people who say: 'Well, why do the extra work when the kids are just going to throw away the food?' And sure, some of them will. And if they don't eat it today, OK, they didn't today. But down the road they will. You have to take pride in what you do and what you put out there for these kids."

Pride is one thing. Money is another. And a lack of federal funds is the perennial reason for the piles of cheap processed food that end up on children's trays. And so I asked McCoy: Where would West Virginia get the money for new equipment, better ingredients, and free lunches for all low-income students?

"I don't know," she said. "They're just going to find it."

It's a nonanswer. But, in a way, it doesn't really matter. What does is that state and county leaders in West Virginia now agree that good food in schools is so important that they'll find some way to put it on students' plates. Or, to put it another way, remaking school food is more about leadership than cash. While chef-advocate Alice Waters and others would like to see the federal government spend $5 per student for organic, sustainable, and local school lunch, the Cabell County school district is proving that it's possible—with dedication and a little ingenuity—to put out tasty, from-scratch meals that both kids and a discriminating food writer will happily eat.

That's not to say that more money wouldn't help. Doling out money is how Congress leads. And school food would be a popular cause if children suddenly got the vote. But the experience in Cabell County proves that sometimes what schools need most is a push to change. "If I had to do it my way, we would have gone slower," McCoy told me. "But now that it's all done, I think, yes, it was worth it."

Grabbing Dinner

Bill Heavey

Since Jody Meche's wife is working late and since Jody and I will be out frogging until midnight or so, we need to get enough calories into Bryce, the couple's fourteen-year-old, to hold him until his mama gets home. Thus it is that my introduction to the art of frogging takes place in the drive-through line of the McDonald's in Henderson, Louisiana, about twenty-five miles east of Lafayette.

Like many froggers in the Atchafalaya Basin, Jody is not a fan of gigs and mechanical grabbers. He prefers to catch his frogs bare-handed. For one thing, gigs and mechanical grabbers aren't the most reliable things. They also kill the frog, and while a dead frog must be iced immediately, a grabbed frog can be kept alive for several days. As we inch forward toward a Number Four Value Meal, Jody explains that you locate frogs by shining them, since their eyes reflect light. We'll each wear a hard hat rigged up with a powerful sealed-beam lamp. Once Jody spots a frog, he'll point it out to me and drive the boat over, putting the frog on my strong side (right), if possible. At which point I, kneeling in the front, will reach down and grab the frog. Jody's not sure whether the frog is stunned by the bright light or simply has too much faith in its natural camouflage. Either way, he says, you can generally get pretty close to a frog before it dives for cover.

Of course, there's more to it. You need a frogging attitude, a mind-set, if you expect to come home with enough frogs to feed your friends, which is our goal this night.

"Now, Bill," Jody tells me, "you got to remember something when you go to grab that frog tonight." He greets the lady inside the squawk box and places Bryce's order. "You're not petting that frog," he says. "You're not slapping that frog. You got to . . ." He presses his lips together, searching for something that will illustrate his point. His eye comes to rest on an empty coffee cup in the truck's holder. "You got to grab that frog." As he speaks, a large right fist shoots out, seizing and crushing the Styrofoam cup so quickly and completely that it basically explodes inside the cab. The noise alone is extraordinary. Even Jody seems somewhat abashed at the violence he has wrought.

"Well, OK then," I say as evenly as possible, picking shards of the cup from my lap.

Frog season in Louisiana runs year-round, with the exception of April and May, when it closes to allow the amphibians to breed undisturbed. While it's possible to catch frogs all year, Jody says late winter and early fall are best. Late winter is good because the lilies haven't greened up yet and it's easy to spot the frogs. Late summer and early fall are good because the water in the Atchafalaya Basin falls, concentrating the frogs. Ideally, you want days that are warm but not too warm, followed by nights that are cool but not too cool. "Frogs feed on the crawfish under the lilies right after dusk," Jody explains. "When they're full, they float to the surface and kind of lie there." Today we had a daytime high in the mid-eighties, which should drop to the mid-sixties after dark. Jody reckons we should have excellent frogging. A friend of his caught more than two hundred the other night and sold them for two dollars apiece.

We get Bryce's order and head home to drop him off. I ask if there are alligators where we'll be frogging. "Oh, yeah," Jody says. "Lotta gators. Most of 'em are small, six feet or less, but there are a few big ones around. They'll be out, hunting frogs same as us. Frog eyes are kind of white or sometimes have a little green tinge to 'em. Gators have red eyes. You don't want to grab anything that has red eyes." Right, I think. No grabbing red eyes.

EATING WILD

When I asked Jody how much of his family's meat is wild game, he initially said "about half." Upon reflection, he bumped the number to 70 percent. Jody has two small freezers. In them we found the following: fourteen frogs, four squirrels, more than a dozen ducks, some rabbits, some leftover wild turkey, as well as five pounds or more each of smoked deer sausage, regular deer sausage, and ground deer meat. There was also some shrimp that he'd caught. His wife, Tracy, likes to have shrimp year-round. Jody sounded almost apologetic at having so little on hand, explaining that the family prefers to "eat fresh." During crawfish season, for example, they eat the crustaceans about twice a week, but he almost never freezes any. They tend to eat frogs fresh as well. The fourteen he has frozen are on hand as gifts. "Everybody loves frogs," Jody says.

At a boat ramp fifteen miles east of Henderson along I-10, Jody backs his nineteen-foot aluminum skiff off the trailer, jumps in, runs the boat up on the bank, walks the four-inch gunwale forward, and parks the pickup. Trucks rumble and hum along the interstate thirty feet above our heads. Although the temperature is pleasant, the twenty-five-minute run to Upper Billy Little Lake will be cold, so I put on a slicker. Jody hooks up his sealed beam to a twelve-volt car battery at his feet, and suddenly the night is banished. The headlamp sends out a beam of light you could hang clothes on. "Jesus, Jody!" I blurt. "You look like the Statue of Liberty. What exactly is that thing?"

"Just a regular sealed beam," he says. "Comes with a GE 4405."

"What's a 4405?" I ask.

"A kind of bulb. It's pretty good. But I put in a TC 7512."

"Which is?"

"The navigation light they use on airplanes." Of course.

He guns the engine and we're off, flying along down a canal as straight as a rifle barrel with the divided lanes of I-10 above. Jody's light darts everywhere as he tries to pick out the eyes of deer in the woods and turtles, frogs, and gators along the shore.

A few minutes later, we turn off into a smaller canal, then into an even smaller waterway, called a "road" but really more like a tunnel through the overgrown swamp that Jody and a few others keep open with chainsaws. Jody slaloms between broad-trunked cypress trees with Spanish moss hanging as if placed by set designers. Night herons crouch on logs and helicopter skyward just as we get close enough to touch them. I'm having a hard time processing this. A moment ago, the swamp was pure chaos. Suddenly it's vivid and picturesque, a Discovery Channel highlight reel.

Jody suddenly shifts into neutral and the boat settles into the water. I put on my helmet, clip the ends of the wire to the battery at my feet, and soon my forehead projects its own godlike light. Meanwhile, Jody is already calling out frogs. "Little one over there, two more over there. Little gator by that log." I register one of the frogs but have trouble seeing the others. And then, I make out the glowing red embers of the gator. "They're not afraid of the light, are they?" I say. "Not most of 'em," he says. "Nice frog by that brush there." Clearly, Jody is not bothered by gators.

"Ooh, good frog! See him?" He shines a bush sticking up among lilies. I catch a momentary flicker, then it's gone. "Gonna put him on your right side, Bill. Get ready now." I still can't see the frog. "He's right in the middle of my light," Jody says. Maybe so, but it's a huge light. "He's right there!" Jody says. "Right next to the boat!" At last I see the frog, motionless in the pads, all of eighteen inches away. The damn frog is the size of a rotisserie chicken. I don't even know that my hand will fit around him. I stab down at him and the frog executes a single, almost sluggish kick. I catch a glimpse of its legs fully extended as it dives. They are ridiculously long.

"Aw, Bill, you got to be more aggressive," Jody says sadly. "You're not trying to be his buddy. That's your frog, know what I'm saying? He can't hurt you. And they're tough, you don't have to worry about squeezing him too hard." OK, I tell him. I know I blew that one. I'm nodding my head now, psyching myself up. You can't half-ass this frog grabbing. You have to commit. The truth is that I'm more afraid of disappointing Jody than anything else.

"Here comes another one," Jody says. "Good frog. See him? I'm gonna put this one on your left side, Bill."

"I don't see him," I say.

"Right there. Right in the middle of my light. Look in the middle of my light!" A note of frustration has entered Jody's voice.

"I'm looking, I just don't . . ."

"Right in the middle of my light!" Jody says. And then I do see it. This frog's not quite as gargantuan as the last one, and I resolve to nail this beast or die trying. I lean until I'm halfway out of the boat to get a good angle, arm raised and ready as I gauge our speed. When we're a foot away, I pounce. I grab the frog across its back and pluck it from the water. It's so big that my grasping hand has slid down, kind of across the frog's waist. It's a handful. I've got part of the body and one leg, and the rubbery creature is kicking hard in an effort to escape. I clutch the frog to my belly with both hands.

"There you go, partner!" Jody calls. "Now you froggin'!" I stagger aft and transfer the frog to Jody. He slips it into a crawfish trap, a rectangular envelope of rubber-coated wire mesh, and folds the top over to prevent the frog's escape. I look down at the frog, sitting motionless save for the faint thrumming of its throat. A pang—guilt, remorse, or both—suddenly courses through me. I don't really want to kill this thing. "He looks so . . . cute," I blurt out. "I feel bad about killing him."

"He'll look even cuter fried up on my plate, partner!" Jody shoots back.

My grabbing average picks up and I start to get some confidence. A couple of our targets dive before we get close. Jody calls such frogs "wild." Then I grab one that feels dead or at least deathly ill. It's limp when I grab it and remains limp in my hand. "This guy's hurting," I start to say. But at this moment the frog, evidently sensing the lessening of hand pressure, makes a break for it, jumping out of my hand and onto the deck, where it immediately starts jumping hard. I practically fall on the thing, pinning it with both hands. I hear Jody's deep laugh as I struggle. "That's one of Mr. Frog's best tricks!" he says. "He'll play dead until whatever's got him drops its guard."

We cruise on, the slough opening into a lake. By now, I've got the proper predatory mind-set and am catching nearly every frog I try for. "You're doing real good, Bill," Jody tells me. "You've got an interesting motion. I sort of smash-grab, you know. I'll push that frog down another six inches when I grab him, but you sorta pluck him out like an eagle." It's shameful how gratified I am at these words of praise. I am a grown, widely traveled man. I have caught a 150-pound tarpon, killed a bull elk with a bow and arrow, and survived an audit by the IRS. But at this particular moment, I would rather be counted a good frog grabber than anything I can think of.

FRY 'EM UP

The next morning I drive back to Jody's house to butcher the frogs for a gathering scheduled that night at another crawfisherman's house. Jody has kept a wet tarp over the cage, where the frogs are now sitting atop each other. As he picks up the trap to carry it to a cutting board placed on his boat trailer, some of the frogs let out a sound like a cat mewing, only louder and more plaintive. It spooks the heck out of me. Jody is set up for work. He's wearing the bibs of his rain suit and has a knife, a sharpening steel, and a pair of pliers designed to remove the skin from catfish at the ready, as well as a hose, a bucket for frog guts, and another filled with water for the finished frogs.

For my benefit, he narrates as he works. "You gotta get rough with him first," he says, plucking a frog from the trap. "You grab his front legs, pull back, and kind of push his head flat." Then there is a brief, last muffled grunt or exhalation by the frog and a crunching sound as Jody saws the head off with a single forward-and-back stroke. The head rolls a couple of inches and settles such that it is now looking back at its own body. "Then you cut the legs at that last joint," Jody says, "just up from the foot." He starts with the right front foot and turns the frog counterclockwise as he cuts the others. "You spin that frog," he says, hands deft and precise. With the legs removed, he inserts two fingers between the loose skin and the frog's back and uses the catfish pliers to strip the skin off with a single, practiced motion. He does the same thing on the front side, then pulls out the diaphragm and innards with his hand. "Your last move is to split the pelvic bone, same as you would a deer. It takes a little strength," he says, pressing until the faint crack can be heard. "And there's your frog."

I watch for a while and finally say that I've got to do some. I steel myself, resolving not to think a conscious thought until I've decapitated my first frog. Once I'm past that, I find—I almost don't want to admit to this—that killing frogs I'm going to eat becomes increasingly easy. After I've done my third, it hardly bothers me. For one thing, the process of butchering requires a lot of focus. It takes me four or five times as long to do one as Jody, and now I see just how skilled he is. It's hard for Jody to watch, and even as I work I can sense him struggling to let me continue. He doesn't relax until I turn the knife over to him again. Then he's content, cutting and spinning each frog on its way to dinner. "You got to be efficient," Jody explains. "You want your tools right at hand. You don't rush, but every motion has to count, you know what I'm saying?"

We have the meal at the house of Mike Bienvenu, another crawfisherman. Mike has cooked up some of the frogs in a rich sauce piquant that we eat over rice, savoring the light, sweet meat and the sauce and picking out tiny bones. There are also fried frog legs, which have the same flavor but also a kind of riverine bass note, wild and clean. I am weighing the merits of each when I hear laughter out back. Jody is telling the group how tentative I was at first but that I got into it as the night went on. "He was leaning so far out the boat I thought he was going in. But he wanted that frog. He was grabbing 'em pretty good. And after about an hour and a half, I asked if he was ready to go, and he says, 'Yeah, my ass is wet.'" Jody laughs his big laugh and everybody else laughs, too. I suppose people who make their living in the swamp take having a wet ass for granted. I'm fully aware that I'm an outsider at this party and always will be. At the moment, however, having acquitted myself well as a novice frogger, enjoying a dry butt and soaking up the last bits of frog and sauce piquant in the rice on my plate, I'm feeling pretty comfortable.

Hogzilla

Dan Baum

One does not hunt in order to kill; on the contrary, one kills in order to have hunted.
José Ortega y Gasset, Meditations on Hunting

When I called the Texas Parks and Wildlife Department to ask about pig-hunting regulations, the lady who answered the phone said, "There aren't any."

"Excuse me?"

"You need a hunting license; a five-day will cost you forty-eight dollars."

"What's the season?"

"Year-round."

"What's the bag limit?"

"Ain't none. Shoot all you want."

"Males? Females?"

"Take them all, big and small."

"Wait. Have I reached the Texas Department of Wildlife?"

"Yes, sir."

"Any restrictions on what kind of gun I can use?"

"Nope."

"Do I have to wear orange?"

"It's a good idea, but not required."

"Time of day?"

"Jack them at night with a spotlight for all we care. As long as you shoot a lot of them. What you want to do is take and shoot the sow first. The piglets will stand around for a minute, and you can pick all of them off, too."

Say what? In thirty-five years of hunting I'd never encountered an official attitude like this. In Montana, for example, where I've done most of my hunting, regulations were published in a thick booklet that divided the state into more than a hundred tiny hunting districts, each with its own fussy rules about species, sex, weapon, the permissibility of vehicles, day of month, time of day, and antler points. Forms had to be filled out and boxes checked. A tiny mistake could invalidate the application. Getting a deer tag was as complicated and tedious as doing taxes, but the process imparted a message: deer were a precious resource, to be managed with care.

My hunting partners extended the ethic into the field. They taught me to stalk on tiptoe, "glass" animals through binoculars for their legal characteristics before placing a shot, and butcher with the exactitude of a surgeon so as not to waste a mouthful of meat. The hip thing to do in Montana was to rub a little tobacco on the dead animal's fur to thank its spirit for the offering. The whole exercise was wrapped in reverence.

Reverence, though, was not the guiding principle in Texas when it came to wild pigs. The lady on the phone directed me to an online pamphlet called *The Feral Hog in Texas* that read less like a wildlife primer than a multicount indictment in a death penalty case. It established straight off that hogs had no business running wild in Texas in the first place. They'd descended from barnyard stock that first escaped from settlers' pens three hundred years ago. The import of Russian boars in the 1930s for hunting had seasoned the stock.

The result: as many as a million and a half feral hogs rampaging through Texas, growing as big as sofas, tearing up farmland and creek bottoms with their root-rooting snouts. They gobbled up baby lambs and caused car wrecks. They carried pseudorabies, swine brucellosis, tuberculosis, bubonic plague, tularemia, hog cholera, foot-and-mouth disease, kidney worms, stomach worms, liver flukes, trichinosis, roundworms, whipworms, dog ticks, fleas, hog lice, and anthrax. Their tusks were "razor sharp," the pamphlet said, and their gallop as fast as "lightning." Lest some shred of sympathy stay my hand from indiscriminate slaughter, the pamphlet threw in the lurid detail that feral sows had been known to eat their own young.

No spirit-worshiping, tobacco-rubbing sanctimony here. By the time I finished reading about Texas feral hogs, I was drooling on my shirt and growling, "Lemme at 'em."

■　　■　　■

Until the early '70s, a banner hung over Lee Street in Casey Gunnels's hometown: GREENVILLE, WELCOME. THE BLACKEST LAND, THE WHITEST PEOPLE.

"That's how it was," he said as he steered his car through town on the way to his grandpa's land. Casey, a twenty-four-year-old high school Spanish teacher, was broad-shouldered, with a substantial belly he'd acquired in college and hadn't yet gotten around to losing. He had a round face, almond-shaped eyes, and spiky black hair.

"People always ask me, 'You Asian?' I know there's Indian or a Mexican back there somewhere," he said. "That must be it."

Casey invited me down after we met through TexasHuntingForum.com, and I figured that as we drove to his family's hunting cabin, he'd teach me tricks for finding wild swine. Instead he wanted to talk about the Church of Christ, in which he'd been raised, and detail the rigors of a faith that took the Bible literally. No alcohol, no instrumental music in church, and no church suppers—for didn't Paul ask in 1 Corinthians 11:22, "What? Have ye not houses to eat and drink in?"

"We'll have whiskey at the cabin, don't worry," he added with a quick laugh. "I believe the Bible forbids only drunkenness. It's full of references to wine."

He lapsed into a pained silence—it was his opinion about alcohol that had set off a recent swivet at church, and I got the impression that one reason he'd brought me down was to process it with someone from outside—an agnostic East Coast Jew seemed to fit that bill. The civil war at church had touched off when he taught his interpretation of the alcohol question to a Sunday School class. The congregation, already divided over whether God used the terms *thee* and *thou* when addressing mere humans, had blown up over Casey's apostasy. His parents, disgusted by the vitriol of the anti-Casey and pro-thee-and-thou factions, had decamped with half the congregation to another church, many miles away. Casey's wife, Megan, though—whom he'd known from church since they were four years old—wanted to stay put with her parents. Sundays were excruciating. I told him the joke about the lone Jew stranded for years on an island, whose rescuers can't understand why he'd built two synagogues.

"That's the one I go to," he tells them. "And that's the one I *don't* go to." Casey laughed and laughed. "That may be the first Jewish joke I've ever understood," he said, wiping his eyes.

As Casey piloted the truck through the rolling East Texas country between Greenville and Cooper, he tried to play the redneck he figured I'd expected. He told me stories about dipping snuff, driving big trucks, and shooting guns, but his heart wasn't in it. The cantankerous intellectual in him kept rearing its head. The master's thesis on which he was working posited that football was ruining high school education in Texas, a topic that was likely to get him tarred and feathered. At a gas stop, he took off his jacket and rolled up his sleeve to reveal a big tattoo: NOT ALL WHO WANDER ARE LOST, from *The Lord of the Rings*. And he kept bringing up Dante's *Inferno*, which he'd first discovered in ninth grade and devoured.

"Being a hell-bound sinner is a big concept in the Church of Christ," he said.

Casey had fallen for guns when visiting his Uncle Charles in Amarillo as a little boy. He would disappear for hours into the attic, where he pored over fragrant and tattered back copies of the *American Rifleman*, *Shooting Times*, and *Guns and Ammo*. Even before he could read, he loved sitting cross-legged on the floor in his short pants, leafing through 1950s ads for Marlin rifles and Colt revolvers. Everything about the shooting world appealed to Casey long before his dad let him hold a gun. Firearms were for serious, virtuous, and technically competent adults of the type Casey wanted to be—like his dad. The men who smiled at him from the pages were rugged and wholesome. The accounts of hunting and target matches were stirring and cinematic. And the guns themselves, rendered in crisp black-and-white photos, were complex, elegant, and manly.

Dad kept a loaded five-shot .38 Smith & Wesson Chief's Special in the house. He showed little Casey where it was—on top of the bottom pair of blue jeans on Dad's closet shelf—and while Casey was forbidden to touch it on his own, he had only to tell Dad he wanted to look at it and Dad would stop what he was doing, unload it, and place it in Casey's small hands. If Casey wanted to shoot it, Dad would take him out behind the barn and let him knock cans off a fence. There was no fear attached to the gun, and no taboo. It was a piece of equipment, like the cream separator or the baler, and Dad was happy to have Casey know how to work it. He drew the line, though, at letting Casey join Grandpa in the ramshackle trailer he kept as a poor man's hunting cabin. It wasn't the guns that bothered him; it was the thought of Casey's young lungs cooped up in that little trailer with the thick miasma of cigarette smoke that followed Grandpa everywhere.

"Grandpa drove a truck for Safeway his whole life, and saved a little bit out of every paycheck to buy land. He had parcels all over," Casey said as he turned off the highway onto a long dirt road. When, at age eleven, Casey was finally allowed to join his grandpa on a deer hunt, it was like being baptized all over again. They stalked the woods as the sun rose and returned to the trailer for a big breakfast of bacon, eggs, biscuits, sausage gravy, and coffee, which they ate standing outside under a cottonwood. It was Casey's earliest lesson in what it meant to be a man in Texas: to lean your rifle against a tree at dawn and, in reverent silence, sop gravy from a tin plate with other men.

Casey received a Remington 870 shotgun for his twelfth birthday, then he was given a sporterized 1891 Argentine army Mauser that he used to kill his first white-tailed deer the following year. He waited until ninth grade, though, to buy his first handgun: a stainless-steel Smith & Wesson 686 .357

Magnum revolver. He was too young to buy it himself, but Dad was willing to do the paperwork and buy the gun with Casey's savings—a technical violation of the "Don't lie for the other guy" rule, but hell, this was Texas, and Casey was a responsible boy. Dad imposed no rules on Casey when he handed him the revolver. He didn't order him to lock it up or shoot it only under adult supervision. A man's guns were his own business, Dad believed, and caring for them safely was part of what it meant to be an adult in a free country. One day, a kid announced in class that he'd captured a wild hog, and the class decided to barbecue it. Casey brought his .357 to school in his backpack the next day to dispatch the pig, and though it was only a year after the Columbine High School massacre in Colorado, it didn't occur to anybody to draw a connection. This was Greenville, Texas, after all—a million miles from places where teenagers misbehaved with guns.

Casey said he saw no contradiction between his love of guns and his love of Jesus. Portraying Jesus as a skinny little pussy was a lie, he felt; a first-century carpenter would have been a big, strong man accustomed to felling trees with an ax, splitting them with a hammer and wedge, and sawing them into boards by hand. Jesus understood the uses of violence; he'd chased the money changers from the temple with a whip, after all, and, according to the Gospel of Luke, he'd told his apostles to prepare to defend themselves. "He that hath no sword, let him sell his garment, and buy one." Turning the other cheek, Casey was convinced, didn't mean letting people beat you up; it meant moving into a defense posture.

The cabin stood in a clearing at the end of a muddy driveway—one room, with a sheet-metal roof and, inside, unfinished plywood walls. Casey lent me a lever action .44 Magnum carbine that his grandpa had given him. It was no longer than my arm; it had a shockingly big bore; and its cartridges were as plump as baby carrots. He shouldered a scoped AR-15.

"I'm trying this out," he said with a sheepish shrug. "I'm still not sure about these things."

As we stepped outside, Casey inhaled deeply. "Smell them?" he asked, waggling his fingers in front of his nose. "Nothing else smells like that." I smelled nothing.

The land around Grandpa's cabin was a lovely expanse of open oak-and-hackberry forest, but the trees were laced with thorny vines that tugged at clothing, at exposed skin, and, I feared, at the exposed triggers of firearms. We hadn't walked a hundred yards when four dark shapes sizzled through the fallen leaves to our left. My heart burst through the roof of my mouth. By the time I recovered, the monsters were gone.

Casey was in full stalk, crouched forward, gun up, urging me forward with commando hand gestures. He froze and passed me his rifle. "Use this one; they're about sixty yards out," he whispered. I raised the scope to my eye, but with all the foliage, I couldn't find the pigs.

"Come on, come on, *Jesus!*" he whispered as I feverishly tried to place crosshairs on swine flesh. The pigs vanished with nary a rustle. As I handed back the rifle, I expected Casey to unleash that vilest of Texas insults—*For Christ's sake, you're hunting like a middle-aged Jewish man from New Jersey!*—but he was a paragon of politesse. "Not a problem, not a problem. I just want to get you one."

The pigs may have vanished, but their handiwork was everywhere. Great swaths of forest looked stomped by giants, the earth so thoroughly churned that small trees had toppled. "They can tear up a ten-acre cornfield in a single night," Casey said. "They'll kill this forest if we let them. My grandmother's hiring a guy with a helicopter next week to come shoot as many as he can. Last year, he got almost twenty." He smiled, his round face lighting up like a little boy's. "I imagine it would take a very long time for *that* to get boring."

Casey jerked to a halt and pointed at a swishing stand of ragweed canes about fifty yards ahead. A sow and half a dozen hefty piglets emerged, sunlight glinting off their backs. "Nice blond one," Casey whispered, taking a knee. "I'm going to count 'one, two, three,' and we'll shoot on three." But there was a tree blocking my shot, and then a tree blocking his. We waited and waited, and finally I landed my sights on a tan flank. I pulled the trigger and up went a squealing like old truck brakes. Pigs exploded in every direction. Casey leapt to his feet, ejecting brass shells into the blue sky—*Bam! Bam! Bam! Bam!*—as a huge, shovel-faced black sow made the fatal mistake of dashing across a clearing to Casey's left. He followed her with his rifle and shot once. The sow shoulder-rolled beside a big oak and didn't move again.

All God's children got wings, but this one also had brush-bristle fur caked in mud and crawling with bugs, jagged three-inch tusks emerging from a ripply grimace of a mouth, and the aroma of a musk-and-feces milkshake.

Of the pig I'd shot, the only sign was a tablespoon of blood on crispy leaves. I began walking in outward concentric circles, searching. "They're not like deer," Casey said as he got down on one knee beside his pig. "They've got a layer of fat that seals up the wound and makes them hard to track." I kept at it, loath to let a wounded animal get away, while Casey did something that nobody I knew would dream of doing with a dead deer. He used his dead sow to test ammunition.

Standing over her, he shot several bullets into her flank, then several more, of various types. "Nice," I heard him say as he dug with a knife through the meat of her hip. "That cheap Russian hollow-point fragmented like I wanted her to!"

I was relieved to find my pig, a young male three feet long, about a hundred yards away, dead of a lung shot. He was proportioned like a smallmouth bass—about one-quarter head—and was as heavy as a sack of Quikrete. Casey estimated he was two months old. I'd have gutted, skinned, and hauled him out, but Casey said not to bother. "If you want meat," he said, "just take the backstraps."

I opened the piglet's hide like a valise and sliced out the backstraps—the tender fillets that run along the spine. I didn't enjoy the feeling. Where I came from, a carcass stripped only of backstraps was the work of a poacher.

■   ■   ■

All 1.5 million of Texas's pigs lived within a mile radius of us, it seemed. As I packed up the fillet meat in a Ziploc bag, another clan came crashing out of the brush in a long line. Accustomed to quiet stalking and single-shot placement, I was amazed to see Casey take off after them at full tilt, firing into the underbrush as he ran. I caught up with him as, panting, he drew his pistol on a writhing pig. "I'm wasted on cross-country!" he laughed, quoting Gimli from *The Lord of the Rings*. "We dwarves are natural sprinters, very dangerous over short distances!" He leaned over and casually shot the pig between the ears.

I looked back as we walked away. The pig lay on its belly, looking comfortably asleep. Leaving a dead animal unprocessed: again, a strange feeling. We ran into another hog family down by the creek, and Casey killed two more before I could even raise my carbine to my cheek.

For about ten minutes, I stalked a deep rustling in the brush, until a foot-long armadillo came waddling out, laughing at me. Then a big sow materialized from nowhere and, for once quicker on the drop than Casey, I took a shot and seemed to hit her; after some squealing and scuffling in the scrub, a deep moaning echoed through the woods. It was late now; the sun filtering through the oaks made long, spooky shadows. I couldn't place the direction of the moaning, and as I crisscrossed the area, it stopped. Casey called to me to come on—there was one more spot he wanted to try before we lost the light.

My every impulse was to keep searching, with a flashlight if necessary. The worst thing a hunter could do, according to the ethic I'd learned, was lose a wounded animal: It was cruel, it wasted meat, and it messed up game management, because no tag went on the kill. But, good Sunday School teacher that he was, Casey explained patiently and repeatedly: "That's not what we're about here." To reinforce his point, he pulled me from the woods into a pasture thoroughly bulldozed by hogs. If it had been my pasture, I'd have wanted the hogs dead, too.

"It's primal; we like to kill things," Casey said of our species as we headed back to his cabin in the gloom. "You got to be careful how you say it, but it's true. It doesn't make us sick. It's just the way we are. The reason I like pig hunting is, I get to kill a lot of pigs. It's the distilled essence of the thing. If you told someone you went out and killed seven deer and let them lie there, they'd put you in jail. You tell them you killed and let lie seven pigs, they're like, *Badass!*"

My mistake may have been to think of Texas pig hunting on the same spectrum as Montana deer hunting. All of the outward elements were there—tramping the woods with a gun, figuring out the nature of the quarry, reading sign, and of course the shooting and the blood. I'd started hunting because of the gun, but I realized with Casey that my reasons for loving the hunt had changed. For me, the shooting and the killing were no longer, as Casey would say, "the distilled essence of the thing." I still loved being in the woods with a rifle in my hands. But for me, hunting was more about the unworldly relationship with one special animal that gives himself over in return for the care you've taken to understand him and his habitat. Then his flesh becomes your flesh, sealing the bond.

At the same time, though, I couldn't find anything wrongheaded or immoral about the way Casey hunted pigs. Through carelessness, people had created the problem of the feral hog, and now it was up to people to ameliorate it. To focus on the cruelty of shooting individual pigs, when we were ruining habitat and causing extinctions from the Arctic to the Great Barrier Reef, seemed a little silly. And a state dependent on agriculture couldn't afford an overpopulation of flesh-and-blood bulldozers. Somebody had to kill them, and it made more sense to let sportsmen pay and enjoy it than to spend public dollars to have rangers cull the herd, as Rocky Mountain National Park had done recently to manage an oversupply of elk (to the outrage of Colorado hunters). The pity in Texas was that tons of useful protein—local, free-range, organic, lean pork—rotted in the woods because a raft of laws banned the selling of wild meat.

Gunning down Texas pigs with Casey was, in the end, a gas—the greatest moving-target shooting I'd ever done, even if it wasn't, for me, *hunting*. It was more like football—our team against theirs, with a score posted at day's end.

We walked on, doubling back past the spot where I'd lost my sow. A sinister rustling came from our right, and a dozen buzzards rose heavily into the treetops like a panel of black-robed judges. "They found your pig," Casey said. "You can stop worrying about it now."

A Taste for the Hunt

Jonathan Miles

The greatest meal of my life involved a Triscuit.

At the age of eleven, you see, I came into possession of a .177-caliber Crosman air rifle. The rifle shot mushroom-shaped lead pellets, and if you pumped the rifle a dozen times or so, to the point that a pneumatic/mechanical explosion felt dangerously imminent, it shot them pretty hard. One afternoon, bored with plinking cans, I took lazy, purposeless aim at a mourning dove perched upon a branch in the next-door neighbor's yard. Perhaps I meant to scare it, to startle it skyward, I don't know. In any case I felt certain I couldn't hit it.

I hit it. The way the dove dropped, in an awful flutter of wings, mirrored the state of my insides; my heart collapsed in free-fall panic. As a boy of the suburbs, I'd never killed anything before, or even considered it; my imaginary targets had always been Nazi infantrymen. I leaped the concrete-block wall dividing our yard from the neighbor's, only obliquely aware, at that moment, of how severely forbidden was this terrain. (The neighbor was a middle-aged mumbler, schizophrenic if you trusted neighborhood rumor, who was fond of sunbathing nude on the roof.) No matter: I dashed across his backyard to where the fallen dove was flailing in the shade. Desperate to end its misery, I pumped the rifle to its airy maximum and shot the dove point-blank in the head. The stillness that followed didn't console me. My eyes soaked, I shot it again, and then again, sobbing, and then again and again until I was finally out of pellets.

I could have left it, or buried it. But something inside me, with a wise and moral voice like Obi-Wan Kenobi's, said I had to eat it. Wasting it, said the voice, would only compound the sin. As a latchkey kid, as we were called in those days, I'd become proficient at making Triscuit pizzas in the broiler, to feed myself after school, but this recipe, cadged from the Triscuit box, marked the beginning and end of my cooking chops. With a pocketknife, then, I cut the dove open, not knowing what to look for but finding a small wedge of purple breast meat from which I carved a few mangled slices. I heaped them atop some Triscuits and watched them sizzle under the red electric coil, my tear-smeared face staring back at me from the oven glass. And then, alone at the breakfast counter, I ate them.

I don't wish to overstate the moment, but the greater risk, it seems to me, lies in understatement. With each sniffling, tentative bite came an ever more profound understanding of the natural world, an epiphanic realization of what it meant to eat meat, to eat flesh, to eat animals, of the way death begets life, the way death feeds and nurtures life, of the cruel and beautiful order under which we all operate, boy and dove alike. If design, as the teleological argument goes, is how God makes His presence known, then here at the breakfast counter was God, speaking to me from a Triscuit pulpit. And though I wept throughout that meal, in hot shame and terror, something else occurred to me as well, a sensation at once irreconcilable but undeniable: the dove breast, seared from the broiler, unadorned with even salt and pepper, was . . . delicious. Here was pain, at seeing the world's dark heart revealed, but here, too, was a new and riveting pleasure, a taste unlike anything I'd encountered before.

For almost thirty years now I've been trying to re-create that meal. With doves, of course, shot over sunflower and millet fields in Mississippi and Georgia, but with ducks too, lifted gently from the mouths of wet Labrador retrievers in the Arkansas Delta and elsewhere, and with wild turkeys, and with squirrels, and with a musky-flavored wild boar I shot in the Tennessee mountains, and plenty of deer as well: all in the service of a single memory, a singular truth. Just recently I read about Facebook founder Mark Zuckerberg's vow to eat only the meat of animals he's killed himself, which he's been doing on a California farm. This is commendable, if a bit unwieldy (he can expect some awkwardness while traveling), and may just be the next logical frontier in the locavore and ethical-eating movements that have been blessedly spreading throughout the nation. For hunters, however, this is no frontier. It's something every hunter comes to understand, whether by shooting his or her first squirrel under grandfatherly tutelage (as my eight-year-old son plans to do this fall, with his Pop), or accidentally shooting a dove over a concrete wall: that only by killing, by enacting (or at least observing) the transformation of animal to meat, can we own up to our appetites with anything like honesty. "Man is a fugitive from Nature," wrote the Spanish philosopher José Ortega y Gasset, and, as we all know, the fugitive's life is necessarily constructed upon lies. Meat is not an abstract protein; that's the lie, subconscious but toxic all the same. It's the lie we abet every time we toss out a cellophane-wrapped package of meat that went neglected in the refrigerator's way-back, stung by the waste of money if stung at all. For the thoughtful hunter there is no such blitheness. Grandiose though it may sound, the hunter afield is stalking more than game; he's stalking truth.

But why wild truth? This is where pleasure bleeds in, admittedly, but also something deeper. It's become fashionable of late for restaurateurs to extol the provenance of the meat on their menus—what farm the pig came from, who fed it—in order to tell a story of how that pork shank made its way onto your plate. These have become the dinnertime equivalent of bedtime stories, designed to lull you into virtuous enjoyment. And while they're a necessary corrective after decades of industrial storylessness, these stories are inevitably about the farmer, not the animal. What we hear about the animal is what was or wasn't done to it. With wild animals, it's different. The story belongs to the animal, except for the ending, when the story turns briefly to the hunter. At a deer-hunting camp I used to frequent near Crystal Springs, Mississippi, we used to perform something we called "the autopsy." The idea was to determine just how the deer had died—where the bullet had hit, what precisely it had done—but, out in that low-ceilinged tin shed, gathered around a pendent whitetail carcass, our whiskey breath visible in the autumn-chilled air, we'd learn a whole lot about its life, too: what it'd been eating, what the scars on its hide revealed, how that hairline fracture on its hind leg was what had prevented it from springing away fast enough to beat a clumsy shooter. This is not to suggest we lounged about the deer camp telling stories about our deer in the sacred manner of movie Indians. Of course not; we told dirty jokes like everyone else. But it is to say that the deer were present, not as mere meat, commodities, or God forbid trophies, but as wild and sentient creatures whose lives we had deigned to take—hungrily, but respectfully.

The flavor of game, like its story, belongs to the animal, not to any farmer, and not to the hunter (unless he botched the field dressing or some such). It's contingent on its diet, its age, its sex, its life, and it's owing to this that the flavors can vary so widely, so maddeningly. Yet there's an elemental magic to those free-ranging and often untamable flavors, a direct link to the natural chaos that lies within that grand design I happened upon as a weepy eleven-year-old boy. For a cook, this can be challenging: it took me months to devise methods of making that ancient Tennessee boar edible, and despite valiant and repeated efforts I have yet to charm guests with a bite of Canada goose. Yet this is somehow part of the allure, too. Into the kitchen with game comes wildness, with its infinite degrees of diversity and complexity, and its infinite mine of stories. This is why the oxymoronic farm-raised game is such a wan replica of the genuine article: its life and death are predetermined, its story not its own. "Poetry," said the French critic Denis Diderot, "must have something in it that is barbaric, vast and wild." As a Triscuit once taught me, the same goes for eating.

Eat Dessert First

Robb Walsh

The Arkansas Delta is the mirror image of the Mississippi Delta on the other side of the river; together, the two are known simply as "the Delta." The area is defined by a deposit of black alluvial soil formed over thousands of years in the shared floodplain of the Yazoo and Mississippi Rivers and encompasses some of the nation's most fertile farmland. With its history of cotton plantations, blues music, barbecue, and largely African American population, the Delta has been called "the most Southern place on earth."

In the small town of Marianna, population 5,000, we pulled over at one of the most revered barbecue joints in the South. Jones Barbecue Diner won a James Beard America's Classic Award in 2012. It is located in a small house that looks just like all the others in the neighborhood. The Jones family has been in the barbecue business for more than a hundred years. James Jones's father, Hubert Jones, told an interviewer in 1986 that the family barbecue business began in the early 1900s with a barbecue pit that was a hole in the ground, a grate made from some iron pipes and a piece of fence wire, and two pieces of tin for a cover. Pork barbecued in the earthen pit was sold at a stand called "The Hole in the Wall," where barbecue was dished up from a washtub and passed through a window to waiting customers.

John T. Edge, director of the Southern Foodways Alliance, once wrote that James Jones's pulled pork was "as soft and creamy as rilletes." I figured any barbecue that made a Georgia boy like Edge start speaking French had to be spectacular. But once we were inside the tiny dining room, Jones told Rufus and me that we were out of luck. He didn't have anything ready to eat.

James Jones didn't want to grant us an interview or allow any photos either. He had had enough of journalists and photographers. A writer from a national magazine had wasted forty-five minutes of his time just the other day, he complained. Jones escorted us out the front entrance of the restaurant where we stood, mouths agape, while he turned the Open sign around to Closed. We got in the car and headed for another famous Arkansas Delta barbecue joint.

■   ■   ■

DeValls Bluff is in the White River Valley section of the Arkansas Delta. During the Civil War, DeValls Bluff, with good stores, several saloons, and more than 2,000 residents, was a major stop on the Memphis and Little Rock Railroad. The Union army held the town throughout the war because its port on the White River was more dependable than the port of Little Rock on the sometimes-impassable Arkansas River. The river port and the railroad allowed for easy transport of troops and supplies. Today, the rural hamlet of DeValls Bluff has a population of fewer than 800 and the air of a ghost town.

Rufus and I pulled into the parking lot of Craig Brothers Café (better known as Craig's). Lawrence Craig founded the place in 1947, and the Smithsonian Institution has honored him for his contributions to American cuisine. Lawrence Craig's life story was recounted onstage in 1998 at the first symposium of the Southern Foodways Alliance.

But sadly, Lawrence Craig isn't cooking anymore. Some of his distant cousins run the place now. Someone was tinkering in the building out behind the restaurant where the barbecue pit was housed, but the door was kept locked. I could tell from the woodpile and the ash pile that there was a big barbecue pit in there, but the pitmaster was adamant that we couldn't come in.

The dining room was a museum piece, looking as it did in the 1940s. Gas and electrical lines ran along the cinderblock walls. The interior walls were covered in vintage wallpaper with a wintery motif of snowy woods, ducks, and pheasants. Most of the customers got their sandwiches to go. We sat down at one of the ten or so faux-wood-grain Formica tables and ordered a little bit of everything. The ribs were very tender, the reheated beef and pork sandwiches were a little dry, and the ginger-inflected barbecue sauces were amazing.

Elethea Lewis was managing the restaurant that day. In the kitchen, the cooks reheated slices of pork and beef with barbecue sauce in frying pans. There were three sauces available: mild, medium, and hot. There wasn't any fresh meat being sliced. I felt like we had arrived at a great barbecue place a few years too late.

The usual quid pro quo of the food writer's game is the promise that the publicity will bring more business. And the unspoken fear of interviewees is that the writer will emphasize their failings and make them the object of public ridicule. In most of America, the public is so plugged into the mainstream media machine that people clamor to be in the spotlight. But the Delta isn't like the rest of America. It is the region with the nation's highest poverty rate and the lowest literacy rate, an area whose residents have been systematically deprived of many governmental services. Much has been written about Craig's, and none of it has changed the place. Were the barbecue folk in this part of Arkansas sick of being gawked at by tourists, writers, photographers, and food bloggers? Or was it just us?

That brought up a nagging question: what was the real nature of our project? My wife, Kelly Klaasmeyer, is an art critic who grew up in Arkansas. She has been critiquing my reporting on the American South for quite some time. Every time I pull over to take a photo of a hand-lettered "watermelon for sale" sign or a rusted barbecue pit, she asks me whether this is really a legitimate story, or whether I am "exoticizing rural southern poverty" for the amusement of the affluent.

Strangely enough, I realized after we had been hanging around Craig's for a while that this very barbecue joint had been the subject of one of Kelly's most withering tirades. In August 2004, in an article Jane and Michael Stern wrote for *Gourmet* magazine titled "Hog Wild in Arkansas," the authors wrote, "The best food in Arkansas is served in the worst-looking restaurants . . . you will eat majestically in derelict shacks." They described Craig's in particular as "a shack so unrepentantly dumpy that you've got to love it": "Dim fluorescent lights hang over a half dozen rickety tables. . . . Diner's attire . . . includes an astounding number of giant-size overalls on great big farm folks." After reading the story, Kelly wrote this letter to the editor of *Gourmet*:

> Tour bus passengers pressing their noses against a window at 60 miles an hour could generate more insightful cultural commentary than Jane and Michael Stern did in "Hog Wild." They describe Arkansas with a blend of superiority and exoticism that calls to mind colonial commentaries detailing the bizarre and primitive habits and habitations of the natives. Their descriptions of "farm folk" and their attire ooze condescension.
>
> The Sterns' writing is intensely self-absorbed and ethnocentric, using whatever place they visit as a backdrop to highlight the authors. Your magazine should not provide them a platform.
> *Sincerely,*
> *Kelly Klaasmeyer*

Kelly never mailed the letter; writing it was enough for her to get over her anger. But while the Sterns may have escaped her wrath (up until now), I haven't. We have been married long enough for me to know exactly what she would say about Rufus's and my present situation: "Two middle-aged white guys with smart phones and expensive-looking photographic gear driving around in a geeky Honda Element in the poorest, blackest region of the United States asking a lot of personal questions—gee, I wonder why you aren't getting anywhere?"

In the excitement of launching our road trip, maybe Rufus and I were getting a little overeager. To get our project back on track, we had to recapture the spirit that had got the book started. We had to slow down, take in the landscape, and get to know the people and places we were visiting.

Craig's and Jones Barbecue Diner, the places that had brought us to the Arkansas Delta, had been written about for a long time—and there was nothing we could do about any of that. The family that owned Craig's was related to the Pie Shop across the street, and we had been talking with the proprietor, Mary Thomas, all morning. We didn't intend to interview or photograph her. We were just passing the time until the barbecue joint opened.

While we were waiting for Craig's to open, I could smell something cooking inside the Pie Shop's kitchen, and I guessed it was peach pie. I was wrong. It was barbecue sauce. It turns out Thomas makes Craig's barbecue sauce on her eight-burner stove. I think Thomas uses some of the same spices in the barbecue sauce that she uses in her peach pie. When I asked her about it, she chased us out of the kitchen and refused to speak to us.

We didn't go away. We stood in the tiny vestibule of the Pie Shop, waiting for Craig's to open, because we had nowhere else to go. We read her entire menu of whole pies and fried pies several times. Rufus took photos of the empty white pie boxes. We put our business cards on the bulletin boards with all the others. Rufus photographed the still life in front on a little table under a window decorated with some lace curtains. It was an arrangement of plastic roses in an ornate vase and a very worn Bible sitting on top of a brand-new plastic flyswatter. The unstill part was the fly that kept circling and landing on the Bible.

A minivan parked in the driveway had the name of Thomas's church, Mount Olive Missionary Baptist, written on the side. When she walked by on her way to the Pie Shop, I asked her about the church suppers they served.

The driveway and the former garage that house the Pie Shop are shaded by pecan trees. On her way back, we talked about the lousy pecan harvest that year, 2011, and the horrible drought that was responsible for it. We talked about the wildfires back in Texas and we bought some pies.

After a while, Thomas stopped giving us the evil eye and loosened up. And since we didn't think we were working, we loosened up, too, and started absorbing the whole experience. We were eating pie and getting to know the lady who made it. A few weeks later, Rufus drove back to the Pie Shop from his home in Longview, Texas, and spent another day with Mary Thomas. On that trip she let Rufus take some photos in the kitchen while she made pies. And then she posed for a portrait out front in the doorway. I wish I could say she also gave me her secret piecrust recipe. She swears it doesn't include lard. I wonder if she uses suet? She wouldn't say.

Anyone and Everyone Is Welcome

As told to Francis Lam by Sue Nguyen

My name is Sue Nguyen; I'm thirty-two years old. I'm the owner and operator of Le Bakery Café.

I was born and raised in San Diego—I say raised, but actually I grew up in Biloxi, so I consider myself a Biloxian.

When we moved into the Point Cadet neighborhood, it was very welcoming. I really did enjoy growing up in that neighborhood. I think that was probably the biggest lure of me staying after the storm, because of the sense of community that I have here in Biloxi.

Years after my parents moved down here, they opened an Asian market with imported foods and whatnot. And throughout the years the business changed. With the passing of my father, I more or less took over the family business. We added in a bakery, and it just kind of took off on its own. I think it came in as an added bonus to the market; it was something that I was able to do as a passion. The demand took off on its own. I'm very blessed that it worked out this way. I never realized how much the bakery and café would change the business.

To begin with, our customers were the Asian community, and then we had a lot of Hispanics that came through that wanted certain ingredients that we had at the market. And of course you'd have your food fanatics that came in and wanted to try different ingredients. So by adding the bakery to the market, it was kind of like the launching pad there. It was a built-in clientele right there. As the bakery and the reputation of the bakery grew and people started coming by for the breads, you would see different cultures and different echelons of people—from economically to racially. It was completely mixed. I think that was kind of the lure of coming to this bakery. You should get the sense that anyone and everyone is welcome. I think the binder between it all was the breads.

We mainly do a lot of the French breads. The breads are more of the traditional style, where it's crusty but yet soft on the inside. It's got a wonderful crumb and flavor to it. I think the lure of our breads here is that they are reminiscent of a lot of different cultures' breads. We get that all the time. Like, "this is just like Cuban bread," or "this is just like the bread I get in Puerto Rico," or "this is just like the bread . . ." It's funny, because we hear so many different things. We have a lot of Europeans that come in here, and they love the crust on the bread. And of course, these are the breads that the Asian community is used to. So it's pretty interesting how everybody seems to think that our bread was made somewhat reminiscent of what they used to have growing up, you know?

The name of the bakery is Le Bakery. It's kind of a play on words: my mother's name is actually Le—it's spelled L-E. The restaurant my mom and dad ran in California was called Le Garden, which was named after my mother also. So it was kind of like the natural progression for me to name the bakery after my mom.

But it also has a French connotation. Everybody always says, "Yeah, the bakery on Oak Street," or "the bakery down on The Point," and that's us. I think a lot of people refer to us as the Vietnamese bakery, which yes, we are, but it's not just Vietnamese food. It's a bakery in which we carry different cultures' types of pastries and breads. You know, fortunately for us there's only one bakery here.

Right after the storm, I think we were in more or less a survival mode. I lost my house, and we lost the business here. We own the building, and of course you're faced with: Do you relocate? Do you not come back at all?

No matter what, we had to start cleaning out the building. And then to see the community outpouring of basic support. . . . And I had people who actually came by my house to make sure we were OK, because they knew I had lived in that neighborhood and that neighborhood was devastated. I had letters from people that lived from different areas to make sure that my family was OK. And then the next question after that was, "When is the bakery opening up?"

The decision to come back was hard, not knowing the future of this neighborhood and this area. And it is heartbreaking to see everything that you worked so hard for literally go out the door.

I love it here in Biloxi. We had the choice to leave, and we decided not to because this is our life. This is where we're based. Whether it was the wisest decision to come back, if another storm comes by; I don't know. I guess I'll face that as it comes.

When we reopened five months after the storm, there was a line out the door for bread. I was completely taken aback. I had people tell me, "This is the first sense of normalcy." We're talking about people who, at that time, were beginning to get FEMA trailers and get out of tents and things like that. They're finally getting the sense of normalcy from their daily stop at the bakery. And to be a part of that was a very great feeling. It was an overwhelming feeling to know that we were able to do that for people.

Five Ways of Looking at
Southern Food

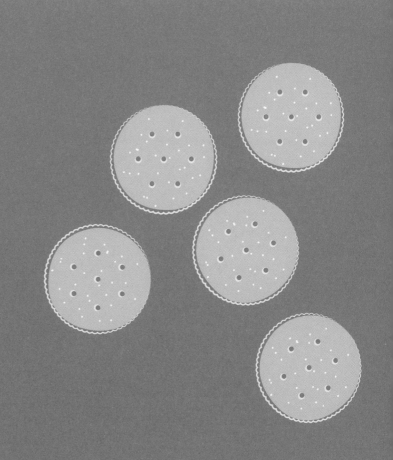

The Great Leveler

Julia Reed

I have been trying really hard to think of something new to say about Southern food, a subject that I (along with a host of other people) have written a whole lot about.

I have written about funeral food and pimiento cheese factions and George Jones versus Jimmy Dean sausage. I have attempted to prove the superiority of Southern cuisine by the all-too-easy comparison of our Junior League cookbooks with those from the North (*Talk about Good!* versus *Posh Pantry*; Aunt Margie's Better than Sex Cake versus Grape Nuts Pudding). And I am still trying to prove the existence of the lone Mexican who introduced the hot tamale to the Mississippi Delta, where I grew up.

Whether or not this mythic figure ever actually roamed these parts is immaterial. The existence of the Delta tamale itself proves what I have long known, that Southern food is the Great Leveler. Hot tamales are beloved by rich and poor, black and white, and they are easily accessible at roadside stands, cafes, and restaurants. A dozen hots wrapped in shucks at either Scott's Hot Tamales in Greenville or the White Front Cafe in Rosedale sells for eight dollars. The ones wrapped in paper at Greenville's Doe's Eat Place (my own personal favorites and the first solid food I ever ate) sell for a little more than ten dollars. But then, pretty much all great Southern food is cheap. Wyatt Cooper, the late, Mississippi-born husband of Gloria Vanderbilt and father of Anderson Cooper, once wrote that, "The best French restaurants in the world are wasted on me. All I want is a few ham hocks fried in bacon grease, a little mess of turnips with sowbelly, and a hunk of cornbread and I'm happy."

If this was Cooper's menu of choice, then he was not only happy, but rich—even without Gloria. On my last trip to France, I dined at two of "the best French restaurants," L'Oustau de Baumanière in Les Baux and Le Grand Vefour in Paris, and the bill for four people at each place put me in mind of what my father once said about a particularly pricey family ski trip to Aspen: "Next year, we don't even have to go—I can get the same effect standing in a cold shower burning up thousand-dollar bills." France in July might not have been as chilly, but each *l'addition* was considerably more than the entire tab for a brunch I gave for a New Orleans debutante the weekend after I returned home. The deb in question was Lizzy Cordes, the daughter of my friend Elizabeth, and her special menu request was for an hors d'oeuvre I make consisting of a piece of bacon wrapped around a watermelon pickle and broiled. I was delighted to comply—these little bundles are not only inexpensive, they are salty and sweet and pair extremely well with the ham biscuits and pimiento cheese sandwiches I also passed around. The main course, 250 pieces of excellent fried chicken from McHardy's Chicken & Fixin' on Broad Street, cost me exactly $240.90. Lizzy and her fellow debs had just been introduced to what passes for high society in my adopted city, but they seemed not just content but really, really happy to be munching away on some crispy chicken that cost less than a dollar per piece, and all the thank-you notes mentioned the food.

If Southern cuisine acts as a leveler by reducing the differences between race and class, the culture itself reduces the differences between—or the distinctness of—other cuisines introduced in our midst. Those Delta hot tamales bear little resemblance to Mexican hots, which, I'm pretty sure, are not bound together by lard and beef suet and, in the case of Doe's, porterhouse steak drippings. Just as deep-fried, bacon-wrapped, butterflied shrimp drenched in hot pink sweet-and-sour sauce on top of a ton of sautéed onions bears absolutely no resemblance to authentic Chinese cuisine. That particular item was my favorite thing on the menu at Henry Wong's How Joy, another Greenville mecca, and it was what I thought Chinese food tasted like until I left home for school at sixteen. Morris Lewis, a prominent wholesale grocer from Indianola, not only left home, he was invited to China on a trade visit just after Nixon opened up the place, but he was still convinced that How Joy was the real—or at least the tastier—deal. Upon his return, Lewis said, "I've been all the way to China and I've still never tasted Chinese food as good as Henry Wong's."

Sadly, neither Henry Wong nor his restaurant is still with us, but almost all of my other favorites are very much around. And a lifetime of eating and cooking them has enabled me to come up with a few new things to say. For example, Southerners who put sugar in cornbread are impostors, or criminals, or both. I love skillet cornbread, fried hot water cornbread, and cornbread muffins, but to add sugar to any of them is an abomination. Which does not mean I am a purist. I love "Mexican Cornbread," which, much like our tamales, does not come from anywhere near Mexico, but from a cookbook called *Bayou Cuisine* put together by the Episcopal churchwomen of Indianola, Mississippi. Among its ingredients are canned cream corn, marinated cherry peppers, Wesson oil, and shredded Kraft sharp cheddar.

Its utter deliciousness brings me to another important point: there is no shame in the occasional canned or packaged ingredient. Nora Ephron put packaged onion soup mix in her justifiably famous meat loaf, and hundreds of hostesses across the South were at a complete loss when Kraft quit making its jalapeño cheese roll (most often referred to as "nippy cheese"), the key ingredient in Spinach Madeleine. The spicy spinach dish was invented by St. Francisville, Louisiana, native Madeline Wright in 1956, and when it appeared three years later in the first edition of *River Road Recipes*, published by the Junior League of Baton Rouge, it immediately put the cookbook on the map. "If there were an Academy Award for cookbooks, the Oscar for Best Performance would go hands down to *River Road Recipes*," pronounced no less an expert than Craig Claiborne.

Then, of course, there is the mighty Ritz cracker, without which at least half of my mother's repertoire would be decimated. She fries eggplant and green tomatoes in crushed Ritz crackers, uses them in place of bread crumbs or the lowly saltine in squash soufflés, and puts them on top of pretty much every other casserole she makes, including her own now famous spinach dish, V.D. Spinach. So named because she served it to every "visiting dignitary" (from Bill and Pat Buckley to Ronald Reagan) who passed through our house, V.D. Spinach was chosen for inclusion in *The Essential New York Times Cookbook*, despite the fact that it includes frozen chopped spinach, Philadelphia cream cheese, and canned artichoke hearts.

I've also learned that Arkansas Travelers may well be the best tomatoes in the world, and all tomatoes are improved by peeling them. This latter point has been driven home to me all my life by my mother, who once peeled several hundred for the Katrina refugees who had evacuated to Greenville's convention center as accompaniments to—what else?—fried chicken. More recently, my friends Ben and Libby Page hosted a brunch in Nashville at which they peeled and served huge platters of various heirloom varieties alongside their collection of Irish crystal saltcellars containing salts from around the world. This added a decidedly chic element to every Southerner's favorite summer pleasure. When I visited Ben and Libby at their Tennessee farm afterward, we had tomatoes from their garden with two or three different salts, as well as skillet corn and squash casserole, a revered summer trinity that leads me to my last point: Southerners have been doing "farm to table"—mostly by necessity—since long before the phrase was taken up by every foodie in the land.

There is a reason, after all, that Mark Twain sent a lengthy bill of fare home ahead of him after he'd spent so much time in Europe. Among the things he'd missed the most were: "Virginia bacon, broiled; peach cobbler, Southern style; butter beans; sweet potatoes; green corn, cut from the ear and served with butter and pepper; succotash; soft-shell crabs." I am reminded again of Wyatt Cooper, as well as of the fact that pretty much the only thing I remember from my aforementioned meals in France was a side of tiny *haricots verts* just picked from L'Oustau de Baumanière's garden and drenched in fresh butter. And then there's the exchange between Katherine Anne Porter and William Faulkner that occurred at a swanky French restaurant that was probably Maxim's. They had dined well and enjoyed a fair amount of Burgundy and port, but at the end of the meal Faulkner's eyes glazed over a bit and he said, "Back home the butter beans are in, the speckled ones," to which a visibly moved Porter could only respond, "Blackberries." Now, I've repeated this exchange in print at least once before, and it is hardly new, but I don't care. No matter who we are or where we've been, we are all, apparently, "leveled" by the same thing: our love of our sometimes lowly, always luscious cuisine—our love, in short, of home.

The Post-Husk Era

Robert Moss

A lot has happened in the Charleston dining world since last summer. Of course, one could make that statement every year. Old restaurants close their doors and new ventures take their places. One chef gets tossed out of a noted kitchen, and another is lured away from a rival to fill the vacancy. This time around, though, it's more than just the usual turnover in an ever-changing industry. Something fundamental has shifted in local dining, and we've entered a new phase of our city's modern culinary history.

We might as well call it the Post-Husk Era.

When Husk opened its doors just before Christmas in 2010, it was the most anticipated and celebrated launch of any restaurant in our city's history. By now we all know the story: heirloom varieties, a celebration of purveyors, no ingredients produced outside the South, and lots and lots of pork fat. The buzz created a multiweek wait for reservations, and it transported Sean Brock into the high firmament of celebrity chef.

Husk's intensity created a thunderclap that is still reverberating through the local restaurant industry. In breathless pieces exploring the new lardcore thing, visiting writers passed over without even a mention of many of the restaurants that once routinely topped the lists of Charleston's best. Long-time chefs parted ways with established downtown restaurants, each for an individual set of reasons, but all involving a perceived need for change.

In this post-Husk era, dining has entered a new mode, one in which elegance and service take a backseat to the food—the bigger and bolder the better. Smoke and flame are the order of the day with wood-fired ovens, grills, and rotisseries letting chefs cook in a big, elemental way. From soft-shell crabs to hog snapper, the seafood served on downtown tables has never been fresher. There's a laser-focus on the ingredients—fresh, local, and heirloom preferred—and an embrace of traditional smoking, salting, and pickling to further concentrate the already-intense flavors.

A steady tide is rolling up King Street, wiping away the boarded-up furniture stores and menswear shops and leaving in its wake fantastically gleaming new restaurants. Kevin Johnson made a splash with The Grocery, where his wood-fired oven kicks out a dazzling array of dishes, ranging from tiny bites of beets to a whole roasted snapper for the table to share. Just one block south, Nathan Thurston is on the verge of opening Stars, where a custom-made, wood-fired grill and rotisserie will be the centerpiece of the kitchen. The pending arrival of The Ordinary, an oyster bar from FIG's Mike Lata and Adam Nemirow, has local foodies buzzing months in advance of its scheduled fall opening.

As if that's not enough, I'm told by folks with the inside scoop that we ain't seen nothing yet. Outside capital is pouring in to fund a range of even loftier and more extravagant ventures, so expect a continuing parade of big-ticket restaurant launches in the year to come.

And that raises an important question about the future of this flourishing dining scene. Not too long ago, I was drinking cocktails at the Belmont with a couple of guys from New Orleans, and we were talking about Charleston dining and all the recent restaurant openings. Finally, one of them paused over his Tiger Paw Sour and asked the pertinent question. "Charleston really isn't that big of a town," he said. "Who's eating at all these new places?"

Tourists, was my immediate answer, noting that events like Spoleto and the Southeastern Wildlife Expo pack our restaurants with out-of-towners. Plus, the coastal charms attract empty-nesters and retirees from far off with plenty of money to spend on fine dining. But even as I said it, the explanation didn't quite ring true.

Last year was a good one for tourism, rebounding from the recession dip with surging hotel occupancy rates. But according to figures from the College of Charleston's Office of Tourism Analysis, hotel occupancy was down 2.6 percent this May over last year, suggesting that the flow of tourism dollars won't be ever-rising. Our population has increased a little—about 15 percent over the past decade—but it's hardly a boomtown expansion.

Will there be enough of a market to support this surge of new high-end restaurants, or will it spark a Darwinian battle where an increasing number of competitors vie for the same limited resources?

There's something more than economics to be wary of. I keep getting glimpses of a warning light blinking somewhere off in the distance. Or, to put it a little differently, despite all the heat of our booming restaurant scene, there's still something that leaves me a little cold.

It's a matter of culinary identity. What is it that makes Charleston special? What do you get when you dine out here that you can't find in, say, Atlanta or Raleigh or Nashville? Are all these lardcore trappings nothing more than window dressing, the style of the moment?

The real risk is that Lowcountry cuisine is giving way to a more pan-Southern type of food. After all, the real innovation of Husk was not to be hyperlocal— that hundred-mile-radius thing—but rather hyperregional in focus.

When outsiders look at Charleston these days, they see not the Lowcountry but the South. "Why all the fuss about Southern American cooking?" Jeffrey Steingarten asked in a recent glowing profile of Brock and Husk in *Vogue*. "It is simply the finest that America has ever produced."

In the new pan-Southern cooking, anything with a Dixie twang is given equal billing. Thus you get cornbread, bacon, shrimp, collards, grits, Carolina Gold rice, Sea Island peas, pickled ramps, pimento cheese, and fried green tomatoes all lumped together and labeled a cuisine.

But the cooking of the Lowcountry was very different from that of, say, south Georgia or the rural western counties of Virginia. When the Works Progress Administration's Guide to the Palmetto State described Lowcountry cookery in 1941, it talked about shrimp, oyster, crab, "hop-in John," red rice, wild duck, okra and tomato pilau, syllabub, and benne-seed brittle. It didn't mention peanuts or country ham.

Like its accents and dialects, the South's cuisine is multifaceted. And yet today, the menus at our city's most lauded restaurants look almost identical to those of Atlanta, Nashville, or Birmingham.

Here's a fun test. The items below were selected from the menus of four different restaurants, each of which has a chef who has won or been nominated for Best Chef South or Best Chef Southeast by the James Beard Foundation. Each dish, in fact, is the first item to appear on the menu under the entrée section. Can you guess which of the four is from Charleston? (It's from Husk, by the way):

1. Fudge Farms pork confit and housemade sausage with rattlesnake beans, pink-eyed peas, and new potatoes
2. North Carolina guinea hen terrine with English peas, turnips, baby carrots, and roasted garlic mushroom broth
3. Sorghum glazed pork belly, carrot, cabbage, field peas, radishes, peanuts, mustard greens, pickled ramps
4. Duo of Border Springs lamb with Anson Mills Hominy, heirloom carrots, corn nuts, lamb bacon jus

No. 1 is from the Highlands Bar & Grill in Birmingham, no. 3 from Restaurant Eugene in Atlanta, and no. 4 from the Capitol Grille in Nashville. The Husk entrée is no. 2.

There's some virtue in the similarities. Our tight-knit Southern chefs share ideas, inspiration, and ingredients, and there's nothing wrong with that. It's led to a vibrant rebirth of Southern cooking, one that has taken us beyond the stereotypes and clichés and found a new depth and intensity in the produce and preparations of our native soil. In some ways, perhaps, we first had to rediscover the South as a whole before we could rediscover our own little corner of it.

But now it's time to turn our focus back to that little corner. If not, we'll be in danger of losing what once made the cuisine of each subregion of the South so distinctive.

This is not a call to return to the past and limit ourselves by it. We can't stop time at some arbitrary point and preserve it in amber, and it would be futile even if we could. The regional cuisines of earlier centuries were as dynamic as ours is today, a cookery created from the intersection of multiple cultures in a particular time and place with a particular set of ingredients on hand to adopt and adapt.

So this isn't a plea to stay static. Instead, it's a plea to continue evolving but to do so in a more tightly localized way.

When I went to Louisiana for vacation over the Christmas holidays, I was struck by the sheer vibrancy of restaurants and dishes that you can find only in New Orleans. Tempting as they looked, we skipped past a lot of hot new restaurants like August and Stella! and Herbsaint, and we missed Cure and Bar Tonique at cocktail hour, too. Why? Because we could get the same kind of meals here at home at Macintosh or The Grocery, and similar craft cocktails at the Gin Joint. Instead, we ate debris po-boys at Mother's, Gulf oysters at Acme, and high Creole at Antoine's and Galatoire's. Happy hour found us sipping Sazeracs at the Sazerac Bar and Vieux Carrés at the Carousel. And when I go back I'll do it again.

Amid the pan-Southern welter, there are some encouraging signs. One of the areas where we are already getting it right is with our seafood. Nothing could be more distinctively Charleston than white shrimp straight from the trawler net or line-caught fish fresh off the Bump.

In fact, I need to make a confession. In my "pick the local dish" quiz above, I cheated. I actually picked not the first entrée from each restaurant's menu but the first nonfish entrée. I had to, because the fish give it away. Highlands Bar & Grill's grilled redfish or the Capitol Grille's pan-fried red mountain trout aren't going to be mistaken for a Charleston dish, and no chef in Raleigh or Atlanta is having deep-sea fishermen deliver them stuff that was caught fresh that morning.

Our local cooks have so much more to work with than pork fat and bacon. After years of avoiding them as a tourist cliché, some of our best chefs have reclaimed shrimp and grits, putting their own deft spins on an old local staple. She-crab soup is long overdue for a similar treatment, for it's a genuine but long-suffering Lowcountry creation with the potential for elegance and grace.

My hope is that this wild flourish of creative energy—and the influx of investment capital that's making it a reality—comes more tightly into focus. The elements are all here: unique local ingredients, a long and rich culinary history, and a close-knit community of chefs working together and sharing ideas and inspiration. These may well converge to create a mode of dining that is unique to our particular place and time. And then, as they arrive in town for their annual treks, our nation's food writers will rave not about the wonders of Southern cooking but rather about the splendid Lowcountry cuisine that can be found only here in Charleston.

Ode to Gumbo

Kevin Young

For weeks I have waited
for a day without death
or doubt. Instead
the sky set afire

or the flood
filling my face.
A stubborn drain
nothing can fix.

Every day death.
Every morning death
& every night
& evening

And each hour
a kind of winter—
all weather
is unkind. Too

hot, or cold
that creeps the bones.
Father, your face
a faith

I can no longer see.
Across the street
a dying, yet
still-standing tree.

■　　■　　■

So why not
make a soup
of what's left? Why
not boil & chop

something outside
the mind—let us
welcome winter
for a few hours, even

in summer. Some
say Gumbo
starts with *filé*
or with *roux*, begins

with flour & water
making sure
not to burn. I know Gumbo
starts with sorrow—

with hands that cannot wait
but must—with stirring
& a slow boil
& things that cannot

be taught, like grace.
Done right,
Gumbo lasts for days.
Done right, it will feed

you & not let go.
Like grief
you can eat & eat
& still plenty

left. Food
of the saints,
Gumbo will outlast
even us—like pity,

you will curse it
& still hope
for the wing
of chicken bobbed

up from below.
Like God
Gumbo is hard
to get right

& I don't bother
asking for it outside
my mother's house.
Like life, there's no one

way to do it,
& a hundred ways,
from here to Sunday,
to get it dead wrong.

■   ■   ■

Save all the songs.
I know none,
even this, that will
bring a father

back to his son.
Blood is thicker
than water under
any bridge

& Gumbo thicker
than that. It was
my father's mother
who taught mine how

to stir its dark mirror—
now it is me
who wishes to plumb
its secret

depths. Black
Angel, Madonna
of the Shadows,
Hail Mary strong

& dark as dirt,
Gumbo's scent fills
this house like silence
& tells me everything

has an afterlife, given
enough time & the right
touch. You need
okra, sausage, bones

of a bird, an entire
onion cut open
& wept over, stirring
cayenne in till the end

burns the throat—
till we can amen
& pretend
such fiery

mercy is all we know.

Mother Corn and the Dixie Pig
Native Food in the Native South

Rayna Green

Native food is in the news. Every day. All over the country, except in the South, farmers, chefs, environmentalists, and food writers are excited about Native food and foodways. That excitement usually comes from a "discovery" (or rediscovery) of the many virtues of old "slow" foods in the now hip vernacular—local, fresh, and seasonal foods that are good for you, good for the land, and good for the small food producer. Often, these rediscovered foods come from "Native" varieties that seed savers, naturalists, nutritionists, and Indians have propped up, from animals that regulators, commercial producers, and advocates have brought back from the brink of extinction, and from habitats redeemed from under middens of waste and neglect.

Some Native communities, in revitalizing their own cultural histories and economies, have begun again to raise, catch, and market crops and critters long associated with them but just as long ago replaced. Hopis and other Pueblos farm and market native varieties of corn, beans, and other vegetables to provide a better diet and income for their people, while Ojibwas do the same with wild rice in the Great Lakes. In the Plains, where once the death of bison was synonymous with the defeat and death of Indians themselves, buffalo herds now thrive on tribal and public lands. Northwest Coastal people fish for salmon, pack and ship it to an audience eager for it, and serve it at salmon feasts, some for the communities, some for the income generated by cultural tourism.

In spite of the good press, Native food and foodways are, as ever, subject to massive assaults on their maintenance and survival. What hunters, hatmakers, the cavalry, miners, and trains didn't deplete or destroy in the eighteenth and nineteenth centuries, industrial and domestic polluters, ranchers, big farmers, dams, cities, and roads rolled over in the twentieth century. Modern tribal efforts at resource revitalization still meet resistance because they interfere—as Indians always have—with large non-Indian economic and cultural interests. Native people and park rangers in the Plains fight ranchers over the renewed presence of brucellosis-carrying buffalo in proximity to the huge cattle herds that graze, subsidized by federal money, on public lands. Northwest Coastal people struggle against international agency regulators, Japanese fish factories, and sport fishers for the right to catch the fish emblematic of their survival as a people. Always, Native Alaskans battle with the state and federal governments and with animal rights activists to continue their traditional subsistence diet and thus maintain cultural skills and legal rights. They all know, out there in Indian country, that the loss of traditional diet and the cultural skills needed to maintain it has killed more Indians than Andy Jackson. And they all know that the food fights, like the struggles to restore language and ceremony, are modern fights for survival. Where they are known to be central to the economies and cultural histories of the entire region, Native food and the politics that govern Native resources are at the top of regional discussion.

Native food and foodways in the South, however, attract neither the rabid enthusiasms nor wild resistances of other parts of the country. Four hundred years ago, the settler-saving "gifts" of Indian food and food production technologies, along with the salvation of an English adventurer by the Indian chief's beautiful daughter, anchored colonial mythology; three hundred years ago Indian corn and tobacco centered the new growth economy; two hundred years ago Indian food resources still constituted, in essence, the base diet of the region. Yet this history seems nearly irrelevant today—as do Indians themselves—to popular conceptions of the South.

It was not always thus. Native food was once the only food story. Early travelers and colonists of the Americas spoke at length of the abundance and richness of the natural environment, the good that Indians made of it, and the absolute dependence of the would-be colonists on Indian mastery of that environment. Archaeologists of Jamestown and other Southern sites echo and reinforce these early accounts, confirming that Natives in precolonial Virginia and North Carolina, the Upland South, coastal Mississippi, Florida, and Alabama ate well and often from a huge and diverse larder. In most instances, they cultivated appropriately and well, renewing their resources by methods of complementary planting, crop rotation, nutritional enhancement, and resource-restorative rules for the gathering of plants and hunting of animals. Meat, fish, shellfish, vegetables, fruits, and nuts made for a better, richer, more abundant, and more nutritious diet than available to most of the Anglo-Europeans that journeyed to the South and a more dependable, consistent, diverse diet than most Indians elsewhere (except those in the Southwest and Pacific Northwest).

From their indigenous relatives in Mexico, Southeastern (and Southwestern) Indians had centuries ago learned the knowledge and skills associated with cultivating corn, which they shared with receptive settlers. Essential Native practices included combining corn and beans to create protein- and amino acid–rich meals; consuming hominy, corn breads, soups, drinks, and mushes (grits, tamales) made from limed corn (nixtamalization); using nitrogen-enriching leguminous ash in various corn dishes; interplanting corn with nitrogen-replacing or nitrogen-enriching varieties (e.g., legumes); and rotating nutritionally exhausted croplands with alternate crops. It didn't take the Spanish very long at all, merely twenty years into their sixteenth-century invasions, to substitute many of their own imports for Native food resources. But well into the seventeenth century—in the remainder of the British-occupied Southeast—Native diet and Native knowledge formed the core of the new Southern foodways even as the British process for amending and replacing that diet, Native knowledge and skills, and Indians themselves escalated. It took nearly a hundred years for the agriculturally and hunting-challenged British, in particular (at least the classes of Brits who first came to the Southeast), to begin amending the Native larder and food technologies for their own foods and technologies from home. It took two centuries more of dismantling Indian food technologies and land management skills to understand the errors of doing so, with once good agricultural lands farmed out and eroded by 1900, the population plagued by niacin deficiency, and pellagra reaching epidemic proportions.

By the eighteenth century, when most colonists had succeeded in breaking the exclusive hold that the Native diet had on their survival, the "new" foods from Europe (Spain, France, the British Isles), Africa, and the Caribbean merged with native staples to create the complex mélange that is today's Southern cuisine. These changes affected Indian and non-Indian alike. From Indians the new Southerners had developed the taste for and habit of eating more vegetables, particularly greens (fresh and cooked), than did other Americans. These native vegetables, both gathered and cultivated, joined Spanish-imported produce such as melons, peaches, and peppers. African food tastes and habits reinforced the Indian vegetable/greens complex and brought in new and healthful crops such as sesame and okra, and legumes such as black-eyed peas and peanuts thrived in the Lowland and southeastern climate. From Africans many also acquired the taste for hot peppers and spices and for the technique of frying. Later, all would adopt dairy products—as they were able to raise the dairy cattle, wheat flour, and sugar when they could afford them—and more liquor when they could make it. Pigs, introduced in the sixteenth century, rooted their way into Indian communities in the late eighteenth century. Women, the primary farmers of the Southern Indian world, first resisted the feral beasts that ravaged their fields and crops, but they eventually accepted the domesticated (and wild) food source that meant meat on the Indian table. And Indians, like other Southerners, learned to use pigs not only as their main meat source but also a source of cooking grease, side meat, and flavoring. They "nativized" the once-alien animal, just as the newcomers once normalized and accepted the American animals and plants new to them, and incorporated pig into dishes featuring Mother Corn alone. These foods remain some of those most beloved by Southern Indians.

Indian removal in the 1830s was supposed to settle the resource dispute first begun in the seventeenth century. Cherokees, Choctaws, Creeks, and Chickasaws stood in the way of land-grabbers, gold seekers, and farmer/landowners with cash crops based in a slave economy. The forced land cessions accompanying Indian removal did indeed take most of the prime farming, hunting, and fishing lands held by Indians in the South, leaving behind many small communities with little but the weakened cultural skills essential to their survival. Those removed retained something of the skills and knowledge regarding the basic foods and foodways, which they tried, only partially successfully, to restore in Oklahoma. Indian losses would be the miner's canary, as they always were, for the environmental and economic disasters that were yet to unhinge large parts of the agrarian South.

The small group of Choctaws, once stellar farmers, who managed to stay in Mississippi were eventually reduced to the poorest of sharecroppers by the turn of the twentieth century. Their hunter-fisher-gatherer Houma relatives, in the Louisiana bayous since the late seventeenth century, would become French speaking, forced to take protective cover in the ways and manners of their neighbors. They and the Seminoles and Miccosukees, who had fled to Florida before removal, had become masters of their environments, subsisting on food sourcing from small farms and watery habitats into the twenty-first century. But Houmas, unlike the Seminoles who resisted assimilation in any visible way, would remain unrecognized and relatively obscured as Indians to the world around them. Cherokees who avoided removal in North Carolina remained in the hills, as poor and isolated as their Appalachian neighbors but able to continue a reasonably successful survival exploitation of the environment left to them. The menu from a 1949 feast given for anthropologists suggests not only how deeply Cherokee foodways had burrowed into the now all-but-Native diet of the Upland South but also how natural, how unexotic, how Southern that diet was.

Other remaining Indians in the South—in South Carolina, Virginia, and North Carolina, in particular—faced a fate different from their removed relatives. Fragmented into small, isolated communities, impoverished, collectively landless for the most part, with no federal treaties and a continuing lack of federal recognition, they most often "disappeared" as Indians. They kept what they could of the old ways and blended through intermarriage and interaction, as they always had done, with white and black folks, with Christians, with English speakers. They ate more and more like the people with whom they lived, just as their neighbors had once learned to eat like them. But they remained at the edges of that society, further and further segregated into smaller units, with their identity as Indians virtually erased after the Civil War, the end of slavery, and Reconstruction by the South's primal obsession with black and white. Indian extinction had not succeeded; marginalization had.

Virginia's Indians, for example, so essential to the founding identity of the place and so embedded in its historical memory, found themselves without any viable social niche. In 1924, via the Racial Integrity Act, they found themselves in a state that declared most Indians nonexistent or illegal entities. This declaration of their legal nonexistence drove Virginia Indians to rise up and insist on repeal of the invidious law that separated them from their historic identity. One of the ways in which they did that was to reenact the historic relationship, forged in Native food, between them and the colonists. In the Colonial era, "Powhatans" (a collective term for all Virginia Indians of the day) had delivered tribute deer to the governor of Virginia every year in lieu of taxes on lands held by Indians. Continuing this practice into the late twentieth century reinforced the survival and continuity of Virginia's Indians, several groups of which eventually obtained state recognition. Relatively recently, that recognition resulted in the restoration of their right to use the land's more abundant larder so praised by early colonists for more than 350 of the last 400 years. By 2005 Pamunkeys and Mattaponi could again hunt deer and fish for shad off their state reservations and collect oysters from the bay without a state license. Still, the Mattaponi in Virginia currently are trying to stop a proposed reservoir that would divert water from the Mattaponi River, endangering their shad fisheries and the shreds of the traditional life they have remaining. Still, much-loved Virginia spring shad feasts, like those offered the colonists four hundred years ago by Virginia's Indians, have come to be reserved for Virginia political events that exclude Indians (and women). In many ways the complex relationship of Virginia's citizens to Indians, as expressed through the acceptance and rejection of Native food and foodways—as well as Virginia natives' persistence toward their food and foodways—may act as a paradigm for the Southern Indian story.

A few Native dishes never passed into the mainstream Southern culinary repertoire and remain distinctly and exclusively Indian, very much a part of Native identity, cherished and propped up in a public way, served to strangers and friends and certainly in revitalized Green Corn or stomp dance communal dinners. Bean bread and *so-chan* among the North Carolina Cherokees are dishes likely not found elsewhere in Appalachia. Choctaws and Chickasaws in Oklahoma eat *banaha*, a tamale-like corn mush with field peas and/or pea shell ash, and hominy in every form it comes in, including *tamfula* (often pronounced "tomfuller"), a hominy and hickory nut soup/cream unlikely to be on a restaurant menu even in Oklahoma. *Sofkee*, a soup or drink of soured cornmeal, links Seminoles and Miccosukees in Florida to Seminoles, Yuchis, and Creeks in Oklahoma and is never found outside Indian communities. Many of these precious foods listed above may indeed have been the staples of the long-ago diet. Others, such as the various corn-and-pig dishes or berry dumplings (often "cobblers" or "pies") that have characterized Indian cooking since the late eighteenth century, represent the beginnings of dietary change long ago, yet they became enshrined within their communities as uniquely Cherokee, uniquely Choctaw, uniquely Indian. Today these foods and foodways belong to the communities that cook and serve them, in spite of the profound changes they represented when first introduced. Some foods maintain the ancient Indian relationships with and responsibilities to plants and animals, and most Native communities worry about passing on their skills and tastes, just as they worry about the death of language. Even when they can get canned hominy, frozen corn, bottled grape juice, and four different kinds of greens at the grocery store, they still organize cultural camps and plant native gardens where younger Indians can learn traditions that now represent physical and cultural survival.

In the late 1970s the United States began to look with favor on marginalized cuisines. Ethnic pride and cultural rights movements of the 1960s demanded acknowledgment for the cultural contributions of those once repressed. The long tradition of African American foodways became a distinctive and redemptive badge of cultural pride, and the new term "soul food" became synonymous with both traditional African American cuisine and the best of "Southern cooking." Thus, soul food, Cajun food, so-called white trash cooking, and good old country cooking started to have their day alongside plantation (antebellum) food, French-Creole traditions, and Lowcountry haute cuisine. The new Southern food historians, a multivocal collection of people of good faith, mind, and heart, respectfully acknowledge the many peoples and ethnicities that have created and amended the delightful fusion that is Southern cuisine. But discussions based solely on black and white relationships still dominate, and roiling underneath the civilities of new acknowledgments remains the intensely Southern spat over which group really gave the most to this beloved food, planting old and ever volatile claims to the kingdom right in the middle of a plate of barbecue.

No Indian claims to a rightful place within Southern foodways surfaced in these tangles, and no one has made any claims on Indians' behalf. Indians have not established restaurants that serve up ethnic pride along with the foods that underpin the Southern diet. No public relations campaign, protest, or demand for respect has accompanied the recent elevation of grits and greens to nearly sanctified status in New South cuisine. Some might say Southern Indians have been too busy putting their cultural and physical survival, their very existence, on the agenda to pursue a more substantive acknowledgment of their historic contributions. But could the focus on Native food provide more than simply some suggestions for what historical curiosities might be served to interested patrons at the casino restaurant or for what might amount to just a little more political correctness regarding Native people by the next cookbook writer? Just what might a little attention to Native food history in the South be worth, and to whom might that worth be manifest?

It is true that Southern Indians and their foods do not have the competitive edge granted Indians in the West with their national attachments to the charismatic megafauna—buffalo, whales, seals—so emblematic of Native place and history in the West and Far North. But a different kind of repatriation might do us all good, and we could start by bringing back those native varieties that appear lost, to say nothing of showing interest in the reasons that certain foods were not lost to Native communities. The new small farms and farmer's markets, the new chefs that care so deeply about the restoration of Southern food, might want to join forces with the oldest farmers to their mutual benefit. We could start in Mississippi, where a Choctaw woman recently sold Mason jars filled with a kind of shoepeg hominy she had raised and processed without a subsidy. Getting her grits on the menu somewhere would do more than simply lend chic credibility to this revitalized Southern cult food. We might all find ways to support and extend the kinds of *so-chan* and ramp gardens that the Eastern Band of Cherokee Indians has started in North Carolina. The story (and the action that needs to follow a good story) is missing in the South, where Native food might bring good news. And with that news could come a cultural construct that might be surprisingly useful—a region of the mind called Native South—a good name, perhaps, for the chain of restaurants that could appear in Indian casinos. The food served there would be shockingly familiar, albeit a tad underseasoned, to all good Southerners, and once again Indians would welcome everyone to eat. Come on in where you see the neon cornstalk flashing over the smiling Dixie pig.

Every Ounce a Man's Whiskey?
Bourbon in the White Masculine South

Seán McKeithan

> *It is about the aesthetic of Bourbon drinking in general and in particular of knocking it back neat. . . . The joy of Bourbon drinking is not the pharmacological effect of C_2H_5OH on the cortex but rather the instant of the whiskey being knocked back and the little explosion of Kentucky U.S.A. sunshine in the cavity of the nasopharynx and the hot bosky bite of Tennessee summertime.*
>
> Walker Percy, "Bourbon"

In a 1975 essay bluntly and beautifully titled "Bourbon," Walker Percy asserts that "the pleasure of knocking back Bourbon lies in the plane of the aesthetic but at an opposite pole from connoisseurship." For Percy, it is Bourbon's aesthetic condition rather than its chemical composition that makes the drink so distinctly appealing. "Knocking it back neat" serves a transportive function, immersing the Bourbon drinker in the rich cultural imagery of the American South: woody, sunny, and romantic. The hot bite of the Bourbon sensuously connects the body of the drinker to nation, region, and locale, enjoining his experience with those of imagined historical bodies, soaking up space and place in the slow burn of what appears an endless Southern summertime. For Percy, a Southern doctor, author, philosopher, and social critic, Bourbon drinking serves as an existential, even religious, act that connects the drinker to an imagined history, an act that ultimately provides an "evocation of time and memory and of the recovery of self and the past from the fogged-in disoriented Western world."

Like Percy, I am a drinker of Bourbon. Although I (and no doubt Percy as well) appreciate both its chemical and symbolic capacities, I am primarily concerned with the symbolic, its aesthetic relation to issues of personal and cultural identity. Percy's personal history with Bourbon began as a child in the Prohibition 1920s in his family's Birmingham basement, as he watched his father age his own product in a charcoal barrel. The personal narrative he recounts in his essay binds Bourbon consumption to episodes of heterosexuality, homosociality, and UNC football games. My personal history with Bourbon begins much later, in the suburban 2000s, at the parties of Virginia Beach schoolmates whose parents were out of town.

At this point, my interests in men like Evan Williams, Jim Beam, and Kentucky Gentleman were primarily physical, corporeal, chemical. I privileged their bodily, pharmacological capabilities over their symbolic and welcomed their presence in my stilted, surreptitious social life with the same wide arms, open mouth, and ready chaser as any gin, vodka, or crème de menthe that we could prize from our parents' liquor cabinets. I trace the first stirrings of my symbolic appreciation of Bourbon to my second romantic relationship in college, with a white Southern man who preferred it to any other liquor. During the time we spent together, I sensed something decidedly self-conscious in his choice of drink and began to conceive of it as a sort of play, a means of both challenging and asserting his place within a specific narrative of white Southern masculinity, in which he was at once bound by his North Carolina lineage and excluded by his sexuality.

Back then I did not articulate his liquor choice in the same historical, theoretical terms that I do now, but I did see it as somehow ironic, an act that called into question some unspoken rules of who can drink what. In my time with this man, I began drinking Bourbon as a matter of choice and of taste, although at first I rather disliked the way it tasted. I drank Bourbon in a spirit of transgression that I could not pin down but felt that, in so doing, I took some nebulous stand against the heterosexist assumption that women and queer men drank from glasses that came with umbrellas, instead of only with ice. As I looked around me, at the fraternity parties I inevitably attended, the dorm rooms in which I inevitably found myself, and the bars into which I inevitably snuck, I realized that the self-consciousness I saw in his consumption was present in everyone's. It dawned on me: there was something political in Bourbon drinking.

Walker Percy and I are both Southern white men of relative economic privilege who have consumed Bourbon in the company of other men and in the same social spaces at the same Southern university. Still, our respective approaches to the Bourbon aesthetic differ greatly. Percy approaches Bourbon as a straight white man, the son of a prominent Birmingham lawyer and his Birmingham wife, in many ways the prototypical Southern gentleman by birth. As a queer white man from suburban Virginia Beach, the son of a working-class North Carolina father and an immigrant Irish mother, I approach Bourbon as a less prototypically Southern, differently gentle man. Despite our differences, or perhaps because of them, we are both drawn to Bourbon as the symbol of a distinct Southern aesthetic.

Bourbon's relationship to the American South is long and storied, rising literally out of the soil of the region and into its culture, both popular and private. To understand the role that Bourbon plays in the psyche of today's white Southern man, it is important to understand its history—economic, cultural, and agricultural—and its relation to the history of the South. Understanding these histories allows us to see how Bourbon drinking can serve as a bridge into the past, allowing a drinker to tap into centuries of culture with a simple consumptive act. Finally, once we understand the ways that Bourbon drinking ties consumers directly to histories of race, gender, class, and sexuality, we can see how distinct individuals—Percy, me, or any other—can function within the Bourbon aesthetic. Consequently, we can begin to understand Bourbon's potential to maintain, negotiate, and challenge existing power relations in the contemporary Southern social landscape, one drink at a time.

DRINKING OUR WAY INTO THE PAST

In popular imagination, the Southerner has long been seen as a social creature, one that lives to eat, drink, visit, and tell stories. Indeed, Southern historian W. Fitzhugh Brundage observes that "Southerners, after all, have the reputation of being among the most historically oriented of peoples and of possessing the longest, most tenacious memories." The methods and mechanisms through which individuals and groups carry out their remembering are diverse, encompassing shared stories and oral histories; public monuments and memorials; cultural rituals and artistic practices; and of course eating and drinking traditions, among others. By these varied recollective practices, groups and individuals pay homage to the past while establishing their identities in the present, as shaped by the history—either real or imagined—to which their remembrances refer. Although the analysis of any group's eating patterns, or foodways, can be quite valuable in understanding its culture, the American South is especially suited for a study of consumption. As Southern foodways scholars such as Marcie Cohen Ferris and John Egerton have shown, politics, poverty, and oppression have shaped the culinary traditions of the South, so these traditions are distinctly imbued with great cultural weight. In the continuously changing, constantly globalizing contemporary South, foodways have survived as largely intact markers of historical Southern identity, even as many of the concrete sociopolitical institutions of the Old South have faded into, well, history.

In today's South, where it seems young men can travel to Bangkok about as readily as Baltimore, Bourbon remains a piece of masculine identity that Southerners can "put on," much like overalls, a seersucker suit, or a North Carolina twang. Bourbon adds an even deeper dimension to the "putting on" of identity because it is literally taken into the body of the drinker, affecting him in both image and consciousness. As the epigraph illustrates, a drinker feels the Bourbon's "bite," which connects him sensuously via literal consumption, as well as aesthetically via symbolic consumption, to a narrative of imagined rurality, of nostalgia for a South that is no more, and can be recalled only with a few straight shots of Kentucky straight Bourbon whiskey. In putting back a few shots of the stuff, we "perform" identities, identities tied to race, class, gender, sexuality, and, ultimately, history. Such performances of identity give us insight into the ways people not only present themselves, but also perceive of themselves, know themselves, and know of others. By studying these performances in a given cultural context, we can begin to see which identities are privileged and which are policed in that culture. To understand Bourbon's function today, it is thus crucial to understand its history, as bound to the agriculture, economy, and settlement of the American South.

AN ECONOMIC, CULTURAL, AND AGRICULTURAL HISTORY OF BOURBON

The story of Bourbon's ascent from the ripe ground of the Southern colonies into the collective consciousness of today's South is a story of thirst, industriousness, and, perhaps above all, corn. Today's Bourbons follow strict legal codes of composition, bubbling forth with terms both scientifically severe: "produced at not exceeding 160 proof" and charmingly quaint: "in charred new oak containers." Bourbon's early ancestors, however, were born of the efforts of the earliest American settlers and were closer kin to today's moonshine than to anything we might recognize as Bourbon. By the late 1790s, a significant population of Scots-Irish had settled in Maryland and southwest Pennsylvania and had "brought with them the strongly held opinion that whiskey, not bread, was the staff of life, the equipment for distilling, and an expert knowledge of the distiller's art." These settlers quickly took to squeezing liquor out of the land, using primarily local rye, but also grains, fruits, and even vegetables, distilling just about anything that could be made to ferment. As these settlers moved south through Appalachia to Kentucky across the Cumberland Gap, they discovered Southern corn, the region's supercrop.

While rye grew well in Pennsylvania and Maryland, corn grew like wild-fire in Kentucky. Settlers could plant it quickly, even haphazardly, and its yield was robust and bountiful. Kentucky farmers ate their corn, drank their corn, and fed it to their animals. They also quickly learned that the fastest way to turn their excess harvest into extra cash was to distill it, as liquid traveled better than grain across the mountains that hedged in Kentucky's Blue-grass region. The road to Bourbon's prominence in the mind of the South was thus paved with corn, like much of the region's cuisine and resultant culture. Distillation slowly evolved from a by-product of the harvest to its principal purpose, and the rotgut corn whiskey of yore slowly evolved into the smooth stuff we know today as Bourbon.

Accounts of this evolution differ greatly. The most cherished story of Bourbon's conception has it that Elijah Craig, a late-eighteenth-century Baptist minister and the namesake of a small-batch Bourbon today, distilled the first true Bourbon. Legend has it that Craig—perhaps a result of divine providence—decided to age the whiskey that others were drinking green and named it based on its place of origin, Bourbon County. Historians have disproven the story on many counts, chief among them that Craig never distilled whiskey in Bourbon County. More accurately, it was the increasing standardization and commercialization of the Bourbon industry that led to Bourbon's routine aging in charred oak barrels, and to the appealing mellow-ness and attractive ruddiness it takes on after a few years in the barrel. As efficiency in distillation rose, and with it Bourbon surpluses, distillers increasingly shipped their product throughout the South, down the Ohio River en route to New Orleans and along the Louisville and Nashville Railroad to the rest of the southern colonies. Like grits and cornbread, corn whiskey began to settle into the collective consciousness and consumption patterns of the South.

Unlike grits and cornbread, however, Bourbon is of particular importance in the study of white Southern masculinity because of its distinctly constructed white Southern maleness. Generally speaking, much of a culture's food production has historically been the province of its women, and has taken place within the home. Alcohol, however, is an important exception, as its production and consumption have, in many cultures, remained the jurisdiction of men. This was especially true in the gendered Old South, where plantation gentlemen used whiskey to construct a homosocial environment apart from women and children, and common Southern men used it to liven any meal or social gathering. Bourbon, more than other staples in the Southern culinary tradition, thus offers a singular insight into white Southern masculinity. Bourbon is also the only indigenous, distinctly Southern liquor, recognized by Congress in 1964 as "America's native whiskey."

Noting the Southern predilection for the drink, Bourbon historian Charles Cowdery goes so far as to refer to the region as the "bourbon belt." Bourbon thus exemplifies Southern drink, and since Southern drinking has long served in the performance of Southern manhood, Bourbon has been distinctly imbued with the rich historical narrative of the white Southern male. Examined in relation to its representation in popular culture, we learn how Bourbon drinking plays a crucial role in the everyday performance of white Southern masculine identities.

EVERY OUNCE A MAN'S WHISKEY

Over the last few centuries, corn whiskey has thus evolved from rotgut into Bourbon, and from Bourbon into today's Bourbon market glut. What was, as late as the 1960s, a humble market of spirits left almost exclusively on the bottom shelf has become an endlessly niched carnival, with distilling houses now producing Bourbons premixed with cola or honey, aged any number of years, and increasingly designated as "ultra-premium," small-batch, or single barrel. As the market has become more diverse, so have the branded identities that distillers use to drive their sales and shape their target market. Maker's Mark and Early Times emerge as two points on a spectrum, brands that project two distinct, though related, consumer identities: the gentleman and the good old boy. Although multiple factors have shaped cultural images of Bourbon, from film to literature, art to advertising, the latter provides particular insights because of the strategic nature of its image construction, tied both to economic gain and cultural appeal. Brands work to maintain distinctive identities while keeping their representations flexible and inviting enough to allow for the participation of individuals who do not wholly, or even significantly, resemble the ideal consumer. This tension allows for analysis of the ways that real and diverse people interact with Bourbon's historical legacy, as they consume a company's branded identity along with its liquor.

In a region long obsessed by history, it seems only fitting that contemporary performances of masculinity would borrow heavily from their ancestral archetypes. In the case of the Southern white man, two more or less historically consistent tropes emerge: the gentleman, with his roots in the moonlight-and-magnolia planter ideal, and the good old boy, his backcountry cousin. It is important to view these social types not as accurate depictions of the way white men are in the South, but instead as archetypal wells from which today's men draw as they craft and express their identities. Individuals move between, into, and around these types as they adjust their drawl, change their clothes, and switch from Early Times in a pickup to Maker's on the rocks. Even in the Old South, the distinctions between the gentleman planter and the yeoman good old boy were often more imagined than real. According to the infamously quick-quilled Southern social critic W. J. Cash, the gentlemen of yore were really nothing more than the most successful of the backcountry pioneers, the former good old boys. As they gained land and property, they rapidly reinvented themselves as Southern nobility, adopting the imagined customs and habits of the existing European aristocracy.

Bourbon in the 1960s was the drink of the working class. In the Old South, where corn whiskey was the only liquor available, the age and character of the whiskey served to convey class and status. By the 1960s, however, the increasing availability of and American preference for exotic European imports led well-heeled southerners to reach for Scotch or Cognac, in much the same vein of affected Europeanism as the earlier colonial gentlemen. Maker's Mark president Bill Samuels Sr. introduced his product as Cognac's counterpart among Bourbons with an audacious advertising campaign in 1965, closing the gap in the market and retying American whiskey to the patrician planter mythos. Reading the self-consciously classed claims of a 1972 Maker's Mark ad in conversation with those of a 1953 Early Times ad shows the continuity of Bourbon's masculine messaging up to today.

Two burly men, up with the early morning sun, load bait, tackle, and apparently a bottle of Early Times for a day of fishing, a tradition of deep historical importance to the Southern man. The nature of the fishing these two men are about to do, as well as the nature of the image itself, evokes a romantic view of the working man's recreation, which meshes well with Early Times, the working man's drink. They have strong forearms, day-old beards, and are covered in flannel. Like any self-respecting good old boy, these men are dressed not to impress, but instead to fish and drink the day away. By staging the scene on Kentucky's "man-made lake," the ad bestows another dimension of virility on its clientele, unfazed by a lack of lake when he wants to fish. Not to worry, the Early Times good old boy will build his own lake! The Southern man, potent and strong, has dominion over nature and will subdue the world around him for the good time he wants and deserves.

The folks at Early Times go yet a step further in spelling out their message. With apparently little faith in their audience's knack for subtlety, the primary text in this ad tells us in very direct terms that Early Times "is Kentucky's favorite Bourbon because it's every ounce a *man's* whisky." Not only is Early Times Kentucky's favorite Bourbon and every ounce a man's whiskey, Kentucky actually prefers Early Times because of its manliness. Not only do good old boys from the South love their Early Times, the South loves its good old boys right back!

With its entry into the Bourbon market in the late 1950s, Maker's Mark stands in for the contemporary gentleman, looking down on the Early Times good old boy with self-conscious awareness of the lineage they share. When the product was introduced in 1958, it was priced at almost double the going rate for Bourbons, and with little justification, "especially since it didn't claim any extra age (it didn't claim any age) or any other tangible attribute to justify its price." The product claim is almost absurdly explicit in its transparency: the reason one should drink Maker's is precisely because it is expensive, because it appears refined. Restated, the ad reads: drink Maker's Mark because it makes you look rich. As opposed to the Early Times ad, with its idyllic and explicit portrayal of working-class Southern manhood, the Maker's ad works to impart its Southern masculinity only secondarily to its assertion of class. Above all else, this ad asserts that Maker's Mark is expensive, with the bold declaration that dominates the text. The gentleman-liness of the product does read, however, in the classic simplicity of design and in the message of the smaller block of text. The spirituous secret, we are told, is in the "original old style sour mash recipe" that runs back through four generations of patrilineal know-how. Evoking nostalgia for the agrarian idyll of a bygone South, the address at the ad's bottom—"Star Hill Farm, Loretto, Kentucky"—furthers this ethos of Southern stateliness. Although possible, it seems unlikely that Samuels included the address to solicit post from consumers. More likely, it serves to conjure in the mind of the drinker a nostalgic image of the "Moonlight and Magnolias" South, on a farm (or a plantation) in rural Kentucky, where he might be taken in, sat down, and invited to sip a Julep while the sun sets and time stands still.

A quick look at the websites of each brand shows that the distinct images of drinker circulated by each have remained more or less consistent over the years. The homepage for Early Times appears as a sort of good old boy playroom, filled with totems of blue-collar leisure: an "Early Times" neon sign, a bar with obligatory Early Times bottle, a mounted bass, a tool kit, and a framed poster of a horserace, among other trophies of manliness. To the delight of the viewer, a quick rollover animates the relics; they come to life as if shot in a booze-laden carnival shooting gallery. The aesthetic is rowdy, country, and fun, and the hunting, fishing, and neon motif reads loud and clear. From its earliest years to today, Early Times has exuded unrestrained, unrefined white Southern manhood.

If the Early Times website is a shooting gallery shrine to working-class Southern whiteness, the Maker's Mark website is a vault of gentlemanly heritage: the primary graphic on the page is a magnified image of the brand's iconic bottle, cropped to show only a portion of the neck. As the light plays lambent on the contours of the bottle, illuminating the Bourbon inside, the image evokes antiquity, appearing as fossilized amber. The two tendrils of red wax that drip down the neck appear strangely poignant, eerily resembling the genteel blood that runs through the neck of each Maker's Mark consumer. The differences between these homepages extend to the rest of the sites, with Maker's Mark privileging information, heritage, and gentility, and Early Times privileging fun, machismo, and irreverence. The tool-kit totem on the Early Times website links to a "Tools" page, where the good old boy finds articles with everything to do with tools and nothing to do with Bourbon, save the rugged manliness they share. In contrast, we find the "Tasting notes" section on the Maker's Mark site, which reads as delicate verse. The page assesses the color, bouquet, flavor, and finish of the Bourbon, stating that ideally, the bouquet would present as "full, yet delicate; well-rounded; possessing a distinctive caramel aroma of the charred oak with a hint of vanilla; pleasant and inviting." One can imagine the archetypical good old boy stumbling across this online and wondering out loud why there are flowers in the whiskey.

The irony of Maker's Mark as a bastion of white Southern male heritage lies in its relatively recent arrival into both the market and the mind of the consumer, especially in relation to Early Times, which traces its origins to 1860, about a century before Maker's hatched under Bill Samuels Sr. When the Early Times advertisement circulated in 1953, it was not explicitly targeting good old boys per se, as good old boys were the only boys drinking Bourbon at all. With Samuels's introduction of Maker's Mark in the late 1950s, he worked to craft a timeless image of the brand that effectively introduced, or reintroduced, the idea that gentlemen drank Bourbon. It was Maker's Mark's entry into the industry as the gentleman's choice that eventually forced Early Times to acknowledge and articulate its good-old-boydom as such. In this light, contemporary masculine performances of "gentleman" and "good old boy" appear like the Old South planter and his yeoman kin, bound inextricably and self-consciously, with each defining itself largely in relation to the other. The marketed myth of the Bourbon-sipping gentleman cemented the image of the Bourbon-swilling good old boy.

The market-driven manhood evident in these investigations goes to show the constructedness of any identity, but particularly that of the white Southern man. To effectively approach Bourbon's function in the contemporary American South, however, it is critical to do so within a theoretical framework that lets us understand the methods by which masculine power exerts and sustains itself. R. W. Connell, in his seminal book *Masculinities*, articulates just such a framework, the notion of "hegemonic masculinity." Connell posits that there is no such thing as an objective *masculinity*, universal and innate, observable in men as a whole. Instead, *masculinities* are constructed through relations of gender, sexuality, race, and class and are located in specific intersections of place, time, and culture. Although there is no singular masculinity to which all men subscribe, particular "hegemonic masculinities" will emerge within a particular social environment, exerting various forms of power over subordinate and marginalized expressions of gender, in the ultimate aim of sustaining patriarchy. Although I do not seek to chart a comprehensive cultural analysis of the white Southern man, I do assert that in today's South the gentleman and good old boy, or their performed approximations, are exalted. Although the masculinities projected by Maker's Mark and Early Times vary in their articulations of class, they share a preoccupation with whiteness, history, and homosociality, and an implicit antagonism toward women, people of color, and homosexuality, antagonisms echoed throughout the lingering Southern social order.

Of course, Bourbon alone is in no way responsible for contouring the landscape of today's South, but it is one of many vital and tangible tools in this landscape's maintenance—and, hopefully, its alteration. Each brand has invested significant effort in shaping its identity, but none is so narrow in its articulation that it explicitly discourages consumption by any who are willing to buy bottles. This reality leads to slippages and fissures between the layers of race, class, gender, geography, and sexuality built into these branded identities and leads ultimately to points of entry for those not privileged by these identity markers. True, the gentleman and the good old boy persist as ideals for many in the South, but even these are open to interpretation, contestation, and play. That anyone can drink Bourbon calls into question the notion, articulated outright by Early Times, that it is every ounce a man's whiskey. Is it?

BOURBON'S POLITICAL TURN

To set the stage for Bourbon's political potential, I start at a seemingly unlikely place: the social phenomenon of "icing." For those unfamiliar, icing is a ritual made briefly but wildly popular around 2010, whereby an individual (usually male, often called "Bro") "ices" another (also often called "Bro") by revealing a Smirnoff Ice lemon-flavored alcoholic beverage anywhere in the visual field of the person (Bro) being iced. Bro ices Bro. Upon said icing, the icee must lower to his knee and consume the entire beverage, to the great pleasure and cheer of all present. The practice, which allegedly got its start in and around Southern social fraternities, went on to enjoy significant celebrity, a dedicated website (brosicingbros.com, now defunct), various offshoots (hoes icing bros, hoes misting hoes), and a *New York Times* article.

Though most see this ritual as good-natured, harmless, binge-drinking fun, it does not take much creativity to understand its gendered symbolism, or its implications. A man forces another man to kneel publicly, insert an object into his mouth and consume its sweet contents, while others hoot and holler. Imitations of fellatio, intimations of fruitiness; what a fun party! The power and the play in icing come in its ridicule of (and distance from) men who perform *real* fellatio and exhibit *real* "fruitiness." The particular resonance of Smirnoff Ice in the practice lies in the common understanding that it is a "girly" drink, in the category of those sweet malt beverages colloquially and disturbingly known as "bitch beer." By casting gay sex and sweet beverages to the realm of the ridiculous, icing elevates heterosexuality and the consumption of unsweet beverages to the realm of the sublime.

Besides sharing demographic practitioners, Bourbon drinking and icing are intimately related, as both are performative, consumptive social practices that subtly but significantly shape the ways we conceive of ourselves and of others. There are, however, important differences. The performance in icing is more obvious, more spectacular; it is staged and almost always features a knowing audience. Bourbon drinking is subtler, but is also therefore more insidious, more ingrained, more pervasive; it conveys information subconsciously. Icing is also novel. Though some men (and women) are undoubtedly still icing each other somewhere, the popularity of the practice left us about as quickly as it came. Bourbon, meanwhile, perseveres, gaining cultural clout and market share. Finally, Bourbon is more sacred. It has been written indelibly into the history of the white masculine South, by Percy, Faulkner, and our fathers, through advertising and through our consumption, for centuries. That history, conversely, has been written into Bourbon, and it is that history that we perform, consciously or not, when we drink it.

Returning to Connell's notion of hegemonic masculinity, we can see the importance of culture in considerations of power. Connell's work draws from that of Marxist philosopher Antonio Gramsci, whose notion of hegemony extends traditional Marxist considerations of power into the realm of the cultural. Hegemony is an especially productive frame for a study of identity and consumption because it conceives of power as intricate and interwoven, incorporating not only political thought and economic materialism, but also mundane choices and behaviors as they relate to personal and collective identity. Culture, and specifically the culture of Bourbon drinking, thus becomes an important site to ground explorations of power in the South.

In a region steeped in the history of its own tumultuous past, a past that placed Bourbon drinking (not to mention landowning and voting) in the domain of the white Southern man, Bourbon becomes a politically charged substance. As opposed to the lightness and frivolity of Smirnoff Ice, the very lightness (read: weakness, gayness, girliness) mocked and derided in icing, Bourbon is decidedly heavy, serious. The weight and gravity of Bourbon register both symbolically through the drink's historical legacy and sensuously through its bite—that burn that makes learning to drink whiskey hard work and separates the proverbial men from the boys (and girls, and queers, and people of color). When a straight white Southern man sidles up to a bar for a Bourbon, he is—whether consciously or not—asserting cultural, physical, and material power. When someone of a different background does the same, this person is—whether consciously or not—challenging that very same history and their exclusion from its positions of privilege.

Thus, the painful physicality that makes Bourbon feel and appear powerful also interestingly makes Bourbon appropriable to those who have not featured in its history, and who have been marginalized by and throughout the history of the American South. Anyone of legal drinking age can sidle up to just about any bar in the South and beyond, can order a Maker's Mark or an Early Times, can knock it back neat and brace through "the little explosion of Kentucky U.S.A. sunshine in the cavity of the nasopharynx," and can sink into the "hot bosky bite of Tennessee summertime." Sinking further, anyone can steep in the smoke, the soil, and the sweat of Bourbon's imagined history, tasting its legacy and relishing its grit.

Of course, the politics of Bourbon drinking is messy and murky. By appropriating its legacy we are by nature participating in it; by challenging Southern structures of oppression we are by nature acknowledging them. A different politics might be seen in the unabashed embrace of Smirnoff Ice, the championing of the sweet, the feminine, the sugary. But by choosing to drink Bourbon and to approach its politics, queer, female, black, and other oppressed bodies can problematize accepted notions of power and privilege. By extension, these individuals trouble accepted notions of who can say, do, or think what. In staging these small, mundane performances, we change the character of the spaces we inhabit. By drinking Bourbon in protest, in play, and in pleasure, we can point to new, more complicated ways of understanding identity and living with each other. Looking around us, soaking it in, we can see the walls and contours of a region slowly shifting. In its dually sensuous and aesthetic capabilities, Bourbon drinking becomes an act of both tasting and making history, grappling with a particular past while pointing to possible futures.

The South, Stepping Out

When the Queso Dripped Like Honey

Sarah Hepola

The first time I ate queso was at a cast party for a high school play. I'd been dieting for months, a lonely stretch of rice cakes and Lean Cuisine, and now unencumbered by the pressure of six hundred eyes staring at me from auditorium seats, I could chow down.

"What is *in* this stuff?" I asked my friend, licking the melted cheese off the side of my hand.

"Velveeta and Ro-Tel," she said. It was like learning the passwords to heaven. *Velveeta and Ro-Tel.* How had I lived seventeen years without knowing?

The answer to that question had something to do with my mother, an early health food adopter who baked her own bread, belonged to a food co-op, and refused to keep processed sweets in our modest home. All of this was enlightened thinking for Dallas in the late 1980s, but to me it was pure fascism. I craved Little Debbie snack cakes, all gooey, gummy chocolate, and marshmallow fluff scooped out of the jar with one eager finger. "Why can't we have frozen dinners like normal people?" I would think when she made lentil soup, with its upchuck tint, or when she forced us to eat liver every Tuesday. My kingdom for a Pop-Tart, man.

On sleepovers in middle school, I ate potato chips not one at a time but by the fistful, crumbs decorating my shirt. At my best friend Jennifer's house, I would sneak out of her room in the middle of the night and dip into the cookie dough her mother kept in the freezer, warming ball after ball of it in my bare hands before popping it in my mouth. I was rebelling against my mother's hippie-dippie ethos, but there was something compulsive, too.

Later I would learn the term for it—binge eating—but back then I only understood the behavior as embarrassing and all mine.

Where did it start? What was I trying to fix? I had been a healthy kid, active in soccer and gymnastics. But I was sideswiped by an early puberty. Boobs arrived when I was nine years old, as weird and unwanted as feathers growing out of my back. I gained fifteen pounds of awkward adolescent chub that year and became quieter, harder to know. Middle school was hideous— it is for everyone—but I coped by retreating to an empty house and medicating with food. I traded after-school athletics for watching *Oprah* alone on the couch. Both my parents worked, and it was in these lonesome, unsupervised hours that the refrigerator called to me. In other people's kitchens, I would have gone for Double Stuf Oreos and cold pizza. But in my whole-grain household, I rooted around for decadence among the natural peanut butter and eggplant.

What we did have was cheese. My mom kept a block of medium cheddar in a drawer inside the fridge. I found that I could eat quite a bit without anyone noticing, and I also found that it was a knockout when lightly melted. My ritual was to cut off a hunk, give it seven seconds in the microwave, and rescue it right as beads of oil bubbled up on the orange skin and the surface tension collapsed. I did this into my teenage years, a secret kink, and if you had called me on it, I would have denied it, without being able to articulate why it mortified me so. It just seemed wrong. Cheese came in dainty squares speared with a toothpick. It wasn't supposed to drip like honey from your fingertips.

And so queso blew my mind: It was a bowl of melted cheese. *Forbidden* cheese, no less, since Velveeta was among my mother's blacklisted items. It was nearly scandalous, this endless supply of unadulterated badness out in the open. By my senior year, I had lost those extra fifteen pounds twice already. I had learned to understand food not as pleasure or sustenance but as a series of numbers that needed to be crunched on the way to a thinner, happier me. A cube of cheese was one hundred calories. A hundred calories! And a cube was not much. Which is another reason I loved queso: it was unquantifiable, bottomless. A vat. How much queso did you eat? Who could even tell?

In college at the University of Texas in Austin, queso practically ran like a river through town. It poured out of the spigots. It rained from the skies. I continued to binge, but it took new forms. I was a beer drinker, a wanton lush who applied the same lack of caution to Dos Equis as I did to romance. That came with its own aches and pains, and queso was the perfect reparative. My friends and I would drive (unwisely) to the Taco Cabana at 3 a.m. and plunk down our last $3 for the freshly made tortillas and queso, which we'd use to sop up six hours of debauch. Or we would gorge on chips and queso at Tex-Mex restaurants near campus, sucking down frozen margaritas and Camel Lights till 2 a.m. Salty, rich, and blessedly cheap, queso was the perfect accompaniment to a life lived immoderately.

When I moved to New York at the age of thirty-one, there was no such thing as queso. The concept did not translate at all.

"Queso?" friends would ask. "You mean, like the Spanish word for cheese?"

Yes, it is the Spanish word for cheese, but like *salsa* is the Spanish word for sauce. I mean something very specific when I say it. New Yorkers believe they have a monopoly on everything good—if it doesn't exist in the Big Apple, it isn't worth knowing about—and I took it as a personal challenge to convince them how wrong they were.

But when I explained queso, my friends wrinkled their noses. Didn't I understand that Velveeta was a radioactive substance made of one-part capitalism and three-parts obesity epidemic? Wouldn't it be better to make queso with a sharp aged cheddar? A sophisticated mix of gouda and gruyere? Hey, look, you can make your fancy yuppie sauce a million ways, and I will eat it all, but it's not queso. It's like if someone said: let's make Coca-Cola with chocolate and pixie dust. Would that be amazing? Well, maybe, but it wouldn't be Coca-Cola. Plus, Velveeta melts smoother than other cheeses.

When I got together with other Texas transplants, we mythologized queso. (Also breakfast tacos, though that is another story.) It spoke of lusty afternoons with no responsibility and meals paid for in quarters and dimes. It was the opposite of New York, which required seventy-hour work weeks and exorbitant rents and careful arithmetic just to use the G train. I discovered a place in Williamsburg, Brooklyn, run by former Austinites, that served queso, and I told my friends about it like I'd found the cure for cancer. When I was hung over—and I was often hung over—I would order tacos and queso from that place, coughing up $20 for the privilege of devouring nostalgia. It was never as good as I wanted it to be. I couldn't tell if the queso was different—or I was.

It's a drag when a fix you have relied upon all your life stops working, but that is what happened to me. I'm not just talking about queso, I'm talking about all of it: the total indulgence, the way I would drink to ease the anxiety of a bad day and then eat to ease the pain of a hangover and drink to ease the shame of eating too much. The endless cycle of medicating yourself only to poison yourself instead. My body and my bank account suffered in predictable ways. I was fat. I was broke. I was so, so tired. More than anything, I was sad—and there was not enough queso in the world to save me.

Earlier this year, I moved back to Texas. I joked that I would never stop scarfing down Tex-Mex once I returned, but the truth is, I rarely eat it at all. As I've gotten older, the idea of eating and drinking till it hurts has less romance in it. It never fixed what I wanted it to, anyway. I crave balance and moderation more than evenings I'll regret. I don't smoke anymore. I don't even drink. It's a sign of boring maturity, I suppose, to recognize that you don't have to slap yourself silly in order to feel alive.

Not long ago, a friend visited me from North Carolina, and I took him to a Tex-Mex place I have always loved, painted in garish purples and yellows and pinks.

"Should we get queso?" he asked.

I could hear the anticipation in his voice; I had been telling him about queso for years. I felt that funny swell of nervousness and excitement: What if he didn't like it? What if it didn't measure up? The menu had two kinds to choose from, including a version crammed with chorizo and guacamole, but we chose the classic. Velveeta and Ro-Tel, baby.

"Mmmm," he said when he took his first bite.

"Mmmm," I said, when I followed suit. And it was good, though I detected a certain plastic twinge that had never bothered me before, though I noticed the bowl congealing too quickly and turning an alarming neon orange.

I got a few delicious bites out of it. It was neither magic nor an abomination. By the time the waitress checked on us again, the bowl was still half-full, but we let her take it away. We'd left room for whatever came next.

Willie Mae Seaton Takes New York

Lolis Eric Elie

Why had they seated her so far from the stage?

She will be 89 come July. Didn't the organizers have her biography right there in front of them?

Even if they hadn't seen the holes cut in her work shoes to accommodate the gnarly bunions of her feet, they could have guessed that a long walk would not be easy for a woman her age.

That huge, New York hotel ballroom, the stage aglitter with bright lights and star chefs, and there she was seated way in the back.

But isn't her long walk up to the front a fitting metaphor for what is about to happen?

       ■   ■   ■

In the old days, there were the other states of the Union, and then there was Mississippi, at the back of the pack in all things progressive.

And at the back of the back—in the back of the buses and at the back of the lines—were that state's black citizens, one of whom was Willie Mae Seaton, nee Johnson.

She was born in Crystal Springs, fifteen miles from Jackson. "I'm a country girl," she will tell you firmly, even though she has lived in New Orleans since 1940. She means by this that she knows all about hard work and country cooking, the taste of home-smoked hogs and preserved blackberries.

She might have gone to college, had she not gone to high school with L. S. Seaton.

"He was a handsome-looking guy, and popular with the girls, " she recalls. "He was olive complexioned with light eyes."

She fell for him and they eloped when she was 17 years old. She came to the city during World War II, when her husband got a job at Higgins Shipyards.

By then she had four children, Lillie Mae, Eddie, L. S. Jr. and Charlie. "I've been through the mill," she says. "You know I drove a cab out here for five years? And I went to school. I'm a licensed beautician.

"And I worked in the cleaners a few years. I was a silk finisher at Shrewsbury Laundry and Cleaners," Seaton says. "I used to do clothes for all of those movie stars from California. Mr. Jim Mozan, he had that business.

"I've been through the mill, baby. Like you see this old lady, I've worked hard. I haven't just now started in the restaurant business; I've been in that business all my life."

It is her cooking, not those long-ago other jobs, that is responsible for her being in New York among the other great chefs at the May 2 [2005] James Beard Foundation Awards.

The house lights are dim now. The focus is on the stage, on the voice of the presenter.

"In 1957 or thereabouts, Willie Mae's Scotch House, a corner tavern, opened in the Treme neighborhood of New Orleans. The proprietor then, as now, was Willie Mae Seaton," he says.

"Willie Mae Seaton has earned a sterling reputation for forthright cookery of unimpeachable quality. She has done so quietly, one platter of deep-fried chicken at a time. And in the process, she has transformed her restaurant from a place one eats to a place one belongs."

It is time for her to stand up now. She is not a tall woman. If you are scanning the audience for a standing figure, you see no one at first.

■　　■　　■

Her restaurant is like that, not imposing or even easily found. It rests in a long, one-story, shotgun double house on the corner of St. Ann and North Tonti streets. It is across the street from Phyllis Wheatley School and one block from the Lafitte public housing development.

There is a sticker in the window indicating that the Underground Gourmet once visited. He did so at the behest of Dr. Frank Minyard, the Orleans Parish coroner.

But that was long ago. The sticker is well-faded now.

"I tell somebody that my great-grandmother has a restaurant, and sometimes they don't know where it is or they never heard of it," says Kerry Seaton Blackmon, twenty-five, who has worked at Willie Mae's for about two years.

"Their body language or their response is like, 'Oh well, I never heard of this li'l restaurant.'

"To me it was like, 'You never heard of it, but evidently somebody important did. And you're going to hear about it.' That's how I felt."

The big food writers have dined here: John T. Edge, author of a series of books on emblematic American foods; Jeffrey Steingarten from *Vogue*; Ed Levine from *The New York Times*; Calvin Trillin from *The New Yorker*; Rudy Lombard, author of "Creole Feast." They have all praised her food.

And it is a favorite with local dignitaries. Former Public Service Commissioner Irma Muse Dixon is there most days. Mayor Ray Nagin is a regular as is bandleader Dave Bartholomew and a host of lawyers and judges too long to list.

The name Willie Mae's Scotch House is a vestige from the old days when Seaton owned a bar at the corner of St. Philip and Treme streets. Scotch and milk—specifically, Johnnie Walker Black label scotch—was her signature cocktail, and with that there was no problem.

The problem was with selling beer. She had applied for her permit, but it hadn't yet come.

So late in 1957, after briefly leasing that corner bar, she moved her operation to its current location.

The St. Ann Street front of the building was leased to a hairdresser. The bar was in the back, with its entrance on North Tonti. On the other side of the shotgun double, then as now, was a kitchen where Seaton cooked her family's meals while she tended her bar.

Her customers smelled the food, then asked for it, then tasted it, then made a suggestion.

"My customers said, 'The way you cook, you should open a restaurant,'" she recalls. "I said, 'You gave me a good idea.'"

When the hairdresser got ill and closed shop, Seaton turned the front of the building into a restaurant.

For roughly three decades she has operated her thirty-seat restaurant. In the old days, the menu was long.

"Baby, we used to fix sandwiches—all kinds: shrimp, oyster, hamburger, ham and cheese, hot sausage. All of that, baby," she says. "And we used to cook turkey wings, meatloaf, barbecue ribs, macaroni and cheese. I used to cook stewed hens on Sunday—I used to be open on Sunday—string beans with potatoes, mustard greens, turnip greens, spinach, sweet potato pies, coconut cakes from scratch and all that."

Time has taken its toll. The menu is smaller, consisting mostly of red and white beans, fried chicken, fried pork chops, smothered chicken, smothered veal chops, and, on Fridays, fried trout and shrimp.

Some things haven't changed. The rice is still real rice, not the hard, flavorless, parboiled stuff served at most restaurants these days. The French fries are made from freshly cut potatoes. The bread pudding, when they have it, is silken and sweet.

All the dishes arrive at the table seasoned with the love of a grandmother's kitchen. But it is the fried chicken that soars above the versions of that dish prepared by even the most loving of grandmothers.

You may ask the secret of the dish. "I'm the only one in the city who uses a wet batter for my chicken. I make it myself," Seaton will tell you. Beyond that, she has little to say.

It is not the chicken recipe she grew up with in Mississippi. She learned it from a friend whose restaurant was closing. He refused to divulge it, then relented after exacting a promise from her that she would never tell the secret to anyone. It is a bargain she has kept.

Slowly, she emerges from a row near the back. Slowly, her great-granddaughter Kerry supporting her on her left side, a kind stranger on her right. She's hunched more than usual. A day of walking around New York has exacted its revenge. Her knees have not been the problem, she explains as she walks. It's her feet that have troubled her for years. But now her knees have conspired to act their age. She is limping more than walking. Limping slowly.

■   ■   ■

What a trip it has been, from back-of-town to Broadway, from North Tonti Street to the James Beard Awards.

After checking into the Marriott Marquis on Times Square, she has a late lunch, then it's off to her first appearance. *The Oxford American: the Southern Magazine of Good Writing* is having a party to celebrate its food issue. The KGB bar, the scene of the party, is a small, second-story room.

By the time Seaton arrives, it's standing room only. A dozen people walk out onto the landing as she makes her way up the stairs. One foot steps up; the other joins it; they pause, and then take another step. Someone vacates a seat for her.

From the podium, it is announced that Willie Mae Seaton, a winner of the 2005 James Beard Foundation's America's Classic honor, is in the house. Attention focuses on her, this gray-haired woman who has come from New Orleans to collect her award and receive her fans.

Would she like a drink? Jack Daniels and Coke.

The rest of the evening is a fast-paced blur of parties, hors d'oeuvres, and champagne.

Bon Appetit and the Chef's Warehouse are hosting parties.

John Besh, the chef at Restaurant August, is a nominee for the Beard award for Best Chef of the Southeast. His food is deliciously intricate, but he wants to meet Seaton, this country girl who can talk to him about cracklin' cornbread and the other dishes his grandmother made for him when he was a country boy on the north shore of Lake Pontchartrain.

Champagne and sushi are being passed around. Seaton indulges heavily in the former and lightly in the latter.

She is a night owl. Though she is best known for her cooking, she has also enjoyed her fair share of late nights as a bar owner and bar patron.

The night grows old. Still, she resists the efforts to send her to bed early.

"Ooh, boy, I'm so excited. And oh, baby, it's just beautiful. I'm enjoying myself to the highest degree," she says.

"People are just so warm and treat you so nice. This is the nicest thing I ever went to in life. I really didn't expect all this warmness and all these parties."

The next morning, the day of the awards ceremony, Seaton begins her day at the Fauchon café in the Drake Hotel on Park Avenue, the pink and black monument to French-style living. It is one of the few places outside Paris that you can get Fauchon tea and coffee.

It is the only coffee Seaton approves of during her trip to New York. It costs $5 a cup.

Lunch is at the Union Square Café, where, told of Seaton's presence, celebrity chef Michael Romano comes out of the kitchen to greet her.

She pays him high compliments in plain language. "You have a beautiful place here," she says, having finished every drop of her soup du jour. "And you were so nice to come out and see us."

You see her, struggling slowly toward the stage, and you understand. The distance she has traveled is best measured not in yards or miles, but in years.

The America's Classic award is for those venerable restaurants that, while not white-tablecloth establishments, have maintained the traditions and standards of American food.

Willie Mae Seaton is a symbol to you then, a symbol of those mothers and grandmothers and aunts who nurtured their families with food. A symbol of all cooks whose food has been the backbone of this country's culinary heritage.

Your applause, which started as polite acknowledgment, grows louder, more enthusiastic.

This evening is dedicated to the memory of Julia Child, the woman who brought French cooking to Middle American kitchens. But step by step, it becomes clear. This moment belongs not to her, but to Willie Mae Seaton.

Slowly, Seaton ascends to the stage. The announcer lightly touches his finger to the corner of his eye.

If she had been able to compose herself, so many things could have gone into her acceptance speech. For the members of that New York audience longing to taste her food, she could have assured them that she has no intention of closing her restaurant.

"I don't want to retire, " she could have said. "You know why? My clientele is so good and my customers just don't want to hear me say I'm going to close. My customers love me dearly and I love them, too. The rich and the poor, the black and the white, doctors and lawyers and the regular folks, too."

She could have spoken about her son Charlie Seaton, who works by her side these days, taking orders and keeping the building in good repair.

Or she could have talked about the fall of 2002.

She had been sick then. But, newly released from the hospital, all she could talk about was opening the restaurant again.

It was Kerry, Charlie's granddaughter, who interrupted her graduate school studies in public administration to help re-open Willie Mae's.

But the character who stars in all conversations about the restaurant is Seaton's late daughter, Lillie Mae. That part of the conversation begins in lively fashion.

Sexy and sassy, Lillie Mae had a quick-witted answer for every flirtatious customer. And she could cook.

She was the one who made the sweet potato pies. She was the one who, side by side with her mother, scrubbed chitterlings and cooked them to the delight of civil rights movement heroine Oretha Castle Haley.

From the restaurant to St. Rita of Lima Church, to the shopping center to the grocery store, mother and daughter were inseparable.

Seaton speaks freely, gaily of these things, then her tone takes a somber turn.

Seaton has lost two children. Both Lillie Mae and L. S. Jr. died in 1991. "Every holiday, " Seaton says, "I take flowers to their graves, my daughter and my son."

Father's Day, Mother's Day or birthdays, they both get flowers, she says. "When I take care of one, I take care of the other."

It is the loss of Lillie Mae that weighs heavily on her. Charlie and Kerry, they work hard. But they are not Lillie Mae.

She has reached the podium now. She tries to compose herself, but behind her glasses, her eyes are filled with tears.

She opens her mouth to speak. First nothing comes out.

What she says then will be remembered for its plainness and honesty. It will be talked about for the rest of the evening.

"I'm just so full, " she says. "I didn't want to break down. It's just so great. It's just such a good feeling. I just can't explain it. I do my best to try to serve the people."

With those words, her speech is ended.

Her gentle conquest of the New York food world is complete.

Mississippi Chinese Lady Goes Home to Korea

Ann Taylor Pittman

Music blares from a doors-open car about twenty yards away from where a woman dances in an open, grassy spot. The tune is a Korean folk song, twang and strings and a tinny singer, and the petite dancer glides across the grass as wind whirls the trees about. She is wearing a *hanbok*, a traditional Korean formal dress—hers a cropped, fitted white jacket over a billowing red skirt with intermittent white flowers. She twirls and ripples her outstretched arms gracefully, skirt following in crimson waves. Every now and then, white satin slippers peek out from underneath. Cars drive past. I can't see if their occupants are staring, or even interested.

It's a spring day in Korea, and I am here with my brother, Tim, enjoying this unexpected performance with some wonderful people I've just met. They are my family. My uncle, Chi Bong, has driven us to the lakeside spot, and his wife—whose name I don't even know—is the dancer. Before pulling over, she confided, "I'm a little shy, but I have a surprise for you and your brother. I rented a dress." Now Chi Bong whoops and claps and encourages, and his wife begins to dance. I do not know this woman, but she has overcome her shyness to dance for us, people she has barely met and will likely never see again. I well up: I think she is showing us we are Korean.

By being here, by being connected to these lovely people, seven thousand miles from home, by the mere fact of it, Tim and I are finally Korean. Gratitude for this feeling takes me back to the moment, six months earlier, that led to my decision to come here. I was sitting in an elementary school cafeteria in Birmingham, Alabama, with my six-year-old twin boys. An older child, maybe a second-grader, looked at us on his way to put up his tray. He grinned and said, "Hey, Chinese lady!" It was a stab to the heart, not much different from words I sometimes heard as a seven-year-old girl growing up in the Mississippi Delta, sitting in my own elementary school cafeteria, listening to friends who puzzled over my otherness. They knew white and they knew black, but they certainly did not know what I was. Nor, exactly, did I.

A LIFE IN THE SOUTH

I am the daughter of a beautiful woman from Busan, South Korea, and a blond-haired, blue-eyed farmer's son from Mississippi. They met on a blind date in 1967 while my dad was stationed in Korea with the Army. That, anyway, was half of the story. Turns out that the date, arranged by a friend of my father's, was more serendipitous than blind. My mom, as it happened, was my father's barber, so they had met before. Now they really talked for the first time. "I knew within the first minute of talking to her that I was going to marry her," says my dad. The barber said no to the proposal several times before agreeing. They were married in a peculiar ritual that I always loved hearing about: first, they went to the U.S. embassy in Seoul. "Suzie was outside the room, and I got married to her," explains my dad. "Then, we went to Seoul City Hall. She went in, and I went to a coffee shop across the street. And she got married to me." Afterward, they went to a Methodist church where my mother's uncle was pastor for a wedding attended by friends and relatives.

Then they moved to the States, where they would raise my brother and me in small towns in which there simply weren't many others like my mom. I was born in Winona, Mississippi, which listed my mother's state of birth, on my birth certificate, not as Korea but, bizarrely, Manchuria. My mother moved through this strange landscape quietly and, to me, bravely and gracefully, and I can't recall her complaining that she ever felt like an outsider. But we'd be in the grocery store, and her accent would prove too foreign for the clerks or cashiers to bother with. They would raise their voices and lock eyes with the little girl whose Luke Skywalker or Bandit T-shirt implied sufficient Americanization, waiting for me to translate. In those moments, blood rising in my cheeks, I resented both sides: the clerk for not trying, my mother for just being Korean. I'd go home and imagine that I had blonde hair and blue eyes and looked like my friends and had a mother who could speak and be understood.

Of course, as a Southerner does, I love the South, long for Mississippi, feel the South ever-present in my blood and my soul. During my elementary school years, we lived in the Delta, whose bleakness I still find mysterious and beautiful whenever I go back. I remember, as a child, passing sharecroppers and seeing white families picking cotton together while a combine stirred up dust in the next field. The poor, dark, tragic, funny, beautiful South: I remember hard dirt clods loosened by the plow in my grandparents' garden that were perfect for pitching at my cousins; angry crawdads waving in the ditches after a rain; people of at least three colors loitering outside the tamale stand; tiny razor cuts painfully discovered at bath time after running through the corn patch; a pail of purple-hull peas in the breezeway waiting to be shelled; the delicious salt-lick brine of boiled peanuts at a ramshackle gas station.

These are the scenes and the foods of my childhood, yet they are bracketed, as none of my friends' lives were, by other memories and different flavors: the joys of slurping up slippery cellophane noodles whenever my mother made *japchae* (noodles with vegetables); my clumsy fingers trying to control tangled chopsticks as they chased a muddy-colored crowder pea across the plate into a pile of sticky rice; the shiny Korean clothing sent to us by our relatives for special occasions; the frightening pungency of kimchi.

Southern to the bone, I don't look it. I look Korean or, as I sometimes still overhear in the South, "some kind of Chinese." But I speak no Korean and, before going on my pilgrimage, knew embarrassingly little of the culture. To me, Korean heritage was mostly about food: the traditional dishes my mom would cook every now and then, after driving up to Memphis for ingredients at the closest Asian market. We loved some of the dishes she made—especially sweet-salty marinated meat and any kind of noodle dish. But she also made funky soups, always in this little gold-colored pot. The rest of us wouldn't join her, wary of the burly flavors.

Those were dishes my mother made for herself: comfort and consolation, taken in solitude. I imagine how it must have been for her to make food alone and not have anyone to share it with—sad for any mother, especially in a place where no one spoke her language and where this was the only part of her culture she could re-create. I ask her now if this hurt her feelings. "No. No, noooo," she says. "Because the food was so different. So strange from what Westerners are used to." My mother, I discovered, didn't have the luxury of learning to cook from her mother; instead, she taught herself to cook in America. "I just guessed," she says, "remembering the taste I had a long, long time ago." She adds, with a confidence that makes me proud, "I'm pretty creative, you know."

Our family never went to Korea when I was a kid, and later I assumed this was because Mom, having escaped, was in no hurry to return. Fine by me. I didn't want to go. I was ruled, well into high school, by a childish hunger to just be like everyone else. But as my dad now explains, "We just didn't have the money to do it."

It wasn't until college that I began to use the K-word to define myself. That's also when I started researching and cooking Korean food, working—

as my mother did—from memory rather than instruction. Finally, at forty-two, having long been immersed in the world of food, I figured it was well past time for me to go to the place whence, through my mother's side of the family, I half-came. Food would be the obvious door-opener. On the web, I easily found food bloggers and experts who would welcome me. I would eat my way around Seoul, nibble through the coastal city of Busan, where my mother is from, and then head to the small town of Hapcheon, where I would finally meet my Korean relatives.

CITY OF WILLOWY WOMEN

In Seoul, no one spoke to me in Korean; apparently they knew by glancing at me that I was not one of them. This was a bit of a disappointment. I decided that, at five feet eight inches tall, I am simply American sized.

Seoul: flanked on all sides by mountains (Korea is 70 percent mountainous), its impressive business and apartment towers are interrupted by an occasional old temple or palace. It's home to ten million people, and to Samsung, LG, Kia, and Hyundai, who ship cars and smart phones and flat-screens and refrigerators to us, while we ship our fast-food franchises to them: Dunkin' Donuts, Pizza Hut, McDonald's. I found four Starbucks within a one-block radius of my hotel.

Seoul's energy is not so unlike that of New York; imagine a Manhattan where your iPhone doesn't drop its calls and the Internet runs a lot faster. What struck me the most, though, was the beauty of the ten million: willowy women with luminous, clear complexions, dressed in flowing chiffon and exquisitely tailored dresses (no décolletage, but the shortness of some women's short-shorts scandalized me). Men were equally beautiful and well outfitted. And everyone seemed to be skinny. Yet, to my delight, I learned that these thin people eat like horses and drink like fish.

The Seoul citizen's obsession with technology outdoes our own, yet her food is surprisingly traditional. With a few exceptions, experimentation and fusion do not seem to interest many chefs or their customers. The cuisine involves a set of repeating flavors: variation and themes, narrowly framed, not unlike the food of Tuscany in that regard. "This framing makes Korean food special," says expat food writer and Korean food academician Jennifer Flinn, who showed me around the city, "and the Koreans who eat it special by extension." Those of us who eat Thai one day and gumbo the next may find that dull, but Koreans don't, and I detected a deep pride about the cooking from the locals. The flavors are anything but subtle: fiery, salty, sweet, pungent, and sometimes very fishy.

At the center of it all are the pickles, and at the center of the pickles, *baechu kimchi*, cabbage fermented with chili and garlic and often referred to simply as kimchi (though the term refers to hundreds of varieties of pickle). As important as sauerkraut may be to a German, it's reasonably certain that no culture reveres pickled cabbage (in this case, Napa cabbage) quite like Koreans. "You know," a cooking teacher named Ellie Hyewon Lee told me when I visited her at the Food and Culture Korea Company in the Jongno-gu district to learn how to make *kimchi jjigae*, a pickle-based soup, "Koreans cannot live without kimchi. We eat kimchi every day." The quality of her soup, she noted, entirely depends on the quality of her kimchi: "For the best taste, use sour kimchi, the more fermented one." With this superpotent cabbage (whose smell can fill a house), Ellie likes to make kimchi fried rice and kimchi pancakes, too.

"There is a typical debate," says Joe McPherson, an expat food writer from Alabama and president of ZenKimchi International, Korea's longest-running food blog, "about whether all Koreans eat kimchi because they like it or because they feel obligated by culture. It's so closely tied [into the culture] that I still occasionally get gasps of surprise from some Koreans when I eat Korean food. It's as if one can only be born a Korean to eat Korean food."

My father had not acquired a taste for kimchi in Korea. "I do not care for the smell of garlic," he says now. "I never did like kimchi. I would not eat those things, so you and your brother wouldn't, either." My mother still acts surprised when she sees me eat it now, though I love its tangy pong: "You really like it?" she'll ask in disbelief. I think now of her there, alone, eating this touchstone of her world, this apple pie of Korea—and us refusing.

Dining out is social sport in Seoul, and the eating is lively. All food is shared at the table and often cooked on the table. A wave of *banchan* (side dishes) arrives, and just when you've rearranged your drink and your chopsticks and think the table can't accommodate another thing, the main dishes arrive. *Banchan* typically include kimchi and variations, plus other dishes like seasoned bean sprouts, cold radish soup (actually "water kimchi"), scallion pancakes, and various wilted and seasoned vegetables. Everyone chopsticks little bits out of the communal plates and bowls (one does not order à la carte). It's both intimate and social, and it's how you eat in Korea—many restaurants aren't even equipped to serve single diners.

BEAUTIFUL EGG-SHAPED FACE

Dumplings are one of my great joys, comfort food as much as biscuits and field peas. My first bite in Seoul of steamed *mandu* filled with pork and tofu took me back to my childhood. At a food stall, I enjoyed another version of *mandu*—huge fried dumplings stuffed with pork and glass noodles, light and crisp, skins puffed with thousands of wonderful little blisters. When I was eleven, in Greenville, Mississippi, I recall my mother making a version of these one time—Mom called them *yaki mandu*—half-moons of crispy dough filled with ground beef and vegetables. Not unlike many of the Southern meat pies I'd had at family reunions.

I had bulgogi, of course, the classic Korean barbecue meal of marinated beef cooked on a searing-hot grill. And here and there I did uncover little slivers of modest innovation: at a loud, bustling restaurant called Mapo Jeong Daepo in the Mapo district in Seoul, the tabletop grills have a channel around the outer edge, a trough into which we placed bits of kimchi, after which our server poured on beaten eggs. As we seared meat and morseled it up in perilla leaves with grilled garlic and spicy *gochujang* sauce, a fluffy kimchi omelet cooked on the perimeter. Translator and guide Veronica Kang, a Seoul native, had never seen that before.

There is a variety of chewy little cakes made of rice flour that Koreans adore—wonderfully rubbery "pasta," shaped in disks or tubes, that holds a sauce or glaze. In Seoul, almost every street food stand sells *tteokbokki*, thumb-shaped rice cakes that are often swimming in a crazy-delicious sweet-spicy red sauce. I spent most of a day seeking every rice cake incarnation I could find. In the Shindang-dong area, I found a carb-lover's delight of rice cakes with ramen noodles, rice noodles, and fish cakes. At Tongin Market, I had "oil" *tteokbokki*; it is the only place, Jennifer explained, to find these: marinated in a bit of soy and a lot of Korean ground chili, then stir-fried so that they're irresistibly crisp on the outside, chewy within, and fantastically simple.

As much as Koreans love to eat, they have a powerful thirst that would impress the Wall Street frat boys of downtown Manhattan. It's not uncommon—on a Tuesday as much as a Friday—to watch business-suited men in Seoul staggering, slumped over, or violently hugging after a night of boozing. The agent of their inebriation is often *soju*, a rice-based spirit with the alcohol content of strong sake and the flavor of a sweetish vodka. It comes to restaurant tables quickly, in small bottles, and is usually drunk neat. I had plenty, but I was more enchanted by *makgeolli*, a drink I fell in love with at the Blue Star Pub in Seoul's artsy Insadong district. *Makgeolli* is a milky-cloudy rice beer, a bit sweet, a bit tangy, a bit tingly on the tip of the tongue. At the Blue Star, it arrived, flavored with mugwort, in a ceramic tureen with a wooden scoop and little bowls to drink it from. *Makgeolli* proved a lovely, sociable drink, with its communal pour and its refreshing, gentle effect.

The owner of the bar, Mr. Choi, a stage actor, looked like a Korean version of Patrick Swayze in *Roadhouse*. He knew Jennifer and welcomed us warmly.

They proceeded to have an animated conversation in Korean. It was one of the first times I had heard such lively talk at close quarters. (Although I had often heard my mother speaking Korean when I was a child, it was always over the phone, so I heard only one side of the conversation, interrupted by long pauses.) Unlike the sing-songy cadence of, say, Japanese, Korean is full of low, guttural sounds and hard fricative stops—what sounded to my ear a bit angry turned out to be a friendly conversation about which bar snacks we ought to eat. Although we had already had dinner, we couldn't resist the crisp mung bean pancakes or the little knobby root vegetable pickles. We drank, we ate, we ordered another vat of the brew, this time flavored with persimmon leaf. At Mr. Choi's table, not far away, was a cheery, clean-cut Korean gentleman whose rosy cheeks indicated that he had been enjoying a few bowls of *makgeolli* himself. In English, he professed his love of Jennifer's "beautiful egg-shaped face" over and over, holding out his hands in the shape of parentheses. There was much laughter and more *makgeolli*. I felt as at home here, in this dingy, comfortable Seoul bar, as I do in the great dingy dives of the South.

DEATH COMES TO DINNER

When I was five years old in Mississippi, my father brought home a live catfish in a red bucket, and I named him Fred and played with him, sloshing the poor thing around and refreshing his water incessantly. That night, Fred was dinner, and I cried at what I'd seen, but I nibbled the fish because I felt I had to. Seeing your food killed is not uncommon in the South today, nor in Korea. My mother told me about being sixteen years old and being given the chore of hacking crabs (plentiful in coastal Busan, even for the poor) for a special dinner; she didn't realize they'd be alive and that she was to cleaver them with a quick chop. She ran from the room, crying, and caught a lot of hell for falling down on the job.

Like many American meat-eaters, I am a wimp about these blood matters, despite the imprecations of nose-to-tail chef-philosophers about the importance of communing with what we eat. Not long before I went to Korea, I decided I ought to attend the killing stump that is located on my brother-in-law's property in Mississippi: he would behead a troublesome rooster, I would make rooster and dumplings, and the circle of life would be honorably, deliciously complete. What unfolded was a Southern Gothic scene right out of a Flannery O'Connor story. It was early evening, with thunder sounding low and distant. Mosquitoes buzzed around like bumblebees—and not much smaller. Catching the rooster was tricky, and the animal became stressed. At last Jamie had the bird, and he held it upside down by its feet because, he explained, roosters will go docile when held this way. But a neighbor's nosy blackmouth cur ran up and began to nip at the doomed bird, causing it to wriggle and squawk. A huge crack of thunder roared, and a downpour arrived, immediate and punishing. The rooster was carried to the killing stump, and I swear that when the ax went up, the sharpened edge glinted in a flash of lightning. Head separated from bird, body writhed on the ground. Let me just say with only a little Southern drama that something died within me that night, too. The rooster proved, despite the ministrations of a pressure cooker, a sinewy old thing.

These matters played in my mind at the Noryangjin Fish Market in Seoul, where Veronica suggested we enjoy a raw fish breakfast, which sounded great until I realized that I would be watching more executions. The market consists of stall after stall of clams, mussels, mackerel, skate, live fish in tanks, and live octopus. Many of the stoic, cleaver-bearing female vendors wore full makeup and these fantastic, hot pink, full-length rubber aprons. We settled on a stall, sat at its one small dining table, and pointed to a black fish swimming in the tank. In a flash the vendor had it on the cutting board. *Hwack!* Head now separate from twitchy body, for our dining pleasure. I felt like I might faint.

I warned Veronica that I drew the line at the reputed local practice of eating live octopus. A few minutes later, though, a pile of writhing tentacles appeared, along with slivers of our freshly butchered fish. The octopus wasn't alive, really—the animated tentacles were already separated from the rest of the animal. My brother dragged a wiggly bit through spicy *gochujang* sauce, popped it in his mouth, and reported it good. I felt obliged to follow, and he was correct. We also gobbled salmon-colored sea squirts, which had the texture of foamy oysters and an up-front sweetness that was followed by bitter iodine. Hard, tough abalone was the least appealing thing on the plate, like chewing wood. *Soju* washed all down nicely and at 9:30 started this day with a cheery warmth, despite the deaths.

I am, I think, an adventurous eater, and this story may support the claim to those followers of the Andrew Zimmern school: in Busan, we visit the enormous Jagalchi Fish Market, the largest in Korea, whose seemingly endless grid of vendors inside is matched by a network of outside stalls that extends for several blocks. There we saw a whole floor devoted to dried fish and seaweed. More intriguingly: shallow bowls at many stalls for displaying *echiuroid*, a horror of pulsating, undulating sea worms of scandalous shape. "Well, we have to try that!" I told Tim, and so we had one sea worm with our lunch. Raw and cleaned, the worm consists of nothing more than a thin, cartilaginous flap that rolled up on itself like wrapping paper. The flavor was that of mild seawater—not nearly as tasty as the sea snails we had eaten on a rooftop bar in Seoul, smothered with chilies and scallions and washed down with beer and *soju*.

Of course, I would meet my match: fermented skate. Joe took us to a place in Seoul known for its grilled octopus, part of a set meal that included the legendarily pungent treat. He warned us, apologizing in advance, hanging his head, laughing, and finally revealing, "OK, so Zimmern may have declared this the worst thing he's ever tasted." After the typical parade of *ban-chan* came a tiny plate that let off an astonishing reek. When skate ferments, uric acid builds up in the flesh, so it stinks terribly of ammonia. It's firm, hideously firm, with bones and cartilage—all of which conspire to make you chew for a long time to get it down. It's served with *bo ssam* (steamed pork) and kimchi, and one is instructed to layer the components to get some sort of ideal mix of flavors in each bite. To this half-Korean, it was terrible. The octopus—barely cooked, with a delicate hint of sesame and salt—arrived as sweet relief.

THE GIFT OF THE DANCE

As the time comes to go to Hapcheon to meet our uncle and his wife, I think again about my mother: her life in Mississippi, her life before that. Growing up, I knew very little of her life in Korea; stories were not volunteered, and it felt forbidden—even rude—to ask. When I finally did ask, I heard of the sort of family tragedy and poverty that lurks in the history of so many immigrants. Her mother died when she was twelve years old, and she grew up during the Korean War, "when everyone was so terribly poor," she says. My mother tells of sneaking out to the Red Cross soup kitchen not far from her house, something her father wouldn't have condoned. On a cold day, she stood in the long line for a tiny ration of milky soup. "It didn't even touch my stomach, reach my hunger," she says. She sneaked back for a second serving. "I was wearing an overcoat and two-sided scarf. I wanted to disguise myself, so I took my scarf off and changed it around to the other side, a different color. But I bet they knew. And they knew that little bit of soup wasn't enough. They didn't say anything, just gave me more soup. It was a blessing."

Now, finally, I am to meet my mother's brother and his wife. In the Busan bus terminal, Tim and I puzzle over how to get to Hapcheon. A tiny woman approaches, touches my arm, and speaks rapid Korean. Unlike in Seoul, where no one took me for Korean, the Busan natives would do this, talk to me in Korean. It makes sense, in my romantic interpretation: this is the place my mother is from; I am with my people, and they recognize me as one of them. "I'm sorry, I can't help you," I explain to the tiny woman, and turn away toward the ticket window. Something rings in my ear, though: Did she call me Ann? We go back to where she still stands, smile fading, clutching an orange envelope. She points to me, then Tim, and says our names. And then, in perfect English, she says, "I am Suzie's sister." This is my mother's sister, my Aunt Su Kyong, whom we were told was too frail to travel, to even visit—now come to surprise us! I laugh and choke and hug her with American aggression, and she reveals what she is carrying: photos of her and my mother, my uncle and his wife, a portrait from my brother's wedding, and a blurry Polaroid from 1975 of my brother and me in our fancy Korean clothing. The three of us board the bus, and I wonder what she must have felt in those few seconds when we turned away from her, how her heart must have fallen.

In the small town of Hapcheon, about a two-hour bus ride from Busan, we meet Uncle Chi Bong and his wife and accept a restaurant recommendation from the local taxi drivers. We settle around a table and smile sheepishly at each other—Aunt Su Kyong will speak no more English today—as we await a soup version of *bulgogi*, a local specialty. I notice that my uncle has brought in a pristine calendar from, oddly, 1999. He also has a map of the area and shows us where he has planned to take us: the burial site of our great-grandfather, then Hapcheon Lake, then the rhododendron festival at Mount Hwangmaesan.

The soup cooks on the table as we try to be together without staring (yet we can't help but stare). My uncle taps his index fingers together and says to me, "You and your mother are the same person. You are just alike." He cannot know how this makes me want to cry. After conferring with his sister, Uncle Chi Bong declares that Tim has our grandfather's eyes and brow. Uncle turns to the back of the calendar and shows us a colorful map of the United States annotated with notes about where my brother, my parents, and I live. We slurp the soup, and I love it—slivers of marinated beef in lots of broth with glass noodles and clusters of enoki mushrooms. Uncle Chi Bong goes out to the car and returns with bags of fruit, a knife, and little plastic trays. Aunt Su Kyong goes to work peeling and cutting apples and oranges, preparing them exactly as my mother does. She pushes them our way and keeps nudging until every piece is eaten.

There is much driving until we find the burial site, which calls for a hot hike up the side of a mountain; my relatives are showing us our ancestry. We lay out a blanket and Uncle has cold water and sesame biscuits for us. After a short rest, we wind our way around to the lakeside spot, where we enjoy cashews and almonds and more fruit, this time cold pineapple—and then we receive the gift of the dance. After a winding drive to the rhododendron festival, we learn that we are about a week early; only a few flowers are blooming. Uncle Chi Bong's wife explains, disappointed, that at full peak, the entire mountainside is a breathtaking pink. We decide to walk a little ways up to take pictures by the few blooming bushes, and Uncle buys hot roasted chestnuts for the hike. He seems pleased that we love the chestnuts, which are hot and fresh and sweet and tender. He frets over us the way our mother does. Then it is time to leave.

Many GPS miscues later, followed by stops to ask for directions, we reach the Hapcheon bus terminal for the ride back to Busan. Uncle Chi Bong says, "Lunch is not enough. We go to dinner. Your aunt's treat." We can't accept. We have to get back to Busan so we can pack and take a high-speed train across the country for our flight out of Incheon. Their faces fall at this news. They purchase our bus tickets and stand as a little congregation of three, unsure of how to part ways. I have just met these people, but they have shown me such kindness. I don't know if I will ever see them again, and the goodbye is excruciating. Aunt Mi Yang, my uncle's wife, blurts out, "I love you!" and I am gobsmacked by a realization that is as true as anything I've known: I may or may not be Korean, but I am part of this Korean family.

A week later, when I am back in Alabama, my uncle calls my mother and says he feels terrible about how the day went—that they didn't like how the restaurant served such an oddball version of *bulgogi*, that the lake suffered from drought, that the flowers weren't blooming. The day was a disaster and they had failed. I find this reaction to be very Korean, and very Southern—self-doubt and regret, plus something else, a deep obligation. We Southerners and South Koreans want you to know that we know when things aren't perfect, and we'll always point out the flaws before you do. I reassure my mother that, for me, the day was perfect. The reluctance of rhododendrons is not important when you find, in some far corner of the world, part of your place in the world.

All that day in Hapcheon, my aunt and uncle fed us. Food, of course, is used everywhere to signify the bonds between people, but these people, this food, this place: it all had huge significance to me. *Bulgogi*, dumplings, raw fish, and milky-sweet confusing rice beer felt as much a part of my DNA as field peas and boiled peanuts did back home. Which was why I could stand by a lake a world away from Mississippi and be moved to tears by a shy dancer in a rented dress, knowing that I had been loved.

An Oyster Named Dan

Jack Pendarvis

I'd like to say I knew he was special from the first. The fact remains I had just eaten eleven of his brothers and sisters, finding them delicious but interchangeable. There he lay then, on a shimmering palette of rock salt, ready to be splashed with mignonette sauce and slurped as a gluttonous afterthought.

Fortunately for both of us, the shucker had been off his game. My briny little adversary clung with his admirable adductor muscle most forcefully, almost comically, to his shell. An exploratory sally with the butter knife both distressed and enlightened me. As I prodded the resistant flesh with that cold, dull blade, I felt something prodding back: nothing less than the sea-heavy thrum of life itself. I put down the oyster and regarded him, my fingers twisting in my luxurious beard.

"All right, you win this round, Dan," I said.

No sooner had I pronounced the name than I knew it was correct. Of course, a human name didn't do him justice. Dan was part of something deeper, something I could approach only by means of the sturdy consonant, giving way, as it did, to an almost meditative hum: "Dan. Daaaaannn." He was shapely and dignified without appearing puffed up, and his complexion was flawless. But what I'm not capturing is a certain endearing insouciance. Dan didn't take himself too seriously. With his plump charm, offset by a yolky self-composure, Dan was something special. Yes, here was one oyster I would never eat.

The waiter noticed our connection—it would have been impossible not to. But his training or natural discretion would not allow him to acknowledge it except in the most conventional way: he referred to Dan as "leftover" and asked whether I wanted him "boxed up."

"Yes, that's right, you'd like to put everything in a box, you and your kind!"

I shouted, instantly regretting my outburst. Minutes earlier, I had been no different than the unfortunate waiter; in a way, I too had been "waiting," knowing not for what. The tip I left was fat with remorse.

I made my way toward the exit, cradling Dan in my outstretched palm, the baffled eyes of other diners on me. By every law, I owned this oyster— but as so often happens, the truth was more complicated. I had heard of World War I fighter pilots meeting for reunions long after the conflict had ended—German, British, American, all quaffing punch from the same bowl, bound by experiences no one else could understand, their shared glories and unimaginable terrors, and even their common jests, transcending mankind's petty skirmishes. Dan and I were so much more awesome than they. They were jerks compared to us. We had met on a battlefield wilder and stranger than the sky, a battlefield I call life, where eat or be eaten is the only rule— and we had come to a beautiful truce.

The simplicity of Dan's example amazed and humbled me. What kind of a bum hand had he been dealt? Separated from his parents and numerous lovers on the Florida Gulf Coast, tossed in a crate sloshing with dirty ice that numbed his senses, deposited into the darkness at the back of a truck. Didn't we all go through life that way? Unlike Dan, though, I had no excuse. For the first time in my life, I knew what I had to do. I was taking Dan home. And on that return trip, I was going to show him everything he had missed.

Before buckling him in for safety, I regarded the pool of "liquor," his natural broth, which filled his shallow shell, and in which he so eagerly bobbed. The first speed bump we encountered would slosh that sweet essence onto my seat covers, where it would be of no use to anyone. "Now don't be nervous," I told Dan as I lifted him tenderly to my mouth. I was careful not to brush my tongue or lips against him and give him the wrong idea. We were in this together. Dan was a champ. Only after I had taken care of every drop did I feel right about securing him properly in the passenger seat, in keeping with the state traffic laws.

Dan's juice was seasoned with something more than salt—it was spiked with *rebellion*. I felt it surging in my bloodstream. Old quacks in musty tomes rhapsodized about the revivifying power of the miraculous bivalve. How I used to laugh at them. I was wrong. I felt young again, idealistic, poetic.

"Let's get you out of here, Dan," I said. "I want you to see the wild American night! What do you think of that?"

"Ooooooweeeee," I imagined might be his mental reply.

"You said it, Dan!"

Those are the only kinds of oysters for me, the mad ones, burning, fevered in the mad, American streets of the night of fevered streets of American dreams, roasting only in their secret oyster thoughts of succulent madness. I peeled out of the strip-mall parking lot, flinging pearl-like chips of gravel that pinged against the window of the oyster bar. As we sped down the dark and legendary highways, we took turns swigging from a bottle of black-market aftershave lotion available only in Belize. A hint of saffron lends it an urgent piquancy. Phantom purple trees flew past. Dan and I gunned it south, Florida bound. The only stop I wanted to make was in Collins, Mississippi, birthplace of Gerald McRaney, television's "Major Dad."

"I just know you're going to love the Gerald McRaney Museum, occupying Gerald McRaney's magnificently restored childhood home," I told Dan. "Built in 1922, the McRaney home displays traditional features such as ornate balustrades."

"Ooooooweeeee," thought Dan.

It's funny how you can live just miles from a place, and always dream of going, but never quite make it. I was done putting things off. Dan had already taught me so much. He grew excited as I recounted some of the major plots of my favorite *Major Dad* episodes, like the one where Major Dad decided to take piano lessons despite the mockery of others. Dan and I could really identify with that! Major Dad wasn't shy about exploring other parts of himself, parts that didn't fit in with the "Major Dad" persona that other people were always using to keep him from realizing his full potential as a human being. "Would you like that boxed up" indeed!

Dan was listening patiently, sprinkled with aftershave lotion. He hadn't complained once—another moment with him, another lesson learned—but suddenly I realized how thoughtless I had been.

Any marine biologist will tell you that oysters are the filters of the sea, eagerly gobbling up pollution and impurities, only to poot out fresh, clean water from their buttholes. If Dan were truly to enjoy himself, he needed a more conducive environment. I stopped at a hardware store and got a bucket to put him in, which I filled with water and a healthy portion of iodized salt. Then I threw in some cheese and crackers from a gas station. An inauspicious start, perhaps, but I planned to treat Dan to some spectacular meals along the way. With his alchemical power to transform filth into wholesomeness, imagine what he could do with a nice Waldorf salad, for example. Why, he'd soon be pooting out mystical ambrosia!

In a way, I was envious. Isn't that what we all want: to digest the vagaries of this dirty world and fart out something beautiful? Dan was already so much more *real* than I was and he didn't even know it. That was the glorious thing about Dan, sitting there with his top off. I took off my shirt and threw it out the window. I didn't need shirts anymore. If you wear a shirt you're just a piece of garbage to me and I feel sorry for you.

I blasted some rock-and-roll music. "You ever heard of Dan Fogelberg before? He's got the same name as you!"

"Oooooweeeee," said Dan. I could tell he was digging hard on some Dan Fogelberg.

We reluctantly quieted the radio on the outskirts of Collins, Mississippi, and coasted into town with our headlights off. It was barely past ten but Collins lay exposed, deep blue, and silent. The parks were hung with empty swings pushed by melancholy breezes, the few sidewalks unoccupied, churches and homes alike in a soft blanket of shadow.

Dan and I stopped at the end of Japonica Street and made our way on foot, with a whispering chorus of sprinklers as accompaniment, to number 1625, a deceptively modest two-story balloon-frame house, all white and trim, its one concession to outward glamour a fancifully designed wrought-iron fence topped with graceful swordlike finials of fleur-de-lis.

Having distracted the guard dog with a sumptuous antelope steak I had been saving on ice in the trunk, Dan and I made our way across the backyard. Dan shone in the moonlight, opaline, glinting in the depths of his bucket like the untold treasure he was, magnified and dreamily distorted, his grayness tending to silver.

In a reflective pause before trying the knob, I stared at the window over the sink, as dainty as a dollhouse window, framed by duckling-patterned curtains. I thought about how many times Mother McRaney must have stood in that very spot, drying a dish and waiting with some anxiousness for young Gerald to come home. I imagined her looking like Gerald McRaney in a dress.

I am delighted to report that the back door of the McRaney place was still unlatched, in keeping with the tenets of genteel country living. I knew the house almost by heart thanks to its elaborate interactive web presence. But nothing could have prepared me for the jolt of the physical place, the tactility of it, the McRaney-based smells baked into the fabrics, a wonderful, heady effluvium of cherry-flavored tobacco, and spoiled lard, and hamster feces. The McRaneys were known as big hamster people. The lavish treatment they gave their hamsters was a favorite topic of gossip around the old courthouse square. But who's laughing now? Gerald McRaney on his way to the bank, that's who.

The door opened directly onto that Holy of Holies, the Southern American kitchen. Just inside, in a china closet repurposed as a display case, I found to my utter astonishment the ultimate grail: Devil Crème, a mid-twentieth-century paste made of mutton brains and eel testicles, perfectly preserved in its distinctive coffin-shaped tin. So Dan was a good-luck charm as well as a friend! By putting my interest in the culinary arts in a proper perspective, he had prepared me to recognize and appreciate the most exquisite dining opportunities all the more. He had truly "whetted my appetite" in a way no other oyster had ever done.

I was thrilled to confirm that all the makings of a ten-year-old Gerald McRaney's breakfast were currently on display: not just the precious container of Devil Crème, still technically banned since 1962 by special amendment to the Mississippi state constitution, but also the individual cellophane-wrapped wafers of Melba toast, the condensed milk, and the sorghum molasses. I would also do as my forebears had done, breaking the Devil Crème into chunks and drenching it with the sweet, thick milk from the rusty can. From thence, merely a crumbling of toast and a drizzle of sorghum separated me from a seminal dining experience, time travel on the magical wings of a wooden spoon. Intended by its makers as a lubricant for velocipede chains, Devil Crème was first consumed as a foodstuff during the Great Depression, mainly in Arkansas, though the cult eventually spread as far south and east as Mobile, Alabama, and continued long after mere economic factors would have necessitated. That was the genius of a long-gone populace: subverting cheap commercial products into complex dishes, approaching a kind of makeshift transcendence.

"Dan, you're in for a rare treat," I said. I put his bucket on the stovetop for convenience. I couldn't help but notice that he looked cold and hungry. In my giddy state I had forgotten that some of us don't have the luxury of waiting around for exotic banquets. Some of us don't take comfort and excess for granted. All Dan wanted was a little warmth, and perhaps some hearty fare, a crust of black bread or such, to help him pass the night. I turned on the heat for him. The tiny blue flame licked the bottom of his bucket, and Dan seemed cozy indeed. I could almost hear him sigh with relief. Luckily, the pantry and refrigerator of the McRaney house were fully stocked, whether for authenticity's sake or in preparation for some convivial gathering of the museum's board members. Could be that this bright green parsley was meant for Gerald McRaney himself! No matter. I chopped it up and put it in Dan's bucket to tide him over until I had finished preparing the Devil Crème. No more brackish muck for him. From now on, Dan would eat only the finest and freshest of everything. Again I envied him. Flavors I had long taken for granted would be startlingly new to him. Oh, that we could all taste with Dan's tongue.

"You're going to love parsley," I told him. "Often used as a garnish, it is sometimes overlooked as a mild but effective seasoning."

Butter, garlic, a dollop of heavy cream, fresh sprigs of thyme, and some coarse black pepper—Dan wanted comestibles no fancier than this for his evening's repast, and I was all too happy to oblige him.

Would that I had been capable of like restraint. When I had smashed open the china closet and peeled back the tin lid of Devil Crème, it emitted a red mist that stung my eyes and made me weep the bloody tears of a dying stigmatic. Did I take it as a warning? I did not. I had faith in canning, one of the most venerable of American preservation methods. I was momentarily stymied by the jar of sorghum molasses, stuck as it was to the bottom shelf with its marvelous adhesive power—God himself could not move a jar of sorghum molasses with drippings down the side. I had to bend at an awkward angle to spoon it onto my bowl of Devil Crème. As for shelf stability, sorghum will last forever, like the honey in the tombs of the mighty pharaohs.

My first bite of Devil Crème "country style" revealed astringent undertones, not unpleasant, and caused me to suffer a severe attack of tinnitus. The second bite managed to be both velvety and earthy, and I detected for the first time a surprising note of vanilla. The third bite, I saw ghosts. My innards clenched.

I rolled around on the floor, coming to realize that previous generations had been full of nothing but idiots. Satan had Frenched me that night, and what could exorcize his taste from my mouth? As if in answer, a wafting aroma fluttered down to soothe me.

It was Dan.

He was simmering now, transmuting into something angelic. Dan in his wisdom had anticipated my struggle. Maybe he had even tried to warn me. But I had been too stubborn to listen. So instead he had "stewed in his own juices," quite literally. The cynical may call it passive-aggressive. Was Our Lord on the Cross passive-aggressive? I leave it for the reader to say.

I struggled to my feet. "I can't believe it, Dan! I can't believe you'd sacrifice yourself like this. Let me get a ladle."

It was then that I experienced a blazingly genuine case of the old-fashioned Eisenhower-era diarrhea.

My search for a ladle summarily abandoned, I reached in with my hands, searching for Dan in the soup.

"There you are, Dan! As much as I'd love to eat you, not even that can help me now. In fact, it might even make matters worse. But there is something you can do for me, Dan. Quick, go for help!"

I threw him out the back door, then fell to the cool, yellowed linoleum. He just lay there on the lawn until the dog came along and picked Dan up in his mouth. They trotted off together. Dan didn't even look back. I knew he was leaving me behind.

"Yes," I said. "Yes, Dan. I understand."

Was I sad to see him go? You bet. Yet in so many ways I was becoming the oyster that Dan had made me want to be. What had I done but absorb the foul leavings of mankind's unrelenting gluttony? And now I was pooping out a fiery truth.

We had come to a crossroad and parted there, Dan and I. My journey was over, but his was just beginning. The dog, whose name was probably Red, was already headed down a country lane, taking Dan to Florida. I knew they'd encounter hardships along the way. They'd probably team up to fight off a mountain lion. But there would be good times too. Foiling a bank robbery. Boxcars and campfires. Winning some money on a game show. Red finds a harmonica! Some bad feelings when they both fall in love with the same gal, but even at the time they know it's something they're going to laugh about later. And laugh they do.

Laugh they do.

But a hush falls when they climb the crest of, I assume, the Appalachian Mountains and look down at the lush, rolling landscape of Apalachicola.

Writhing on the kitchen floor in an agony as visionary as it was intestinal, I could see it all. Red's paws are sore by the time they reach the sugary dunes, swollen beyond recognition! But he'd do it all again.

"You're home, buddy," he says.

He drops Dan out of his mouth there at the edge of the gentle surf.

But Dan doesn't answer.

He's dead.

Oh my God in Heaven, Dan is dead.

Red noses Dan into the water, then settles wearily into the sand and watches the Devil Crème sun, red as he is, sink into the bay.

Coconut
The Queen of Cakes

Jeffrey Steingarten

From the day I was born until the autumn of 1991, I baked only one cake. Cakes seemed pointless, bulging, huge, and bloated. They delivered so little sensory pleasure compared with their incalculable calories, their massive weight and volume, their off-the-chart glycemic index. Cakes were effeminate, woman's work, and surely politically incorrect.

And then, in 1991, I was introduced to the Queen of Cakes. We were walking into a restaurant I'd been wanting to try, K-Paul's New York Kitchen, the short-lived outpost of pioneering Louisiana chef Paul Prudhomme, whom I greatly admired. A woman who had just finished dinner stopped us and, with a wide smile, shared the news: "They've got the coconut cake tonight! There's only one piece left—you'd better claim it right away." Which we did, and near the end of an uneven meal, we were brought a vast wedge of ivory and gold. I tasted it twice, then called for more forks, and in the blink of an eye, our kilogram of cake had vanished.

It had apparently begun life as six disks of yellow cake, each one moistened with a coconut syrup and slathered with a thick layer of sweet white filling. Then the disks were stacked up tall and covered from top to bottom with a fluffy white frosting and dusted with sprinkles of fresh coconut. Later I would learn that many cakes native to the American South are enriched with what one cookbook quite unromantically terms a soaking solution, a glaze that is brushed on the surface or poured over it. And it was not unusual that the filling between the layers was not identical to the icing on the top and sides.

What an elaborate production, each molecule in it calculated to give exquisite gustatory pleasure. I needed to possess it, to make it mine. I began telephoning K-Paul's early the next morning and reached the chef several hours later; he couldn't give me the recipe until he spoke with Prudhomme's HQ in New Orleans. I nagged him without mercy until he called them and reported, "They say the recipe's right out of *The Prudhomme Family Cookbook*."

The days that followed were busy with shopping, with the compounding of glazes, filling, frostings, syrups, and batters. The Prudhommes insist upon fresh coconut, and those of us without long experience may, as I did, find the retrieval of coconut meat from its adamantine and ligneous shell to be a long and painful challenge from which one rarely emerges without the spilling of blood.

If the baking had gone well, I would have worn these battle scars with pride. But it didn't. Our idea was to bake three thick cake layers, then slice each of them crosswise for a total of six. But the layers didn't rise much at all and resembled pancakes in the end; splitting them in two required microsurgery. The culprit was undoubtedly a can of exhausted baking powder. Some of the chemicals in baking powder are expected to react with one another to produce carbon dioxide after they're heated in the oven, but they can apparently also react at room temperature, slowly and continuously, on the shelf in your pantry or supermarket, until there's no gas left to make all those little bubbles that aerate a cake and convert it from a biscuit into a cloud.

Sure, our failure was but an accident, yet somehow, whatever the cause, it was our Waterloo, our Battle of the Little Bighorn, and we had lost the will to spend another three days replicating the project. We were still convinced, as are so many bakers and cake lovers, that Southern American Coconut Layer Cake is indeed the Queen of Cakes. And so every once in a while, in the years that followed, we tried a new formula. The most promising of them and thus the most deeply tragic was a fine recipe from Brenda Cooper of South Carolina, the cousin of an old friend of mine. It was a warm day, and we had reached the final steps, stacking up the layers and slathering generous gobs of sweet, creamy filling in between. Then, as we were swirling icing over the very top, we noticed that the layers were not stacked as evenly and neatly as we had thought, and that they were shifting, imperceptibly at first and then really, really perceptibly, the top two layers threatening to slide off. Before we could act decisively, they carried out their threat, and although I lunged to catch them, all five layers and their icing and syrup and filling plopped to the floor. It all happened so fast.

And yet, once we had scooped up several handfuls of cake scraps from the floor and tasted them, and saw how delectable they were, we realized that we had come quite close to creating a perfectly iconic Southern American Coconut Layer Cake. Only our exhaustion, physical and psychological, kept us from trying again the next day, the next week, or even the next month.

■ ■ ■

In the meantime, our spirits were lifted by signs that cake had become less politically incorrect. In my view, cake's connection with Marie Antoinette had always been the chief drag on its prestige. But the truth is emerging that Marie never, ever said, "Let them eat cake" when she was informed that the peasants were starving for lack of bread. Here are the facts: (1) The legend is based on an anecdote in Jean-Jacques Rousseau's autobiographical *Confessions*, which he wrote in 1766, when Marie Antoinette was only ten and living in her native Austria; (2) Rousseau attributed the remark not to Marie but to an unnamed "great princess," who has since been identified as having lived one hundred years earlier; (3) Lady Antonia Fraser, in her biography of Marie Antoinette, quotes from a letter Marie wrote to her family back in Austria that expresses unmistakable compassion for the peasants' plight, which all demonstrates how out of character such a cruel remark would have been.

In any event, Rousseau's quotation was "Qu'ils mangent de la brioche": "Let them eat brioche." There was no mention of cake. The French, in fact, have no precise word for our rotund, fluffy, tall American cakes, which did not exist until baking powder was invented in the mid-1800s. Did Rousseau's first English translator twist "brioche" into "cake"? My investigation at the New York Public Library was inconclusive, and the Library of Congress search engine was broken. I found the e-mail address of a distinguished elderly scholar, a retired professor and Rousseau translator at a leading Southern university. It was late at night by this point, and after several inconclusive e-volleys, he left our chat, saying that he was afflicted with a gravely anemic condition, that his red blood cells were dangerously dwindling, and that he needed to climb back into bed. I was grateful nonetheless.

As you can tell, I've been boning up on cakes, reading widely and deeply, baking a few practice layers here and there, and confecting a tentative quart or two of frosting—all as mere calisthenics in my training for a bold and final assault on the summit, the Kanchenjunga of American cake-baking, the Southern American Coconut Layer Cake! Yes, the moment of challenge had arrived once again. And at my side, a Sherpa Tenzing Norgay to my Sir Edmund Hillary (if you'll permit me to switch mountain peaks), was my assistant, Elise, who has shown an amazing and, frankly, unanticipated facility for generating cakes with a fecundity traditionally attributed to rabbits.

I fearlessly decided to start on square one; that is, to begin with flour, water, air, and fire, and create the universe from there. Plus sugar and eggs and a little dairy. And don't forget the coconut. We followed an elaborately detailed plan. First we reminisced about the dreamiest American Coconut

Layer Cakes we had ever tasted. We wrote down the reasons for our high regard, and these became our tentative criteria, our standards for cake excellence. Then we purchased a half-dozen American Coconut Layer Cakes that had garnered the highest recommendations (in print, in person, online) and sampled and rated them all, while refining our criteria.

To some readers, especially those in the mental-health professions, all this may seem excessive—obsessive, compulsive, depressive, even geeky. But as we will soon come to appreciate, they couldn't be in more serious error.

We agreed that the ideal Classic Southern American Coconut Layer Cake has six or more cakey layers and six or more gooey layers; that the cakey parts should be tender and fine grained; and that the upper third of each layer should be nearly as moist as pudding. Nearly every element should have a wonderful coconut taste (preferably without the help of coconut extract). The icing should be white, creamy, fluffy, neither runny nor sticky nor stiff.

So the baking commenced. If I had not already discovered Elise's hidden talent, I would have limited us to six recipes, but Elise proved indefatigable. We baked the cake layers first and rated them; then whipped up eleven icing recipes and took notes; then finally applied the icings to the cakes. Within three days there were Classic Southern American Coconut Layer Cakes everywhere, all shiny in their snowy frostings.

Some of them were two layers tall and some were three; some were virginal white, inside and out; and some were a rich yellow. Some cakes had coconut—shredded or chopped, toasted or raw—sprinkled onto or pressed into their icing. Some of the icings tasted of nothing but sugar. Some had the flavor of marshmallows because they started out as meringues with lots of egg whites, which are the mother of marshmallows. Several had the tang of cream cheese, which when whipped up with butter and sugar makes for a popular white, generic, nice-tasting frosting. Most had no coconut taste at all. Some cake layers were dry and some were as moist as pudding; some were aerated with tiny bubbles and some with large, indelicate bubbles. Some were tender and some were tough.

Halfway through our baking, I telephoned the Peninsula Grill in Charleston and inquired about their celebrated Ultimate Coconut Cake, which I had tasted on my previous trip to the city. It weighs twelve pounds (enough for twenty-four servings of dessert) and costs $100 plus $97.62 for overnight shipping. It arrived the next day, and yes, it was in pristine condition—deeply frozen and just barely waking from cryo-hibernation, like the spaceship crews in *2001: A Space Odyssey* and *Alien*. Sure, we gouged off little troughs of frosting with our fingertips, but we would have to wait another two days to eat the cake fully defrosted. So there it sat, atop the Roto-Broil

400, rotund and self-important, a monument to Southern baking, vaguely reminiscent of the Jefferson Memorial as seen from the rear.

In fact, it would be no exaggeration to say that every horizontal surface in and near our kitchen (not counting the floor and ceiling) was laden with Classic Southern American Coconut Layer Cakes on round white platters. To our great surprise, my adolescent bitch Jesse evinced an immediate weakness for cake, which forced us to move our productions to horizontal surfaces high off the ground, such as the top of the refrigerator.

It was time for the showdown.

In the end, none of the cakes we baked ourselves lived up to our memories, our hopes—but when we finally cut ourselves some slices of the cake from Peninsula Grill, we agreed that it was close to the best we'd ever tasted. A day later, at room temperature, the Peninsula Grill Ultimate Coconut Cake had reached its prime, and it stayed there for forty-eight hours. Its flavors and textures had merged and melded, the filling and frosting were light, nearly fluffy, and its grain was delicate and tender. We never needed to slice another full wedge from the cake, because everybody who passed by the Roto-Broil 400, even some relative strangers, helped him- or herself to an extravagant forkful of it. In this way, the entire cake, all twenty-eight thousand calories of it, disappeared within thirty-six hours. Twenty-eight thousand!

And now we were *cogido* on the horns of a dilemma. The notion of creating the ideal Southern American Coconut Layer Cake from scratch—that is, from vials of hydrogen, oxygen, and carbon—had proved to be an impossible dream, and perhaps a truly stupid one. Unlike savory cooking and even bread baking, the baking of sweet things is much like chemistry. Small alternations can be disastrous and rarely a source of gladness. Beginning with a good recipe that can generate a family of fine offspring is the best way to start.

If I had tried to reverse-engineer the Peninsula Grill's cake, I might have ended up somewhere on the positive side of approximate. Instead, I appealed to my friend Lou Hammond (whose firm does Peninsula Grill's public relations) to intercede on my behalf and wangle the actual recipe, and a few days later Elise was busy at the stove. The results were good enough but paradoxically not paradisiacal, and I doubt it was Elise's fault. OK, maybe it was. But what she produced did not stack up against Peninsula's mail-order creation or my treasured memories of the original amazing cake from K-Paul's New York Kitchen. Had I idealized it? Was I doomed to disappointment?

■   ■   ■

Thus it was that I asked Elise to shop for and prepare the components of the Prudhomme family's creation, which I hadn't approached since my devastating failure twenty-one(!) years earlier. It had been, after all, only the second cake I had ever attempted. Maybe, just maybe, we had gained enough experience and wisdom in the course of baking forty cakes that success would be ours.

First, we altered the recipe in various places—to stanch the bloodshed, for example, we substituted frozen grated coconut from Thailand for the fresh. Following Shirley Corriher's general findings in *BakeWise*, we added homemade whipped cream to the batter to increase the cake's tenderness, and it worked! And then. . . . I sense that you are perched on the edge of your seat, and so let's leap ahead to the climax, to our very happy ending: it was the finest coconut cake we had ever made and the best either of us had ever tasted.

And if you wonder, What does our Classic Southern American Coconut Cake go with best?, the answer is . . . nothing! It goes with nothing. Not coffee or milk or any alcoholic beverage. Maybe a few sips of water every now and then to keep yourself from choking. Contemporary, up-to-date desserts are expected to be (1) moderate or less in sweetness; (2) sweetened with honey or brown sugar or fruit concentrate or maple syrup, but never with that deadly, toxic sweetener known as white sugar; (3) balanced in flavor between sweetness and acidity (from tart fruit or sweet vinegar). Our classic coconut cake is none of these. It is unalloyedly sweet and as white as a leukocyte. It is not contemporary or up-to-date, and yet it is perfect and unimprovable, unequaled.

The Vicksburg Lebanese Supper

As told to Amy Evans by Mary Louise Nosser

My name is Mary Louise Nosser.

When my daddy came to this country from Lebanon, he was twenty-two years old, and it was August 27, 1920. And he said he arrived in Vicksburg at eight-thirty in the evening with fifty-five cents in his pocket.

My mother came to the United States from Lebanon when she was around seventeen, with other members of her extended family.

Daddy opened his store in 1924, and they were married in '25. And he posted on his little ledger, "May 6th, I got married." That's what he put in his stock book. And so my brother was born a year later, and then my second brother was two years later, and then I came, and then my sister, and that was the crop.

■   ■   ■

I have been involved with the annual Lebanese Dinner at Saint George Orthodox Church since approximately 1968.

For a while I was cochairman of sweets with my cousin, Gloria Abraham. We have an overall chairman and then different department heads: the cabbage, the kibbe, the salad, the setting up the dining room, and so forth.

When Gloria got sick one year, we decided we needed to do a little cross-training so that we wouldn't be caught red-handed with only one person knowing the particulars. So I decided to drop out and let somebody else handle the management of the sweets department. I just picked up boxes and did manual work. Gloria contacted the people about making certain kinds of pastry, and she was instrumental in picking it up and bringing it to the church and so forth.

But with the cross-training situation, I decided that I like being in the dining room during the dinner. It's a hectic job, and if I got paid by the mile, I could retire every year. But anyway, I help with all of the other activities. In fact, we beg everybody to come and help, and we welcome our friends in the community to come and learn. We're proud of our food, and we don't hide our recipes. We're really glad to share with other people.

For a long time, the men didn't help with the dinner, you know. But now they'll get in there and chop garlic and roll cabbage and make kibbe and everything. It takes a strong person to make kibbe, and we need more men to help with that. We're making batches that consist of eight pounds of wheat and thirteen pounds of meat. You're working in one big dishpan, and it takes a lot of strength to do that. And we have to make many of those batches. So it's really good to have the men helping with that.

I help with the kibbe and the cabbage. There's a lot of prep work with the cabbage rolls. You know, we work two or three days on just prepping for the cabbage rolls, and then a couple of days just rolling all of those. We fed 3,420 people last year, and that's a lot of food to prepare.

The tickets to that dinner sell themselves. We don't have to peddle the tickets. People come to get the tickets. And they know what they're going to get. They know the quality is going to be top, and it's a lot of smiles and greetings and best wishes and so forth, and people like to come to the church so they can see everybody else in town.

My brother had a friend who used to have a Taco Bell on Washington Street. And he said the Monday of the Lebanese dinner, he just didn't even open up because he knew everybody was going to be eating at the Orthodox church. I think that's pretty much true.

In fact, when people say, "Oh, it's so good, we should have it twice a year"—well, we'd faint and fall out at that because it's so much work. We truly work a whole month.

Our menu is always the same—only the pastries vary a little bit. We always have the kibbe, and we have rolled cabbages. People ask us, "How do they get better every year," and I don't know. I just tell them, "Honey, it's God's hands in it, because we keep doing everything the same way. And, if it's getting better, it's—it's due strictly to him." The cabbages have gotten tremendously popular. And then the salad, plus the tabouli. And then the snap beans—we cook gallons of that, too, you know.

It was always a citywide thing. We've always opened to the public. But lately, interestingly enough, our people are awfully glad to eat the food, because people don't cook at home anymore like they used to. And I dare say, a lot of the younger girls don't know how to cook any of it.

I can remember when the dinners were two dollars, and I was a widowed little mother, and I could hardly afford to buy a ticket. Of course, that wasn't the only one I had to buy. I bought one for the maid keeping my baby. I bought one for my daddy. And you can't stay up there and work like a dog all day and not eat, so I had to have two tickets. And I'd always get one for the next day. I'd call it withdrawal. I just hate myself when I don't buy that third meal for Tuesday, you know.

I really don't know that our dinner has any relationship to our church services or anything in the old country. I think it's just something that we did out of necessity to raise some money, and it just got to be bigger than we could handle. And it's kind of like catching something by the tail. You're scared to let go of it. I don't think it has any connection otherwise, except that we're very proud of our food, and it's very popular. And we believe you're certainly getting your money's worth.

Soul Food? What Is That?
(From *Simple's Uncle Sam*, 1965)

Langston Hughes

"You heard, didn't you, about that old colored lady in Washington who went downtown one day to a fine white restaurant to test out integration? Well, this old lady decided to see for herself if what she had heard was true about these restaurants, and if white folks were really ready for democracy. So down on Pennsylvania Avenue she went and picked herself out this nice-looking used-to-be-all-white restaurant to go in and order herself a meal."

"Good for her," I said.

"But dig what happened when she set down," said Simple. "No trouble, everybody nice. When the white waiter come up to her table to take her order, the old colored lady says, 'Son, I'll have collard greens and ham hocks, if you please.'

"'Sorry,' says the waiter. 'We don't have that on the menu.'

"'Then how about black-eyed peas and pig tails?' says the old lady.

"'That we don't have on the menu either,' says the white waiter.

"'Then chitterlings,' says the old lady, 'just plain chitterlings.'

"The waiter said, 'Madam, I never heard of chitterlings.'

"'Son,' said the old lady, 'ain't you got no kind of soul food at all?'

"'Soul food, what is that?' asked the puzzled waiter.

"'I knowed you wasn't ready for integration,' sighed the old lady sadly as she rose and headed toward the door. 'I just knowed you white folks wasn't ready.'"

"Most ethnic groups have their own special dishes," I said. "If you want French food, you go to a French restaurant. For Hungarian, you go to Hungarian places, and so on."

"But this was an American place," said Simple, "and they did not have soul food."

"The term 'soul food' is still not generally used in the white world," I said, "and the dishes that fall within its category are seldom found yet in any but colored restaurants, you know that. There's a place where jazzmen eat across from the Metropole that has it, and one or two places down in the Village, but those are the only ones I know in Manhattan outside of Harlem."

"It is too bad white folks deny themselves that pleasure," said Simple, "because there is nothing better than good old-fashioned, down-home, Southern Negro cooking. And there is not too many restaurants in Harlem that has it, or if they do, they spoil everything with steam tables, cooking up their whole menu early in the morning, then letting it steam till it gets soggy all day. But when a Negro fries a pork chop *fresh*, or a chicken *fresh*, or a fish *fresh*, I am telling you, it sure is good. There is a fish joint on Lenox Avenue with two women in it that sure can cook fish. But they is so evil about selling it to you. How come some of these Harlem eating places hire such evil-acting people to wait on customers? Them two ladies in this fish place stand behind the counter and look at you like they dare you to 'boo' or ask for anything. They both look mad no sooner than you enter."

"I'll bet they are two sisters who own the place," I said. "Usually by the time Negroes get enough money to own anything, they are so old they are evil. These women are probably just mad because at their age they have to wait on anybody."

"Then they should not be in business," said Simple.

"I agree," I said. "But on the other hand, suppose they or their husbands have been skimping and saving for years. At last, at the age of forty or fifty they get a little business. What do they want them to do? Give it up just because they have got to the crabby age and should be retiring, before they have anything to retire on?"

"Then please don't take out their age on me when I come in to order a piece of fish," said Simple. "Why them two ladies never ask what you want politely. They don't, in fact, hardly ask you at all. Them women look at customers like they want to say, 'Get out of here!' Then maybe one of them will come up to you and stand and look over the counter.

"You say, 'Have you got any catfish?' She will say, 'No!' And will not say what other kind she has or has not got.

"So you say, 'How about buffalo?' She will say, 'We had that yesterday.'

"Then you will say, 'Well, what have you got today?'

"She will say, 'What do you want?' I have already said twice what I wanted that they did not have. So now I say, 'How about butterfish?'

"She says, 'Sandwich or dinner?'

"I say, 'Dinner.'

"She says, 'We don't sell dinners after ten p.m.'

"'Then why did you ask me if I wanted a dinner?' says I.

"She says, 'I was paying no attention to the time.'

"I said, 'You was paying no attention to me neither, lady, and I'm a customer. Gimme two sandwiches.'

"'I am not here to be bawled out by you,' she says. 'If it's sandwiches you want, just say so, and no side remarks.'

"'Could I please have a cup of coffee?'

"'We got Pepsis and Cokes.'

"'A Pepsi.'

"She rummages in the cooler. 'The Pepsis is out.'

"'A Coke.'

"She comes up with a bottle that is not cold. Meanwhile the fish is frying, and it smells good, but it takes a while to wait, so I say, 'Gimme a quarter to play the juke box.' Three records for a quarter.

"Don't you know that woman tells me, 'We is all out of quarters tonight.'

"So I say, trying to be friendly, 'I'll put in a dime and play just one of them. What is your favorite record?'

"Old hussy says, 'There's nothing on there do I like, so just play for yourself.'

"'Excuse me,' says I, 'I will play "Move to the Outskirts of Town," which is where I think you ought to be.'

"'I wish my husband was here to hear your sass,' she says. 'Is your fish to eat here, or to go?'

"'To go,' I says, 'because I am going before you bite my head off. What do I owe?'

"'How much is two sandwiches to go?' she calls back to the other woman in the kitchen.

"'Prices is gone up,' says the other hussy, 'so charge him eighty cents.'

"'Eighty cents,' she says, 'and fifteen for the Pepsi.'

"'I had a Coke,' I says.

"'The same. You get a nickel change.'

"'From a five-dollar bill?' I says.

"'Oh, I did not notice you gave me a five. Claybelle, have you got any change back there?'

"'None.'

"'Neither is I. Mister, you ought to have something smaller.'

"'I do not carry small change around on payday,' says I. 'And what kind of restaurant is this, that can't even bust a five-dollar bill, neither change small change into a quarter for the record player? Don't you-all have nothing in the cash register? If you don't, no wonder, the way you treat a customer! Just gimme back my five and keep your fish.'

"'Lemme look down in my stocking and see what I got there,' she says. And do you know, that woman went down in her stocking and pulled out enough change to buy Harry Belafonte. But she did not have a nickel change.

"So I said, 'Girl, you just keep that nickel for a tip.'

"If that woman owns the place, she ought to sell it. If she just works there, she ought to be fired. If she is the owner's girl friend, was she mine I would beat her behind, else feed her fish until a bone got stuck in her throat. I wonder how come some Harlem places have such evil help, especially in restaurants. Hateful help can spoil even soul food. Dear God, I pray, please change the hearts of hateful help!"

We Shall Not Be Moved

Jessica B. Harris

If the period of the Civil Rights movement began with traditional African American cookbooks extolling the virtues of greens, macaroni and cheese, neckbones, chitterlings, and fried chicken, it ended with a transformation of the diet of many African Americans. By the end of the decade and throughout the 1970s, brown rice, smoked turkey wings, tahini, and tofu also appeared on urban African American tables as signs of gastronomic protest against the traditional diet and its perceived limitations to health and well-being, both real or imagined. One of the reasons was the resurgence of the Nation of Islam.

The Nation of Islam (NOI) originated in the early part of the twentieth century but came to national prominence in the 1960s under the leadership of Elijah Muhammad, who preached that peaceful confrontation was not the only way. In Chicago, Detroit, and other large urban areas, the Nation of Islam offered an alternative to the Civil Rights Movement's civil disobedience, which many felt was unnecessarily docile. It preached an Afro-centric variation of traditional Islam and provided a family-centered culture in which gender roles were clearly defined. Food always played an important role in the work of the Nation. As early as 1945, the NOI had recognized the need for land ownership and also for economic independence and had purchased 145 acres in Michigan. Two years later, it opened a grocery store, a restaurant, and a bakery in Chicago. One of the major tenets of the religion was the eschewing of the behaviors that had been imposed by whites, who were regarded as "blue-eyed devils." Followers abjured their "slave name," frequently taking an X in its place, and adopted a strictly regimented way of life that included giving up eating the traditional foods that were fed to the enslaved in the South.

NOI leader Elijah Muhammad was extremely concerned about the dietary habits of African Americans and in 1967 published a dietary manual for his followers titled *How to Eat to Live*; in 1972 he published another, *How to Eat to Live, Book 2*. As with much about the Nation of Islam, there is considerable contention about Muhammad's ideas and precepts, which are a combination of traditional Islamic proscriptions with an idiosyncratic admixture of prohibitions that seem personally biased. He vehemently opposed the traditional African American diet, or "slave diet," as he called it. Alcohol and tobacco were forbidden to Nation of Islam members and pork, in particular, was anathema. Elijah Muhammad enjoined his followers:

> Do not eat the swine—do not even touch it. Just stop eating the swine flesh and your life will be expanded. Stay off that grandmother's old fashioned corn bread and black-eyed peas, and those quick 15 minute biscuits made with baking powder. Put yeast in your bread and let it sour and rise and then bake it. Eat and drink to live not to die.

Pork is *haram*, or forbidden, to traditional Muslims. Pork, especially the less-noble parts, was also the primary meat fed to enslaved African Americans. Pork in any form was anathema to NOI members, as were collard greens or black-eyed peas seasoned with swine. The refusal of the traditional African American diet of pig and corn was an indictment of its deleterious effects on African American health, but also a backhanded acknowledgment of the cultural resonance that it held for most blacks, albeit one rooted in slavery. Pork had become so emblematic of African American food that the forbidding of it by the Nation of Islam was radical, and the refusal to eat swine immediately differentiated members of the group from many other African Americans as much as the sober dress and bow ties of the men and the hijab-like attire of the women. Forbidding pork made a powerful political statement, but the real culinary hallmark of the Nation was the bean pie—a sweet pie, prepared from the small navy beans that Elijah Muhammad decreed digestible. It was hawked by the dark-suited, bow-tie-wearing followers of the religion along with copies of the Nation's newsletter, *Muhammad Speaks*, spreading the Nation's gospel in both an intellectual and a gustatory manner.

■   ■   ■

Increasing numbers of African Americans chose to celebrate Kwanzaa in the late 1960s and early 1970s as part of a growing awareness of their own African roots. The Peace Corps and continuing missionary work by churches black and white sent African Americans to the African continent, resulting in more widespread knowledge of the African Diaspora and expanded gastronomic horizons, and contributed to a growing sense of shared culinary underpinning. In larger cities and college towns, dishes of African *jollof* rice and Ghanaian groundnut stew began to be found on dinner tables alongside more traditional favorites.

Then, in 1977, the publication of the autobiography of writer Alex Haley, *Roots*, and the subsequent television miniseries based on it transformed the way many African Americans thought of themselves and of Africa. Blacks were galvanized by *Roots*, and large numbers made pilgrimages to the African continent with hopes of discovering their own ancestral origins. (Coinciding with the release of the television miniseries, a travel organization began to offer trips to Dakar, Senegal, for $299, a price that was affordable for many who might otherwise never have traveled to the continent.) They boarded the planes by the hundreds and on the other side of the Atlantic found myriad connections between African American culture and that of the motherland. One major connection they discovered was West Africa's food. They visited markets and recognized items that had for centuries been associated with African American life: okra, watermelon, and black-eyed peas. They tasted foods that had familiar savors and learned new ways to prepare staples of the African American diet like peanuts, hot chilies, and leafy greens. In Senegal, they tasted the onion-and-lemon-flavored chicken *yassa* and the national rice-and-fish dish, *thieboudienne*; in Ghana, they sampled spicy peanut stews; in Nigeria, they savored a black-eyed pea fritter called an *akara*. African Americans began to taste the culinary connections between foods they knew and those of the western section of the African continent.

This new knowledge found its way to a larger public, as the avant garde of African American cookbook authors took a more international approach in their work. *Vibration Cooking: or, The Travel Notes of a Geechee Girl*, by Verta Mae Smart Grosvenor, and *The African Heritage Cookbook*, by Helen Mendes, look at the traditional foods not just of the American South but also of an international African culinary diaspora and contain recipes for dishes from the African continent and the Caribbean as well as traditional Southern ones.

Africa, its diaspora, and their foods, though, were only a part of the expanding African American culinary paradigm; cookbooks of the period also evidence wider-ranging African American attitudes about what to eat and how to eat, like 1974's *Dick Gregory's Natural Diet for Folks Who Eat: Cookin' with Mother Nature*, by the eponymous comedian, and 1976's *Soul to Soul: A Soul Food Vegetarian Cookbook*, by Mary Keyes Burgess of Santa Barbara,

California. The traditional foods of the South were still being written about in works like *Spoonbread and Strawberry Wine: Recipes and Reminiscences of a Family*, by Norma Jean and Carole Darden. Using genealogical research that had been popularized by *Roots* as well as recipe and memoir, the Darden sisters crafted a 1978 cookbook that tells the story of their family through food. It also tells of the diversity of African American food.

Up until the 1970s, the food of African Americans could be loosely categorized by class. The upper classes ate a more European-inspired diet, while the underclass consumed a diet evolved from the slave foods of the plantation South. Regional differences played a lesser role. The South always took primacy of place at the table, but those living in the North and West also had their own dietary habits, like a predilection for potatoes instead of rice or an affinity for beef instead of the more traditional pork.

The 1970s, however, exploded all hypotheses. Certainly many African Americans still clung to the traditional foods of the South. However, after the decades of the Civil Rights gains and with the growing awareness of the African continent and its diaspora, increasing numbers of blacks of all classes throughout the nation began eating a diet that was widely varied and reflected a newly discovered pride in African roots and international connections. The African American diet of this era was one that continued to celebrate the traditional foods; it also encompassed the vegetarianism espoused by Dick Gregory, allowed for the dietary concerns of Elijah Muhammad and the Nation of Islam, reflected the international diversity of the African Diaspora, and even acknowledged the culinary trends of the time. In short, in the 1970s, the food of African Americans began to evolve into a cuisine that honored hog maws and collard greens and yet allowed for West African foufou, Caribbean callaloo, brown rice, and even tahini. Just as Rosa Parks's sitting down on a Montgomery bus changed the face of public America, civil rights workers at kitchen tables, black restaurants in urban enclaves, and four students at a North Carolina lunch counter transformed the African American foodscape and brought it out of isolation. Black food in its increasing diversity was no longer segregated on the blacks-only side of the menu, but squarely placed on the American table.

Fixing on the Next Star

Patricia Smith

*Between 1916 and 1970, more than half a million African
Americans left the South and migrated to Chicago.*

Mamas go quietly crazy, dizzied by the possibilities
of a kitchen, patiently plucking hairs from the skin
of supper. Swinging children from thick forearms,
they hum stanzas riddled with Alabama hue and promises
Jesus may have made. Homes swerve on foundations
while, inside, the women wash stems and shreds of syrup
from their palms and practice contented smiles,
remembering that it's a sin to damn this ritual or foul
the heat-sparkled air with any language less than prayer.

And they wait for their loves, men of marbled shoulders
and exploded nails, their faces grizzled landscapes
of scar and descent. These men strain every room
they enter, drag with them a stench of souring iron.
The dulled wives narrow their eyes, busy themselves
with clanging and stir, then feed the sweating
soldiers whole feasts built upon the okra and the peppered
necks of chickens. After the steam dies, chewing
is all there is—the slurp of spiced oil, the crunch
of bone, suck of marrow. And then the conversation,
which never changes, even over the children's squeals:
They say it's better up there, it begins, and it is always
the woman who says this, and the man lowers his head
to the table and feels the day collapse beneath his shirt.

The Brixton

It's New, Happening, and Another Example of African American Historical "Swagger-Jacking"

Stephen A. Crockett Jr.

Last month, the corner of Ninth and U got a British resident—a kind, three-floor chap: the Brixton. It's the new happening restaurant and bar on the former Black Broadway, appropriately named after a multicultural section of London that lost the gentrification battle in the 1990s.

Look. I get it. The Chocolate City has changed. It isn't what it used to be, and I don't know what's worse: the fact that D.C. was once so marred by murder that it was nicknamed Dodge City or that there is now a hipster bar on U Street that holds the same name. Point is, there is a certain cultural vulturalism, an African American historical "swagger-jacking," going on on U Street. It's an inappropriate tradition of sorts that has rent increasing, black folks moving further out—sometimes by choice, sometimes not—while a faux black ethos remains.

In a six-block stretch, we have Brixton, Busboys and Poets, Eatonville, Patty Boom Boom, Blackbyrd, and Marvin. All are based on some facet of black history, some memory of blackness that feels artificially done and palatable. Does it matter that the owners aren't black? Maybe. Does it matter that these places slid in around the time that black folks slid out? Maybe. Indeed, some might argue that these hip spots are actually preserving black culture, not stealing it.

But as a native of a then Chocolate City, I can remember when a Horace & Dickie's fish sandwich always felt like a warm hug, because they were cheap and we were broke. It felt like the owner knew we were struggling, so he lowered the prices for us. It felt like home.

Their presence makes me feel the same way I felt when my homeboy's dad, who lived on the corner of Fifth and L Street N.E., used to rant about how there needed to be a four-way stop sign at the intersection. Oh, how he would wax about how someone was going to get hit by a car and how the city didn't care about the black folks that lived there. The city turned over and the first thing that showed up on the corner of Fifth and L was a four-way stop sign.

I guess this is to say I am grateful for the stop signs but sad that it took us leaving to have it happen. That it didn't feel important to build until we were gone. That it isn't FUBU (For Us By Us). I know now that I can hit up any of these places and hear the music of my past and walk outside and see a city that I don't know.

Here's a news flash to those who don't know: this place was a place well before you. You didn't discover us. We aren't Indians. You didn't make Ben's; we did. This city was pig intestines after so many left, and we made it into chitterlings. And these places, these fancy places with "authentic" food, aren't homes. They're just rentals.

The bigger question is: Is it possible for a once-black city to experience gentrification while opening businesses that exploit black culture? Yes. Culture is weird in the way that air is weird: you need it, you breathe it, but you don't own air.

You can connect through culture, embrace culture, dance culture, but in the end, you can't be the culture police. Maybe I want to sit at the doors of D.C.'s black culture and check IDs, making sure you deserve to appreciate what Marvin Gaye and Donald Byrd meant to a city that really didn't have much to be proud of when these cats came up.

Maybe there should be a quiz at Brixton about the neighborhood's cultural significance. Maybe there should be a box set sold behind the bar at Marvin. Or maybe these places should just be called something else (Patty Moo-Moo or Farvin for starters, as I believe those are all free). But there is a certain territorial connection that comes with culture that just has to be expected. The District isn't a city or a state, and it was at one point Chocolate City.

It was always a place that was special, with people that made laws during the day and the people that broke them at night. It was Ben's Chili Bowl way before it had a bank line. In order to get food, you had to jockey for position. You had to shout.

You had to let your voice be heard, because it was never just about the chili; it was about the experience—and it wasn't manufactured or re-created. It was organic. If the Ben's at Nationals Park made folks yell to get their orders in, it would feel just as false as these places.

The most conflicting part about these places—Brixton and Blackbyrd,

Patty Boom-Boom and Busboys—is that they are extremely welcoming and well-run establishments. But there is something inherently inauthentic about homemade sweet tea out of a mason jar.

It feels like a rip-off. It feels like watching NWA perform at the Kennedy Center. It feels like something is missing. It just doesn't feel like home.

Southerners Going Home

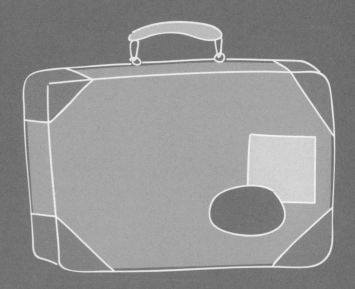

I Placed a Jar in Tennessee

John Jeremiah Sullivan

In the yard of the house I grew up in—I'm looking at it right now on Google Maps, satellite and street views open in simultaneous windows (plus a real estate site that's telling me it wasn't even a full half acre of land)—there grew three fruits. The man who'd built the house was a priest. Our priest, actually, at St. Paul's Episcopal downtown. He baptized me. His name was Fallis, pronounced like "phallus." The doctor who delivered and circumcised me was called Hymen. The Fallis family would have been the ones to plant the trees and bushes, sometime in the fifties. Whether meaning to or not, they'd bequeathed some culture to our small sector of the rolling tract-house development. In the backyard we had a mature peach tree that my mother would visit on summer mornings. She'd slice pieces onto our cereal. There was also an apple tree, with some variety of bitter cooking apple that nobody in our family knew how to prepare—tiny ones, bright green with a brushstroke of bright red when they were ripe. The fruit all went to waste. But at least we watched it grow and talked now and then about how a person might use the apples, my mother confident that there were "people who could tell you how to do it."

About the third fruit, the quinces that grew on a large bush next to the driveway, nobody ever said anything assuring like that. The quinces were weird. We didn't know what to make of them, figuratively or literally. Did people eat them? They could have come from space. In fact on *Sesame Street* there used to be a skit that involved two aliens. They couldn't reach the fruit on their planet's fruit trees. One alien was too short, the other couldn't bend its arms. When that came on I would glance outside at our quince bush. Extraterrestrial nectarines: that's what they looked like. Beautiful, I realize now. Like a cross between a lemon and a pear. (They symbolize fertility.) In the street-view picture, the quince bush was still there, but in the satellite view, taken five years later, you can see it's been mowed to the ground. In the grass where it was there's a pale, almost perfect circle.

I hadn't thought of the quince bush for a couple of decades until I visited an old friend in L.A. last year, one I'd kept in contact with but hadn't seen in several years. I'd flown into town that afternoon and was supposed to leave at dawn—it was one of those situations where it made no sense to go to sleep. You'd just be torturing yourself. Kevin West: a friend from college. We were in his apartment in Koreatown, a nice pad with a view of the city lights, though noticeably smaller than his old place in Laurel Canyon. He'd recently downsized his life. He had a bottle of good rye whiskey and some olives. At one point he was explaining to me that all modern fruit preserving, in cans and jars, descends from a discovery the Romans made—that if you cooked the otherwise inedible quince in honey and sealed it in jars, it became sweet and made excellent jam. Quince in honey, as a preserve, spread all over the world. The Portuguese called it *marmelada*. Marmalade.

Kevin showed up at our small school in Tennessee as a junior, seeming somehow older. He'd spent the preceding couple of years at Deep Springs, the college out West where you grow your own food and herd cattle on horseback while debating Aristotle. Before that, he'd grown up in an actual holler, in East Tennessee, where his family had been settled for nearly 150 years. His self-described "flower child" mother nurtured his love of books and shells. But he had a fashion thing going, too. In my first memory-image of him, he's walking across the quad in safari shorts and a purple neckerchief, his hair as it remains, full-bodied butterscotch. Carrying some kind of satchel. He drove a tiny yellow diesel car and could roll a cigarette with one hand, pouch to flame. Within days one of the wittier campus wags had dubbed him the Jolly Rancher.

But meeting him, the word *pretentious* never entered *my* head. He was too clearly doing Kevin, both doing and inventing him. Two paths were open when he graduated—studying classical languages at Berkeley or becoming an assistant at *Vogue*. He chose the latter and moved to New York, soon getting hired at *W* magazine, where he became their Paris editor. For years you'd talk to him on the phone and he'd have just come back from staying on an island with models somewhere. He partied on separate instances with Prince Charles and Puffy (in the latter case somehow smuggling in a bunch of fellow Deep Springs alums dressed like hippie hobos—the woman at the rope looked dubious until Tom Ford appeared in a velvet jacket and swept them all inside). Hearing his stories, I always pictured old Alfa Romeo Spiders like the one in *Contempt*. "Swimming swimming, sun golden," was Kevin's characteristically gerundive description of those lost weekends.

I won't lie, it was pretty strange to imagine him out there among the pretty people. Not that he didn't belong, couldn't pull it off, but when I knew him best, he was a bookish person. That's how we connected. A mutual friend of ours talked about finding him in the quad one day in tears because a professor was inside "destroying" one of his favorite books. He'd been compelled to run out of the room. When we talked, it was mostly about Shakespeare's sonnet sequence, which he was obsessed with in those days. He had a hopeless confused crush on a beautiful lesbian woman. How was that Kevin surviving the inevitable moral obscenities of the ultra rich? It was impossible not to suspect that the old scholar/seeker/cowboy person was getting . . . not bored, but restless.

He got depressed. He dropped out of the "mag world." He was more or less stranded in California, where he'd been working as *W*'s West Coast editor for a while but had no roots. He started feeling a gut-level homesickness that made him physically ill. But like most of us, he didn't really want to go home. "Do you know that song," he asked, "'How Ya Gonna Keep 'Em Down on the Farm (After They've Seen Paree)'?"

It wasn't east Tennessee he missed, anyway. Not the physical place, in other words. It was something about the life he'd known there, the feeling of your everyday reality being in sync with the natural world in a way that went beyond daytime/nighttime. He found himself thinking about his grandparents' farm. His grandmother had been "a pretty active preserver," he said, meaning of fruits and meat but more than that, too. "She wouldn't have thought of herself this way," he said. "Part of farm life was 'putting up' food." She had a pantry full of hams and bacon. "That part of Tennessee didn't get electricity till the forties," he said, "so within living memory you had a food culture that went back to the preindustrial age." He had nice memories of his grandmother's pickled beets. "Fourteen-day pickles—a fermented pickle. Also, she made this strawberry freezer jam that was really delicious." The canning and jarring moved with the seasons—you had to pick the fruits and berries at the right time. Each batch was a new little chemistry experiment. Things could go wrong. You were always monitoring some jar in the kitchen, observing its changes. It gave the whole house a clock to go by.

One day Kevin was getting ready to have people over for dinner—this was about four years ago—and wanted to serve strawberries for dessert. He drove down to the Santa Monica farmers' market and bought a giant flat of ripe strawberries, ten pounds, many times beyond what the guests would eat. At home he looked at these beautiful berries, realizing with that sort of animistic empathy a child can feel for nonanimal objects that half of them would probably go to rot, and he thought for the first time in many years about the strawberry jam. Waking up the next day, hung over, he started trying to make it. Called home for help with the recipe. Cooked the fruit in sugar.

"Fruit cooked with sugar equals preserves," he said. "The jam was a total mess. Edible, just not very good."

If he could make it taste as good as hers had, recreate the flavor and texture, that would be to carry forward that old life, bringing it into his world. A thread of connection. So he felt.

These days when you say someone becomes "obsessed" with something it usually means they spent four hours reading about it on the Internet last night, but it seems accurate to say that Kevin became obsessed with preserves. It gradually became not only the thing he talked about, but the thing you could tell he was always thinking about. He started making cross-country trips to track down fruits that supposedly "put up" well. He tried to preserve things he'd never seen preserved, stuff that would have made his grandmother have to lie down and fan herself. He sent me a picture of a Buddha's hand citron one time. It was an unearthly yellow and looked like a squid. If one of the ghosts in Pac-Man had been bright yellow and was preserved in a specimen jar, where it got all distended over time, it would have looked like this thing. "Found this last night at the Altadena farmer's market," he wrote. "My first thought was, I wanna get that, I wanna preserve it."

He visited libraries to read old recipe books. He took a cooking-chemistry class, at one point, to know more about what was happening to the fruits and vegetables at the molecular level. He connected with other fixated types out in the world of new-primitive preserving. Mainly, though, he was spending hundreds of hours alone in the kitchen experimenting. I would get e-mails from him about his struggles. Jellies were "temperamental," he wrote. They were like young sopranos singing arias: you had to sit there hoping they wouldn't crack. Especially if you didn't use the commercial pectin, which he avoided, preferring to rely on the fruits themselves for their natural supply. But working that way it was "easy to end up with syrup—that's a failure." He made jams, jellies, and other concoctions out of beach plums, cardoons, cushaw, damsons, eggs, elderberries, fennel, horseradish, huckleberries, limettas, medlars, mulberries, and nasturtium pods. He preserved quince: under the guidance of Oregon pickle-jam guru Lina Ziedrich, he made a syrup of quince, not a disaster-accident syrup but a deliberate one, flavored with rose geranium.

■　■　■

It seemed on one level the kind of life phase your friends go through when you say, "Is it making them happy? 'Cause that's all I care about." But over time it grew clear that something deeper was going on. My wife had a student once, in North Carolina, who went off one spring break to intern on a movie set, and in the midst of it the whole department got a very short e-mail from him that read, "Found my passion y'all." That's what had happened.

With this passion there developed another, quasi-ideological, near-survivalist side to Kevin's interest in that old prerefrigerated world. I have one e-mail from him in which he describes the home-preserving culture he'd grown up with as "a template for how to survive in the post-oil/post-global/post-Apocalypse future. . . ."

> . . . grow your own food, preserve it at home, survive. One of the big issues with climate change is where can we secure access to arable land and clean water in order to grow food, and how to develop the personal skills and connect with a local agricultural context that would allow for true food independence—in other words, reinventing village life. It's the Jeffersonian ideal refracted through the dark prism of contemporary pessimism about the future. I think the remnant agrarian communities in the southern Appalachians provide a viable model. By contrast, not far from my dad's place is a demonstration of one of the gravest errors we've made as a nation, which is to take rich farmland out of production by turning it into sterile suburbs. I could show you where my grandparents' farm was sold and turned into a housing development—some of the streets are named after them, which they would have despised. There's actually a spot where John Riley West Road intersects with Eloise West Road. Bitter . . .

Kevin has written a book about all of it, called *Saving the Season: A Cook's Guide to Home Canning, Pickling, and Preserving*, to be published this summer by Knopf. Part cookbook, part manifesto, and part crypto-memoir, it's literate and lyrical and fanatically well researched. Also probably quite useful, if you're into home preserving or want to be. Even if you're not, though, it's the kind of cookbook you can read for pleasure. Me, for instance—I can't see doing any canning or jarring anytime soon. I want to, I feel the appeal, but a person should know his limitations, and when you grow up on Pillsbury toaster strudel, for breakfast and sometimes lunch (what the hell), even the simple stages of cooking with sugar, sealing the lid, et cetera, can present real obstacles. Even I was able to enjoy the book. It has more than 200 recipes but is shot through with little essays, too—about preserving, food gathering, gardening, family, and what it means to find a second act.

I ordered a couple of boxes of Kevin's jams and pickles, which he sells and barters in low quantities. Just having them has exerted an effect on the vibe of our kitchen and by extension the rest of the house. They're like little jars of distilled sunlight, sitting there on the table. Through them I discovered the beauty of really good jam, namely that if you put it on toast—the most difficult to ruin of all human foods—suddenly, almost without meaning to, you've started your day off well, with a little moment of flavor worth lingering over. My mother visited and ate some of Kevin's Scotch marmalade, saying it gave her strong Kentucky-childhood flashbacks.

My favorite of all the jars, the one I was saddest to see go down to just those sticky smudges of unscrapeable purple scum on the glass, was the boysenberry jelly. I sent Kevin a message asking him about the history of this fruit, which I'd always thought was made up by energy-drink purveyors to describe vaguely pan-berry flavorings. Kevin replied that its origins were more complicated than that. It had indeed been developed recently, in evolutionary terms, but in the 1920s, by a man named Boysen. He served in the army in World War I, and when it ended, moved with his wife to a small farm in California. There he started experimenting with berry hybrids, mixing pollens. He finally achieved the boysenberry—which tastes, to me, like a quintessence of berryness, with a grape-juicy sweetness, but wide enough on your palate not to seem oversweet. "It's one of the bramble berries," Kevin wrote. "It has an obvious kinship with the wild blackberries I picked growing up."

Boysen tried to make a go of his berry. He even started filling out a patent application. He suffered a freak accident, however—fell fifteen feet and broke his back. The farm on which he'd developed the berry got sold. His berry beds all but disappeared under weeds. Only years later did he receive a visit from two men, one of whom was Walter Knott, of Knott's Berry Farm. They'd heard about Boysen's berry from other farmers who'd tasted it, and wanted to try it themselves. He led them out to the old field, where they were able to salvage a few vines for transplant.

Now Boysen's berries were on my table, in some form, or used to be. While the jar lasted, it seemed expressive of something—that what's old doesn't need to be old fashioned. It gets reborn. And with patience and skill you can capture it. You can arrest it.

A Love Letter to North Carolina's Red Bridges Barbecue

Monique Truong

Dear Red Bridges Barbecue Lodge,

It's been ten years since I last ate at your fine establishment, but I can still see the teal blue vinyl that covers your booths and chairs. It's a shade of blue that belongs to a different era, which is appropriate, as so do you. And of course, I can smell the hickory smoke and the sharp jabs of vinegar that accompany every tray that emerges from your kitchen.

It was October 2002, and my husband and I were in your hometown of Shelby, North Carolina—my first trip back there in decades and his first ever—for the wedding of our friends Sean and Kristin. Kristin is a local girl whose parents still live in Shelby. Sean grew up in Connecticut, the same state my husband is from. My husband and I joked that their marriage, like ours, would be a mixed marriage: a Northern boy and a Southern girl, of course.

Back in Brooklyn, where we all lived and still do, Kristin and I had been amazed at and laughed over the fact that I had grown up in neighboring Boiling Springs, and that my parents were both graduates of Gardner-Webb, a Baptist college that is now a university, located in the sleeping heart of that little town. *Town* is perhaps too expansive a word for Boiling Springs. I once called it a "freckle" in an essay. It was the most neutral-sounding, diminutive word I could think of for it. My relationship to Boiling Springs is complicated, but so is my relationship to you and, therefore, the writing of this letter.

Over the course of that long weekend, my husband and I ate at your establishment three times, and that's really saying something given the packed schedule of meals, receptions, and parties that Kristin and her family had arranged for us out-of-town wedding guests. My husband and I attended them all but also made time in our day and room in our stomachs for your Jumbo Plate: pork shoulder, fork-tender from its overnight sojourn on the pit. In the vernacular of your menu, I ordered mine "chopped" with a mix of "white and brown" meat. I didn't know about the "crunchy brown" option back then, which would have added crispy, fat-rendered bits of skin to the mix. I knew enough, though, to order extra sauce.

As you know, yours is North Carolina Piedmont–style barbecue sauce at its finest. If you'll forgive me while I slip into the language of food writers (we too have a vernacular of our own), Bridges, your sauce has a top note, a middle, and a base. What Italian perfumers call the testa, corpo, and fondo. The top is, of course, the vinegar. It's there to invigorate the taste buds; slap them to attention, if you will. The middle note is undoubtedly tomato, either ketchup or paste. It's a velveteen, light touch, a makeup kiss after the physicality of the vinegar. The base note is the reassuring warmth of spices easily found in any American kitchen. Nonetheless, it's your secret, which I've tried to uncover in my own kitchen many times since. I've a deep appreciation for the elusive, a profound respect for flavors that play hide-and-seek with my tongue. I've tried sweet paprika, black pepper, a bit of brown sugar, a wink of cayenne. I've come close but have never matched it. The obvious conclusion, of course, is that your sauce—any barbecue sauce worth licking off your fingers, in fact—does not sing alone. Sauce needs its pig. And there's no way I would try to conjure up your pit-cooked pig in Brooklyn. I'm persistent, but I'm no fool.

But you already know all this about yourself. I suppose I just wanted you to know that I know it as well. It's important to me that you understand how the taste of your barbecue had made me feel right at home, had comforted me in a way that took me by surprise, and had asked me, just like a childhood friend would: Why have you been away for so long?

Can you imagine all that communicated via a plate of barbecue? Okay, three Jumbo Plates of barbecue.

I wrote earlier that my relationship to you is complicated, and you must have asked yourself: But how could that be? You're a restaurant—a local institution, really—sitting proudly at your present location on East Dixon Boulevard since 1953; and I'm a customer, like many others, a patron in search of pork enrobed in smoke and sauce. What could be so fraught about that transaction?

In our case, I think the answer lies in the concept of belonging, which is often expressed as "the sense of belonging." Like the five senses we are born with, the sense of belonging defines the way we experience the world. It demarcates the borders of our known world. *Belonging* is a meaty word, full of meanings, and yet as elusive as the base note of your sauce.

My parents and I lived in Boiling Springs from 1975 to 1978, and yet you and I didn't meet until October 2002. There are two mysteries here: (1) How was it possible that during those years, my family never once drove the fifteen minutes from Boiling Springs to Shelby, parked our silver Chevrolet Nova in your parking lot, and gazed up at your neon sign with the word *barbecue* written out in loopy lowercase letters, except for the middle B, which was a tall, outsize capital, which drew the eye even further upward, like a church steeple? (2) If I had never dined with you before, why did your barbecue taste to me of home, the way dogwoods in bloom or the scent of honeysuckles at dusk always make me think of my childhood in the South?

We've met now, but maybe it's time for me to introduce myself properly. I tell the story of how my parents and I came to Boiling Springs in different ways. There are many places to begin our story, but let's begin this time with our names:

In the summer of 1975, when I was seven years old, my parents and I began using our baptismal names: Charles, Angela, and Monique. Vietnamese Catholics all have additional French names chosen from the roster of saints. The names were required by the church but rarely used in our day-to-day life in South Vietnam. Charles, Angela, and Monique, however, were no longer in Vietnam. In April of '75, we had lost our country after a protracted civil war, escaped as refugees, and had been living in limbo on U.S. military bases repurposed as and renamed "relocation camps."

We were not homeless anymore, though. We had been sponsored by an American family whose home, and thus our home for the next several years, was the small town of Boiling Springs, which as you know is located in the foothills of the Blue Ridge Mountains, toward the western tip of North Carolina. We needed easy-to-pronounce names for this new and unexpected geography. I think that the switching of names was also an act of magical thinking, or perhaps faith. All acts of renaming are about transformation, and all transformation requires faith: in our case, the faith that we would blend in better and be less conspicuous with these Western monikers. "Charles" and "Angela" had the best hope of that; I'm sorry to say that "Monique" remained hopelessly foreign sounding.

In 1975, Boiling Springs had a Baptist college but little else. A short drive away was Shelby, whose signs proudly proclaimed it "The City of Pleasant Living" and the seat of Cleveland County. Shelby was where we attended our churches (for a while, we alternated between a Catholic and a Baptist church because Charles and Angela didn't want to offend either congregation, which had both so kindly welcomed us with donated food, clothing, and an exuberant niceness that I would later learn had a name: Southern hospitality). Shelby was also where we went to buy our groceries and shop for the odds and ends of our new life.

After our first year in the Boiling Springs–Shelby area, my father went to Boston to study for his MBA. My mother was a nursing student at Gardner-Webb, and I was in Boiling Springs Elementary getting the spirit kicked out of me every day. At first I thought my classmates were simply confused by my country of origin, but I soon realized that "Chink" and "Jap" had little to do with China and Japan. They were words meant to wound me, not to identify me. My mother and I sought solace, distraction, and entertainment in our occasional meals out. There wasn't much else that a thirty-three-year-old Vietnamese woman and her eight-year-old daughter could do together.

When we headed for Shelby, we gravitated toward the fast-food chains with the commercials and jingles that were familiar to us from television. To this day, I've never met another person who savors an Arby's roast beef sandwich the way my mother did. She even liked that neon yellow cheese sauce that coated your teeth like glue. Angela was on a tight budget, so we also found ourselves at the all-you-can-eat night at Pizza Inn, an outpost of the national pizzeria franchise, jockeying for position with young men with large appetites.

Angela knew a bargain when she saw one, and the combination of the all-you-can-eat pizzas with that American thing of wonder known as the "unlimited salad bar" was irresistible to her. In Vietnam, Angela had been a lady of leisure. Her parochial school education had taught her fluent French and English, and she had traveled to Europe and returned home with suitcases full of French lingerie and other nonessentials. In Shelby, she was a woman in search of a bargain, in search of American food on a plastic tray or in a paper bag. What Angela was also looking for, perhaps, was the kind of anonymity that these nondescript restaurants offered the two of us. Often located near the highway, these places didn't serve anything besides food, fast and cheap. There was no conversation, no community, no shared history, and no sense of belonging. In that void, there existed instead a kind of parity among the customers. No conversation, community, history, nor belonging meant that no one was included, and no one was excluded.

Now, Bridges, I'm not suggesting that back in the mid-'70s you wouldn't have welcomed us with a smile and the small slip of paper that you call a menu. What I am suggesting is that we feared that you wouldn't, or maybe that some of your patrons wouldn't, and I stand by that fear, because you know that the children whom I went to school with in Boiling Springs weren't born with those ugly racial epithets in their mouths. Someone put them there, and those someones were most likely the adults in their lives. Maybe even some of your best and most loyal customers.

Southern hospitality, my mother and I had learned, had its flip side, and we did what we could to avoid running headlong into it. This protective instinct made Boiling Springs and Shelby even smaller for us. One of the consequences of our proscribed world was that we never had the pleasure of enjoying a Bridges Jumbo Plate together. It would have been a splurge for Angela, but one that I know she would have found addictive. I can assure you that my mother and I would certainly have joined the ranks of your best and most loyal customers.

Vietnamese people honor the pig. In fact, we honor one another by bestowing a pig. A wedding engagement, for instance, is not complete until the groom's family brings a whole roasted pig to the house of the bride's family. My Connecticut-born husband and his family did not fulfill this obligation. This is why, when I'm feeling ornery and wicked, I tell him that our marriage is technically null and void. No pig, no marriage.

Now for the second mystery: the homecoming that the taste of your barbecue bestowed upon me. Some may argue, and I hope you won't, Bridges, that my family and I didn't live in Boiling Springs long enough to make it our home nor to make me a Southerner. But 1975 to 1978 were years that formed me. These were the years when I acquired a new language, the third of my young life. English is now the only language in which I can claim fluency. In Vietnamese and French, I'm at best a writer of haikus or of unintentionally experimental, disjointed prose. In English, I'm a novelist.

The Belgian-born French novelist Marguerite Yourcenar once wrote that "the true birthplace is . . . [where] for the first time one looks intelligently upon oneself. My first homelands have been books, and to a lesser degree schools." Yourcenar is right that for some of us, the word *homeland* isn't singular but plural. She's also right about the critical self-recognition that books can allow us to experience. How else can I explain the homecoming that I've felt on the pages of novels by Harper Lee, Carson McCullers, and William Faulkner? I think there's a connection between how these books and how your barbecue seem like longtime friends to me. Yes, Bridges, I just compared you to Lee, McCullers, and Faulkner. You're very welcome.

The words *homeland* and *home* can refer to a place that may be on a map but does not necessarily exist yet within your heart; a place you have to learn, slowly and with trepidation, to claim because you're afraid that it never claimed you; a place that lies dormant within you, like a seed or a song, waiting. Waiting for words like these to wake it up: "I could smell the curves of the river beyond the dusk and I saw the last light supine and tranquil . . ." (Faulkner, *The Sound and the Fury*). Or waiting for the alchemy that occurs when patience, heat, and smoke coax forth every ounce of flavor that a slab of pork has to give.

Bridges, I'm a writer and I'm food obsessed, so it makes perfect sense to me that homelands—whether dormant or active—can be found in books and in flavors. So much so that I wrote my second novel, *Bitter in the Mouth*, about a young girl who has a neurological condition that causes her to experience the sensation of taste when she hears or speaks certain words. Her name is Linda Hammerick, and she's from the Tar Heel State.

Bridges, I hope you don't mind, but you have a cameo—actually several cameos—in my second novel. I took some liberties: I shortened your name a bit; I referred to your barbecue as "pulled" pork, as opposed to "chopped"; I added perhaps a couple more pigs to your neon sign; and I renamed myself Linda Hammerick and imagined a different life and family for her in Boiling Springs. But otherwise it's a story about tasting and claiming a home in the American South.

I hope you'll like it as much as I liked you.

Yours truly,
Monique

The Missing Link
Donald Link Opens Second Cochon in Lafayette

Brett Anderson

Donald Link barely gave the chickens a chance to stop sizzling before he put his hands around them, subjecting each to a tactile examination that looked like nothing so much as a quarterback blindly feeling his way to a football's seam.

One of the chickens looked like wild game, its flesh darkened by injected Cajun spices vivified by the flames in the wood-fired oven behind it. The other, which had been brined overnight, wore the more typical mottled gold-brown armor of roasted farm-raised fowl. Both stood upright in cast-iron pans, impaled by beer cans. Link appraised them while sucking the grease off his fingers. "Turns out there are a lot of ways to cook a chicken," he said.

That statement of the obvious prompted laughter in the peanut gallery behind him, at the edge of the open kitchen inside Cochon in Lafayette.

The opening of the restaurant, a spin-off of the original Cochon in New Orleans, was still three weeks away, but on this hot August night, Link and his team had crossed the threshold where obsessive planning gives way to undressed rehearsals. Ryan Prewitt, until recently chef de cuisine at Herbsaint, Link's flagship New Orleans restaurant, explained, "We talked about [cooking chicken] for like three hours last night."

"It got pretty heated," chuckled Stephen Stryjewski, who is, along with Link, chef and co-owner of both Cochon locations.

Cochon Lafayette has more than just a name in common with its New Orleans counterpart. The most important similarity is a concept that encapsulates Link's vision of what, to use his words, "Cajun food has become." Not since Paul Prudhomme opened K-Paul's Louisiana Kitchen more than three decades ago has New Orleans seen a new restaurant elicit such a pheromonal response from such an array of diners. That both happen to hang their hats on the food of Acadiana is a topic ripe for academic inquiry.

Evidence of Cochon's success goes beyond the crowds that regularly congest the restaurant's corner of New Orleans's Warehouse District.

Since Cochon opened in 2006, both Link and Stryjewski have won prestigious chef awards from the James Beard Foundation. In 2008, the *New York Times* ranked Cochon the third best new American restaurant outside New York. Link also won a Beard for *Real Cajun*, his provocatively titled cookbook that delves deep into the pot that inspired Cochon's creation. *Gossip Girl* star Blake Lively was so besotted with the restaurant's sweet potato sauce at a recent visit that she tried to persuade staff to circumvent FDA regulations by sending her some inside a disemboweled teddy bear. (The response she received from Cochon, according to *Glamour* magazine: "We are not the drug cartel.")

Still, the new Cochon is a re-creation of the old one, not a straight replication. (An item not central to the New Orleans Cochon repertoire: roast chicken.) The fine distinction begins to explain why Link's journey back to his native Cajun country—Lafayette is its putative capital—has been filled with trepidation as well as joy.

The chef's family roots run deep in the region: he was raised in Lake Charles, on Cajun country's southwestern edge. But as much as Link identifies with the cooking of his—and perhaps as important, his family members'—youth, there is no erasing that he became a big shot in a city whose relationship to Cajun country has dysfunctional dimensions. As Billy Link, a Crowley soybean, rice, and crawfish farmer, put it, "New Orleans is New Orleans, and there's a line between New Orleans and here. They don't mix well, in a way."

Billy Link, who is either Donald's third or fourth cousin (it depends on whom—and when—you ask), was leaning against the poured-concrete counter separating the restaurant's kitchen from one of two main dining rooms. He'd arrived with his wife, Becky, and their two young sons to feast on the dishes Cochon's chefs were fine-tuning while test-driving the new kitchen equipment.

The banquet included the two roast chickens, along with one that had been cooked in an outside smoker built by Dwane Link, another cousin; two darkly crusted pork shoulders; a whole rib-eye roast cut into bite-size strips; a pan of shrimp in a butter sauce spiked with the Brazilian peppers that Donald Link grows in his Lakeview backyard; and smothered rabbit provided by yet another cousin, served with rice that Billy Link is supplying the Lafayette restaurant.

"That's the old Cajun style right here!" Billy Link proclaimed, delighted by the sight of the rabbit, which he called, in an exaggerated French-Cajun accent, *lapin*. "If they cook it like this, they'll be all right."

Billy Link has known his cousin only as a successful chef, having first met Donald at a family reunion six or seven years ago, and relishes his role as an unofficial critic of Cochon's food. He's playfully dismissive of meat smokers as an influence of the Zaunbrechers, the Cajun family on Donald Link's mother's side. ("The Link side? Non-smokers.") He wore a Cochon T-shirt but actually prefers Herbsaint, where the food reflects European traditions as much as Louisiana ones.

The preference could be a simple matter of taste. It also could have something to do with the games Cochon plays on native Cajuns' memory and sense of pride. The phenomenon might be summed up by the review Billy Link said a group of his friends gave the New Orleans restaurant after visiting: "We can cook better than that."

Donald Link responds to his family's ribbings the way he responds to irritants both mild and severe: with a crooked smile that causes him to resemble a cat that just made a snack of a pet canary. While he's no stranger to cameras or laudatory press, by the standards of a moment where chefs can become television stars without ever running a restaurant, Link counts as a throwback to the days when chefs let the food speak for itself. He insists, "I am not trying to be a celebrity chef."

The strategy has served Link well, and not just economically. Anthony Bourdain, the acerbic chef, television host, and best-selling author, has said of Link, "There's no one in the business with more credibility."

The challenge in Lafayette is that credibility earned for cooking Cajun food in New Orleans isn't exactly a recognized currency. In fact, it could be a liability.

"A lot of [Cajuns] know of him who haven't tried his food, but they know of him because he's up here," Billy Link said of his cousin, raising his hand up high to illustrate the chef's exalted status. "And they're waiting for him."

One of the many ironies attending Cochon Lafayette is that its owners don't regard area Cajun restaurants to be their primary competition. Ask Link or Stryjewski what inspired them to open in Lafayette, as opposed to, say, Houston or Covington, both of which were considered, and they will invariably talk with amazement about the crowds at Pamplona Tapas Bar or the slick Japanese restaurant Tsunami in Lafayette's old downtown.

"You need to check that place out on a Friday night," Stryjewski said of Tsunami. The night-clubby restaurant is not the sort one would expect to impress Stryjewski, a tattooed, bearishly boyish man who in plain clothes often appears to have just stepped off a skateboard.

But Tsunami, like Pamplona, captured the chefs' attention because its crowd, particularly on weekends, exposes an indigenous population of young adults whose interests clearly go well beyond—and possibly don't even include—boudin and zydeco.

The opportunity Cochon's chefs see in Lafayette has as much to do with business as it does aesthetics, and it is similar to the one they rode to fame and profit in New Orleans. While the level of attention Prudhomme had brought to Cajun food in the 1980s altered the way Americans eat, the Opelousas-born chef's fame was so widely felt—and his food so widely misinterpreted—that it sparked a debate over authenticity of the cuisine that has yet to quiet.

Stir the Pot: The History of Cajun Cuisine, a definitive book on the subject, debunks the myth that Cajun food was developed in a vacuum; authors Marcelle Bienvenue, Carl A. Brasseaux, and Ryan A. Brasseaux call it a "cross-cultural borrowing of the diverse ethnic and racial groups that have co-existed in the Bayou Country since the late eighteenth century."

Cochon entered into this historical fray by exposing one thing Prudhomme's revolution did not spawn: modern Cajun restaurants that uphold the highest standards of quality and service. The very fact that Link's team drew a bead on Lafayette suggests that this has been the case not just in New Orleans but in Cajun country itself, an implication that steers the age-old debate over authenticity into uncharted, potentially turbulent waters.

Link and Stryjewski are intense students of Cajun cuisine and its evolution. And the chefs' idea of "real" Cajun food around Lafayette tends to be found in the same places Cajun food purists look for it: on home cooks' stoves or in decidedly blue-collar restaurants like T-Coon's and Laura's II, both order-at-the-counter, rice-and-gravy plate lunch places that have almost nothing in common, at least atmospherically, with Cochon.

But in the crowds found at the more modern non-Cajun restaurants, Link sees "an indication of the desire of this city. If you want to feel metropolitan, if you want to go for a glass of wine and a decent meal, where do you go? It's usually fried food and beer and cocktails, and if there is wine, it's not good wine. I think there's a lot more sophistication going on in these small towns that's not being reflected in the restaurants."

Demographic evidence supports Link's hunch. The 2010 Census data puts the median household income in Lafayette Parish at $47,901. That compares to a $35,505 median household income in Orleans Parish, according to data provided by the Greater New Orleans Community Data Center.

But is it possible tonier Cajun-style restaurants are few and far between in Cajun country because Cajun diners don't trust restaurants with wine lists to properly represent a folk-art form born of subsistence living many people still remember?

Pat Mould was the chef at Charlie G's when the restaurant opened in Lafayette in 1985. He remembers raising eyebrows with the restaurant's contemporary Louisiana cooking and sleek interior, which was designed by a prominent Chicago architect.

"Because we had this perception of being a citified restaurant, we got a ton of [criticism]," Mould said. "People were suspicious. We have this jaded perspective that no one's going to cook it better than mama."

That Charlie G's remains one of the region's relatively few high-end restaurants interpreting Louisiana cuisine also points to persistent assumptions about the corrupting effects of elevated social status. In an oral history conducted for the Southern Foodways Alliance by the New Orleans historian (and Lafayette native) Rien Fertel, T-Coon's owner David Billeaud said, "I'm not a chef. I'm a cook. Cooks work hard."

■   ■   ■

In New Orleans, Cochon proves daily that questions surrounding its food's authenticity are matters of semantics and style, not substance. The food's rusticity provides cloud cover to a technical proficiency that is the mark of professionals who regard the chef title as an honor earned through labor. The results—the fried rabbit livers riding pepper-jellied toasts, the hog's-head cheese shaved over fresh peas, the skillet-cooked rabbit and dumplings based on a Link relative's recipe for squirrel—are almost always prettier than anything a Cajun grandmother has ever served.

Link and Stryjewski, after all, are not Cajun grandmothers. They're chefs whose skill sets and sensibilities were formed in restaurants as far away as northern California. But because the ingredients and recipes ground Cochon's food in Cajun country's bayous, prairies, and marsh, Cochon cuts through the social baggage—name another Beard-winning restaurant offering iceberg lettuce salad, unironically—that has weighed on Cajun cuisine since its commercialization.

Diners can reasonably argue that they've never had anything like Cochon's braised pork cheeks in Abbeville, or that it is heresy to charge $8 for an oyster-meat pie, flaky as Cochon's is. But it would be impossible to conclude after eating either dish at Cochon, perhaps with a bottle of Burgundy wine alongside a free cone of fried pigs ears, that the chefs regard their source of inspiration as a backwater.

Still, theories that hold true in New Orleans are being tested all over again at Cochon Lafayette. And Link knows it.

"As a chef your [work is] always on the table. You're always up for discussion," Link said. The difference in Lafayette, he explained, is "everybody is a food critic who could make or break you. It's a whole other level." You can't "PR your way out of" a bad night's performance when there are no waves of tourists coming in behind the diners you may have disappointed on an off night.

"I'm feeling way more pressure performance-wise," Link added, comparing Lafayette to New Orleans, "because it's deeper."

The chef was sitting on the deck outside Cochon after dinner service on September 15, the restaurant's opening night. The task of convincing Lafayette diners that the restaurant is adequately respectful of Cajun cuisine's hardscrabble roots is further complicated by its location in the city's River Ranch development, a model of mixed-use New Urbanism that architecturally looks more suburban than urban.

T-Coon's is only three miles away, but Cochon Lafayette's closest and fiercest business competition may be the Bonefish Grill. Earlier in the night, the River Ranch outpost of the Florida-based national chain hosted overflow crowds, mostly locals angling for a good view of the LSU football game. (Bonefish is also where Link's father, who lives in Lake Charles, drove to celebrate his most recent birthday.)

Cochon Lafayette won't conjure visions of the rural idylls on full-color display in Link's cookbook, but it is beautiful, particularly at night, when its lights cast a soft glow on the Vermilion River running just below the herb- and citrus-tree-lined deck and terrace. At six thousand square feet, the restaurant seats around 250, twice as many diners as its sister location in New Orleans. It also evokes the original, with its pigmented concrete floors, blonde wood accents, and open kitchen.

Beth Hebert ate her lemon-and-garlic-scented oven-baked shrimp at the restaurant's expansive bar, which overlooks the river and suggests what a fishing camp might look like if renovated by an architect specializing in urban lofts. Hebert was in Lafayette visiting relatives from her home in Los Angeles. She declared Cochon's food "not unrecognizable" from what she knew growing up. Still, she said, "I couldn't take my parents here. They're old. They'd be confused." Hebert's friends in L.A.? "They'd absolutely love this place."

If Cochon Lafayette succeeds, bridging this generational divide could be its greatest accomplishment. Cognizant of this challenge, the owners larded the opening-night staff with seasoned Link Restaurant Group operatives. Among them were Stryjewski and Prewitt, who was recently promoted to oversee all of the company's restaurants' kitchens, including Cochon Butcher, the sandwich café and Cajun-style butcher shop in New Orleans.

"One of the reasons we're doing this is to give our people new opportunities, provide them a career and a life," Link said. "If we didn't have the talent to open this place, we wouldn't be."

Together with Kyle Waters III, Cochon Lafayette's chef de cuisine, the restaurant's team built a menu around Cochon classics while, as Link put it, "trying not to appear like we're competing with anyone's grandma."

The smothered chicken nods to a regional mainstay, only Cochon's is smoked and gilded with pickled onions and mustard seeds. One older man told Link he enjoyed the grilled skirt steak "but didn't know what to do with" its side of collard green slaw. (Major difference between the slaw and traditional smothered collards, which are also on the menu: length of cooking.)

The fried redfish collar was certainly familiar to any Cajun fisher who has refused to waste any morsel of a day's catch—never mind that other diners may recognize the dish as a staple of Japanese cooking, too.

Cochon Lafayette's boudin is smoked, its casing charred, the space in the cavity where it's split filled with a pinch of sliced pickled chili peppers. The dish represents a reversal of Link's original vow to stay away from boudin in Lafayette for fear of becoming ensnared in the contentious regional argument over whose is best. So what if his doesn't resemble anything anyone has ever eaten in the cab of a pickup?

"There are a lot of cultures involved in Cajun food," Link said. "No one can really lay claim to it. Why does it have to be one thing? Why can't it be different? Why can't it be in an entirely different context?"

On opening night, Cochon Lafayette was already addressing these and other questions. The restaurant's parking lot was full.

Of Pepperoni Rolls and Soup Beans
On What It Might Mean to Eat like a West Virginian

Courtney Balestier

In the end, it took New York City to make me a West Virginian. There is the technicality of my birth, in Morgantown, West Virginia, my only home until age twenty-two. But I spent those years eating pepperoni rolls and waiting to move to Manhattan, where the mountains are hard, reflective steel and pepperoni is a pizza topping.

In New York, I became that friend from a novelty place, fielding questions about incest and obesity, stereotypes that offer crude attempts at definition, as stereotypes do. Not that I knew the real definition. Until those barbs stirred some latent identity, I'd never felt the need to name it. Then I got a job writing about food, and I started thinking about food in West Virginia. I was, at this point, something of an immigrant. And when you're talking about food, which I prefer to do most always, every immigrant is a minute of stopped time. In foreign kitchens, we cook what's familiar, preserving the recipe, the story, the self. We do this because, when we're uprooted, food is our root. It's also our root long before we're uprooted, long before we realize it.

I started baking pepperoni rolls, those pillows of meat-stuffed bread that began as lunch for West Virginia's Italian coal miners. I breaded and fried chicken like my grandmother's, armed with one of her cast-iron skillets. I shopped New York's greenmarkets and was shocked just to find ramps, the Appalachian wild onions, let alone to find them selling for ten dollars a pound. Back home, you can buy them from a truck bed for practically nothing, and that's if you don't know where to forage them. Not that I do. With parents from Pennsylvania and New Jersey, I'd never considered myself much of a West Virginian. The only things I foraged were extra cheddar biscuits on those special trips to the closest town with a Red Lobster, an honor not then available to Morgantown and one that, from New York, I realized was dubious. From my third-floor walkup, I imagined the broader pastoral of this place I'd left: prideful home gardens, the occasional quiet farm. Yet I'd go back to a town that (while home to a few local-loving gems, like the unimpeachable Black Bear Burritos) was increasingly overrun by the usual casual-dining-at-the-strip-mall suspects. Why this enduring fetishization of endless pasta bowls and value meals, the sodium-spiked suburban faceless-ness? Surely, West Virginia could eat better than this off its own abundance. Surely, somewhere, it already did. I believed that slow-food curiosity to be my motivation.

I believe it to be, at least, a motivation. Either way, it compelled me to spend one August day driving my mother's car to Rock Cave, West Virginia, a cartographic gesture separated from Interstate 79 by twenty miles of country road, in search of a farmer and chef named Dale Hawkins. A note on me and back roads: I love them. I find them comforting. In college, I had a period of something approximating insomnia, and I would spend chunks of midnight hours driving country roads, persuaded by the impression of forward motion. Sometimes I'd drive in one direction until sunrise, then turn around. That this drive made me nervous, in the way that one is nervous to drive in a foreign country, felt a little weird.

My camera was in the passenger seat, and there were picturesque spots along the route—an old gas station, an abandoned restaurant—that caught my eye. I slowed down, and again on the way back, but didn't stop.

When I reached Dale Hawkins, in the kitchen of the Rock Cave IGA, he was packing tomatoes. Hawkins runs a slew of culinary enterprises under the name of the seventeen-acre farm he grew up on, Fish Hawk Acres. Aside from the farm, community-supported kitchen, and CSA, Hawkins's pet project is New Appalachian Cuisine: "global food fused with local ingredients and given a regional interpretation." In the kitchen, he told me that the inspiration for it came from his experience cooking in Florida and seeing the clout that the peasant food of his youth, ingredients like ramps, quail, and rabbit, held on a menu. "We were chichi before we knew it," Hawkins said, laughing. Just ask the Union Square Greenmarket.

A bearishly boyish guy with a welcoming, dimpled face, Hawkins offered to drive me through the farm. We were in his dusty Subaru for about thirty seconds before we hung a right into rows and rows of crops. Hawkins was hoping to plant forty acres before long; he already had squash, tomatoes, melons, beans, greens, peppers. We talked about mono farms in the Midwest growing miles of corn. We talked about the state's bakeries and creameries, businesses that were seeking him out to sell their products. We stopped at the cooling shed and surveyed buckets of tomatoes, birthmarked and Willy Wonka bright. One of his employees showed off a new "chicken condo." Then, Hawkins and I drove to the farmhouse, where we found his brother. Who, naturally, took us to see the goats.

There were baby goats. And puppies, of some snowy-white shepherd breed, whose mother I believe was charged with guarding the goats. When I was in kindergarten, we took a field trip to a local farm; we watched ducklings zip down a slide into a pool and got a swath of shorn wool each and, if I did see a goat then, it was the last time before this day. The whole experience—the incongruity of driving a car through a field, the damn integrity of it all, agricultural to familial—made me giddy. The way a journalist feels when an interview goes well, maybe. But also, I don't know, like I was buying a piece of some village artisan's pottery. A little self-satisfied. A little drunk on the rural atmosphere I no longer inhabited. I am not sure, still, how much of that day amounts to more than vaguely autobiographical tourism.

Months later, I spoke with a friend of Hawkins's, another chef, named Tim Urbanic. Urbanic grew up in a small Pennsylvania coal-mining town. His family lived off the land, and he moved to West Virginia as an adult because it was one of the only places where living off the land remained possible. He runs Cafe Cimino, a celebrated restaurant in Sutton, West Virginia, that sources largely from its own crops and those of friends (including Hawkins), with over twenty Appalachian purveyors supplying regional items like paddle-fish caviar.

I didn't know much about paddlefish caviar, or really what we talk about when we talk about Appalachian cuisine, or whether what I grew up eating constituted it. So I called Mark Sohn, an Appalachian scholar and author of *Appalachian Home Cooking*. Traditional Appalachian cuisine, Sohn said, is a product of necessity: families had what they grew (tomatoes, apples), foraged (ramps, morels), raised (chickens, pigs), and caught (deer, trout). The cuisine, if you will, was so basic that he summarized it with your standard culinary action verbs: snapped (as in beans), boiled, fried, canned, gardened, milked, salted. Chicken was fried. Apples were preserved into butter. Soup beans were simmered and served with cast-iron-skillet cornbread. Sohn's voice bore his Kentucky roots, and in the course of conversation it came out that I lived in Brooklyn and he in Manhattan. We got a kick out of this, the fact that we'd made separate trips across the Mason-Dixon Line to sit in New York waxing about apple butter.

When Sohn spoke of necessity, I thought of my grandmother. Like Urbanic, she grew up in a Pennsylvania mining town. She more or less ran the house in her youth, after my great-grandmother injured herself with an axe while chopping wood. My grandmother made great beans—navy beans—simmered with salt, pepper, and (how I adore her preference for this term) oleo. She did have a cast-iron skillet. She had many, as I learned when I remarked that I'd like to get one myself: she opened the cellar door, where at least five hung from their handles on the wall, and handed me one as if she were passing me a cup of coffee. She used hers mainly for chicken, perhaps cube steak too. Mine was not a cornbread family. I suspect that might be beside the point for our purposes.

Mine was also not a farming family, but most everyone in West Virginia seems to garden, so we had no shortage of neighbors' tomatoes and peppers and zucchini. So it made sense when Urbanic said that what state chefs like him and Hawkins were doing, really, was accelerating a natural shift toward celebrating local food, "by letting people know how lucky they are to be here and pick a tomato, a cucumber, and put it in a salad."

"We're in a very special place," he said.

There was just one problem: I wasn't in that place. When I had been, I hadn't particularly cared. I wasn't exactly in the place I was either, New York, where citizenship is so conditional that years pass before outsiders can claim the place as their own. (And even then, New York is onto them.) It's a curious experience, trying to triangulate yourself between two geographical ideas. It's like parsing out which of your personality traits come from which parent, or wondering where you've put the car keys while you're driving.

Eventually, it creates the sensation of being both embedded in and absent from the same place, a sort of metaphysical jet lag, until that place becomes too conceptual to occupy. Which is how it tricked me. I'd made my involvement in this place of cast-iron skillets and soup beans too complicated, needlessly elusive: I was there. It's a simple matter of fact, which offers an appetizing symmetry, because Appalachian cuisine is so simple. It's almost biblical, really: celebrate what you have. Pepperoni rolls are born of utility, but also of grandparents and great-grandparents and the industry that sustained them. They existed, and now you do. Honor that.

Sohn, the Appalachian scholar, told me a story about a former student of his, whose mom would pack homemade biscuits in his lunch when he was a boy. The boy hated it. He wanted Wonder Bread, because you had to buy Wonder Bread, and that meant you had money. It gets laughs now, because we idolize the homemade and deride the idea of Wonder Bread as status symbol. But it also makes me think of being a kid, crossing state lines to the nearest Red Lobster. Impatient, unconcerned, because I was only from West Virginia, not of it. As if the two should ever be separated.

Pasquale's Hot Tamales

As told to Amy Evans by Joe St. Columbia

My name is Joe St. Columbia. I was born October 30, 1938.

It all began with my grandfather, Peter St. Columbia, coming to America in 1892, and leaving my father, who was a newborn baby—leaving his wife and baby in Sicily. He stayed in New Orleans maybe a few months, cutting sugarcane down there to make some money. Daddy said Grandpa earned fifty cents a day cutting sugarcane, and he earned passage on a riverboat coming up the Mississippi River. And he came as far as Helena, Arkansas, and decided to get off the boat. Daddy said Grandpa's money ran out, and that's why he chose Helena. He was here five years, and he earned enough money for my grandmother, Maria St. Columbia, to come and bring my father, and they came in 1897.

My father was five years old in 1897, and he could not speak the English language very well at all, and the kids would laugh at him and make fun of him when he tried to go to school. So he played a lot of hooky and hung out among business people in the community. As a teenager, growing up in the early years of the 1900s, he learned the ways of the business world—"the school of hard knocks," as we call it today.

In those early days, daddy could speak a Sicilian dialect to some of the Mexicans that came here—there were Mexicans doing farm labor. He learned from them about tamales. My father liked the taste of the tamales. He made friends with them, and they taught him how to make tamales. The Mexicans would get with my family and say, "OK, here's the way we did it in Mexico." So as the years went on, my daddy would make tamales at home with his father. And they formulated their way of doing it.

Grandpa and Daddy would go to the farms and the sawmill companies along the levees and take sandwiches, salami, tamales, different homemade foods—and they would feed the workers out on the farms and at the sawmill so they didn't have to go to lunch. Daddy and Grandpa would pull up there and they had everything for the people. They would buy from them like they do with my food trailer today. It was a thing they could carry—it was hot, fresh, and tasty. They would just hold it in their hand and eat it and suck on the shucks, and it was real juicy. They didn't have to stop their work. And the owners of those businesses liked that, because their workers would not have to leave and spend an hour or two eating lunch.

A young black couple, Maggie and Eugene Brown, came to my father right before the Depression. My father had built a building downtown, and they wanted to rent a space in it, but they didn't have any money. They wanted to open a restaurant and sell soul food. So my father formed a business arrangement with these people. He told them, "Well, if you sell my tamales in there, we'll form a partnership. I'll show you how to make them, I'll buy all the equipment, and you make them. And we'll share the profits of the business."

So they did. They formed a business relation, and the black family did well. In fact, they did so well that they educated their children and sent them to college away from here. They got jobs in Detroit and never came back.

So it survived the Depression; it survived the war. World War II came on, and the business continued making money for both my family and their family. My father helped this man build a little cart, and they would put the pots on it, with a little burner underneath. During the war, they would push it down Walnut Street and Elm Street at night, especially on Friday night, Saturday night. And people would buy it right off the street.

My father could neither read nor write, but he was very smart when it came to business and it came to people. He was very strong in his Catholic religion and believed that if you go to church on Sunday and see God first, then you can go out and work all day, if you want to. And he did.

Eventually, Maggie and Eugene Brown died, and the Elm Street Tamale Shop fell back into my family. My father had died when I was about eighteen years old, so tamale making in the city of Helena became dormant for a while.

I was in the wholesale beer business, and after I sold my beer business, my wife and I brought back the tamale business in the Arkansas Delta. My wife is an excellent cook; she was trained by her grandmother, who was Italian. We took my mother and father's recipe of tamale making and we began to upgrade it, fine-tuning it. Our tamale is made from all-natural foods. We start out with around one hundred pounds of beef. We use top sirloin and chuck roasts. We use real onions, real garlic—no powdered anything. Our cornhusks come out of Mexico. We wrap each tamale—hand-roll them in the corn husks, and then we cook them submerged in a special sauce for six to eight hours on slow heat. The tamale absorbs the seasonings, and the juice makes them real tender and succulent. So that's basically the secret to our tamales and why they're so juicy.

This time, we decided to name the business after my father. His name in Italian was Pasquale, and it rhymed with tamale, so we came out with Pasquale's Hot Tamales. It was in 1987 when we formally established the business. And it's been doing well ever since.

cutting greens

Lucille Clifton

curling them around
i hold their bodies in obscene embrace
thinking of everything but kinship.
collards and kale
strain against each strange other
away from my kissmaking hand and
the iron bedpot.
the pot is black,
the cutting board is black,
my hand,
and just for a minute
the greens roll black under the knife,
and the kitchen twists dark on its spine
and i taste in my natural appetite
the bond of live things everywhere.

Remembering Pitmaster Ricky Parker

Joe York

They buried Ricky Parker yesterday. A few miles down the road from the cinder-block pits where he cooked whole hogs for more than half his life, from the sliding glass window where he sold sandwiches, from the creosote-stained door where he hung the SOLD OUT sign every afternoon to let the latecomers know not to bother, they gathered to say they were sorry, to say good-bye, to say that they didn't know what to say.

They dressed him as he dressed himself. In blue Dickies, a tan work shirt with a pack of Swisher Sweets peeking from the breast pocket, and his burgundy-and-brown ball cap resting on the ledge of the coffin, he went to his reward. The only thing missing was his greasy apron. I imagine it hangs on a nail somewhere back by the pits where he left it.

They came to eat at Scott's Barbecue long before I did. For years it was run by its namesake, Early Scott, who grew the business from a roadside stand into a place of pilgrimage. Along the way, he took Ricky in and he raised him as his own son, though he wasn't. Ricky recalled how he came to live and work with Early in an interview I did with him in 2005:

> "When I was sixteen, me and my dad got into it and I hit him
> with a baseball bat because he was whooping up on my momma.
> I went to school the next morning and when I come back he had
> all my clothes sitting out on the front porch. So I called Mr. and
> Mrs. Scott and I've been with them ever since."

"Ever since" lasted thirty-five years. In that time Early taught Ricky how to cook hogs, how to coax smoke and vinegar into every nook and cranny of the carcass, how to burn down the leftover hickory scraps from the local ax-handle factory into the perfect catalyst for their edible alchemy, how to load the shovel, where to put the fire, when to stoke it, and when not to. Mostly, he taught him how to work and how to wait, the only two ingredients that really matter. Somewhere along the way Early faded into the smoke and Zach and Matthew emerged from it. Ricky taught his boys what Early taught him, and through it all they came.

They came to the tiny glass window and asked for shoulder, and ham, and middlin. They asked for extra slaw and extra sauce. And whether it was Early or Ricky or Zach or Matthew that handed the sandwiches and trays and cans of Coke through the window, it always tasted the same, always smelled the same, and they always came back and came back and came back. And when they ran through one hog, Ricky and the boys would go back and lift another from the pit to take its place.

It was fitting, then, and crushing, that it was those same boys who lifted their father's casket and carried him to the front of the sanctuary at the Sand Ridge Baptist Church in Lexington, Tennessee, yesterday, where the parking lot was so full and the lines were so long that you'd swear you were at Scott's.

They filled the church and they sat quietly as the preacher spoke. They bowed their heads when he bowed his head. They *amen*'ed when he *amen*'ed. And when there we no more words to say, they stood and came one by one to say good-bye to Ricky Parker.

They filed past his body, looking down at the restless man turned still life. I was with them. He was there and he wasn't, more something ready-made for a wax museum now than the man who roamed the pits, who burned more hickory in his fifty-one years than lightning ever did, who spent his days here transforming hogs, and himself, through an inscrutable transubstantiation of fire and smoke into the embodiment of two of our greatest human virtues, patience and hard work.

I paused over him and noticed that in his right hand someone had placed a single cigar between his index and bird fingers. His thumb rested, anticipatory, on the business end of the Swisher Sweet and in that moment I couldn't help but imagine a scene in which Ricky saunters up to Saint Peter, looks him up and down and says, "Well, Pete, you got a light for me or what?"

They will still come to Scott's. The smoke will still rise behind the old wooden store that Early built and passed on to Ricky, that Ricky passed on to his boys. One morning not too long from now, they'll get up before any of us would dream of waking. They'll drive out to the edge of town and light a fire. They'll heave a hog on the pit and shovel a load of coals under it and wait. And when the fire and smoke have done what their daddy told them it would, they'll reach up and grab the greasy apron from the nail where Ricky left it and get to work.

Grace

Jake Adam York

Because my grandmother made me
the breakfast her mother made her,
when I crack the eggs, pat the butter
on the toast, and remember the bacon
to cast iron, to fork, to plate, to tongue,
my great grandmother moves my hands
to whisk, to spatula, to biscuit ring,
and I move her hands too, making
her mess, so the syllable of batter
I'll find tomorrow beneath the fridge
and the strew of salt and oil are all
memorials, like the pan-fried chicken
that whistles in the grease in the voice
of my best friend's grandmother
like a midnight mockingbird,
and the smoke from the grill
is the smell of my father coming home
from the furnace and the tang
of vinegar and char is the smell
of Birmingham, the smell
of coming home, of history, redolent
as the salt of black-and-white film
when I unwrap the sandwich
from the wax-paper the wax-paper
crackling like the cold grass
along the Selma to Montgomery road,

like the foil that held
Medgar's last meal, a square of tin
that is just the ghost of that barbecue
I can imagine to my tongue
when I stand at the pit with my brother
and think of all the hands and mouths
and breaths of air that sharpened
this flavor and handed it down to us,
I feel all those hands inside
my hands when it's time to spread
the table linen or lift a coffin rail
and when the smoke billows from the pit
I think of my uncle, I think of my uncle
rising, not falling, when I raise
the buttermilk and the cornmeal to the light
before giving them to the skillet
and sometimes I say the recipe
to the air and sometimes I say his name
or her name or her name
and sometimes I just set the table
because meals are memorials
that teach us how to move,
history moves in us as we raise
our voices and then our glasses
to pour a little out for those
who poured out everything for us,
we pour ourselves for them,
so they can eat again.

Contributors

Brett Anderson, a 2013 Nieman Fellow at Harvard, is the restaurant critic and features editor at the *Times-Picayune* in New Orleans.

Courtney Balestier has written about food and culture for the *Wall Street Journal*, *Saveur*, *Gastronomica*, and the *Oxford American*.

Dan Baum is the author of four books, most recently *Gun Guys: A Road Trip*, and a contributor to magazines such as *The New Yorker*, *Harper's*, *Popular Science*, and the *Oxford American*.

Burkhard Bilger has been a staff writer for *The New Yorker* since 2001, writing primarily about food, science, and American subcultures.

Jane Black is a food columnist for the *Washington Post* and is at work on a book about Huntington, West Virginia's, effort to change its food culture.

Lucille Clifton (1936–2010) was the author of numerous collections of poetry, a two-time Pulitzer Prize nominee, and the former poet laureate for the state of Maryland.

Stephen A. Crockett Jr., a frequent contributor to *The Root*, is at work on his first collection of short fiction.

John T. Edge is the director of the Southern Foodways Alliance at the University of Mississippi and a frequent contributor to the *Oxford American*, *Garden and Gun*, and *Southern Living*.

Lolis Eric Elie is a writer for print and television and the author, most recently, of *Treme: Stories and Recipes from the Heart of New Orleans*.

Barry Estabrook is a former contributing editor at *Gourmet* magazine and the author of *Tomatoland: How Modern Industrial Agriculture Destroyed Our Most Alluring Fruit*.

Amy Evans is the lead oral historian for the Southern Foodways Alliance.

Rayna Green, a curator at the Smithsonian Institution's National Museum of American History, writes and curates exhibits on Native American history and culture and on food history and culture.

Jessica B. Harris is the author of eleven books on the foodways of the African Diaspora, most recently *High on the Hog: A Culinary Journey from Africa to America*.

Bill Heavey is a longtime columnist for *Field and Stream* and the author of *It's Only Slow Food Until You Try to Eat It: Misadventures of a Suburban Hunter-Gatherer.*

Sarah Hepola is a writer and editor from Texas.

Eddie Huang is the chef of Baohaus in New York City and the author of *Fresh Off the Boat: A Memoir.*

Langston Hughes (1902–1967) was a poet, novelist, and playwright who emerged as one of the leaders of the Harlem Renaissance literary movement.

Todd Kliman is the food critic for *Washingtonian* magazine and the author of *The Wild Vine: A Forgotten Grape and the Untold Story of American Wine.*

Francis Lam is editor-at-large at Clarkson Potter, an imprint of Random House books. He was a contributing editor at *Gourmet* and has written for *Salon*, the *New York Times*, *Bon Appétit*, and *Food & Wine.*

Edward Lee is the chef at 610 Magnolia in Louisville, Kentucky, and the author of *Smoke and Pickles: Recipes and Stories from a New Southern Kitchen.*

Ida MaMusu is the owner of Africanne on Main in Richmond, Virginia.

Seán McKeithan is a doctoral student in Theater, Dance, and Performance Studies at the University of California–Berkeley.

Nikki Metzgar is a Houston native and writer.

Jonathan Miles is a contributing editor for *Details*, *Field and Stream*, and *Garden and Gun*, as well as the author of two novels, *Dear American Airlines* and *Want Not.*

Robert Moss is a food writer and restaurant critic for the *Charleston City Paper* and the author of *Barbecue: The History of an American Institution* and *Going Lardcore: Adventures in New Southern Dining.*

Sue Nguyen is the owner of Le Bakery in Biloxi, Mississippi.

Mary Louise Nosser is a leader of the annual Lebanese dinner at Saint George Antiochian Orthodox Christian Church in her hometown of Vicksburg, Mississippi.

Susan Orlean is a staff writer at *The New Yorker* and the author of seven books, including *The Orchid Thief*, which was made into the Academy Award–winning film *Adaptation.*

Argentina Ortega is the owner of La Sabrosita bakery in Richmond, Virginia.

Daniel Patterson is the chef at San Francisco's Coi restaurant and the author of *Coi: Stories and Recipes.*

Jack Pendarvis is the author of three books. He is a columnist for *Believer* magazine and writes for the television show *Adventure Time.*

Ann Taylor Pittman is the executive food editor at *Cooking Light* magazine.

Kathleen Purvis is the food editor for the *Charlotte Observer* and the author of two "Savor the South" cookbooks, *Pecans* and *Bourbon.*

Julia Reed, whose reporting and essays have appeared in *Newsweek*, *Vogue*, *Garden and Gun*, and elsewhere, is the author, most recently, of *But Mama Always Put Vodka in Her Sangria: Adventures in Eating, Drinking, and Making Merry.*

Sara Roahen is a New Orleans–based writer and oral historian and the author of *Gumbo Tales: Finding My Place at the New Orleans Table.*

Besha Rodell is the restaurant critic for *LA Weekly.*

Patricia Smith is the author of several collections of poetry, including *Blood Dazzler*, a series of poems about Hurricane Katrina that was a finalist for the National Book Award.

Joe St. Columbia is the owner of Pasquale's Hot Tamales in Helena, Arkansas.

Jeffrey Steingarten is *Vogue*'s longtime food critic and the author of *The Man Who Ate Everything*.

John Jeremiah Sullivan, a contributing editor for the *New York Times Magazine* and *Harper's* and the Southern editor of the *Paris Review*, is the author of two books of nonfiction: *Pulphead* and *Blood Horses*.

Gabriel Thompson is the author of *Working in the Shadows: A Year of Doing the Jobs (Most) Americans Won't Do*.

Monique Truong is the author of two novels, *The Book of Salt* and *Bitter in the Mouth*.

Robb Walsh is a Texas-based food writer and the author of *Barbecue Crossroads: Notes and Recipes from a Southern Odyssey*.

Sara Wood is a student in the MFA program at the University of North Carolina–Wilmington and an oral historian for the Southern Foodways Alliance.

Jake Adam York (1972–2012) authored four books of poems: *Murder Ballads*, *A Murmuration of Starlings*, *Persons Unknown*, and *Abide*.

Joe York is a Mississippi-based filmmaker whose most recent feature-length documentary, *Pride & Joy*, explores the diverse foodways of the American South.

Kevin Young is the author of seven books of poetry, including *Ardency: A Chronicle of the* Amistad *Rebels*, which won a 2012 American Book Award.

Acknowledgments

"We Waited as Long as We Could," by Daniel Patterson. Originally published in *Lucky Peach*, no. 4 (Summer 2012). Reprinted by permission of *Lucky Peach*.

"The Homesick Restaurant," by Susan Orlean. Originally published in *The New Yorker*, January 15, 1996. Reprinted by permission of the author.

"Stuffed, Smothered, Z'herbes," by Sara Roahen. Originally published in *Gumbo Tales: Finding My Place at the New Orleans Table* (New York: W. W. Norton and Company, 2008). Copyright © 2008 by Sara Roahen. Used by permission of W. W. Norton & Company, Inc.

"What I Cook Is Who I Am," by Edward Lee. Excerpted from *Smoke and Pickles: Recipes and Stories from a New Southern Kitchen*. Copyright © 2013 by Edward Lee. Used by permission of Artisan, a division of Workman Publishing Co., Inc., New York. All rights reserved.

"God Has Assholes for Children," by Eddie Huang. Excerpted from *Fresh Off the Boat: A Memoir* (New York: Spiegel & Grau, 2013). Copyright © 2013 by Eddie Huang. Used by permission of Spiegel & Grau, an imprint of The Random House Publishing Group, a division of Random House LLC. All rights reserved. Any third party use of this material, outside of this publication, is prohibited. Interested parties must apply directly to Random House LLC for permission.

"You Have to Fall in Love with Your Pot," as told to Sara Wood by Ida MaMusu. Oral history conducted for the Southern Foodways Alliance, March 5, 2013.

"Around the World in Eight Shops," by Kathleen Purvis. Originally published in the *Charlotte Observer*, March 20, 2013. Reprinted by permission of the *Charlotte Observer*.

"That's Your Country," as told to Sara Wood by Argentina Ortega. Oral history conducted for the Southern Foodways Alliance, December 10, 2012.

"Friends and Families," by Nikki Metzgar. Originally published in *Food Arts* 26, no. 1 (January–February 2013). Reprinted courtesy of *Food Arts*.

"The Perfect Chef," by Todd Kliman. Originally published in *Oxford American*, no. 68 (Spring 2010). Reprinted by permission of the author.

"Nature's Spoils," by Burkhard Bilger. Originally published in *The New Yorker*, November 22, 2010. Reprinted by permission of the author.

"I Had a Farm in Atlanta," by John T. Edge. Originally published in *Oxford American*, no. 80 (Spring 2013). Reprinted by permission of the author.

"The Price of Tomatoes," by Barry Estabrook. Copyright © 2007 Condé Nast. All rights reserved. Originally published in *Gourmet*, 2009. Reprinted by permission.

"Working in the Shadows" (excerpt), by Gabriel Thompson. Originally published in *Working in the Shadows: A Year of Doing the Jobs (Most) Americans Won't Do* (New York: Nation Books, 2010). Reprinted by permission of Nation Books and the author.

"The Celebrity Shepherd," by Besha Rodell. Originally published on the *Modern Farmer* website, May 16, 2013. Reprinted by permission of the author.

"The Triumph of Jamie Oliver's 'Nemesis,'" by Jane Black. Originally published on *Gilt Taste*, August 29, 2011. Reprinted by permission of the author.

"Grabbing Dinner," by Bill Heavey. Originally published in *Garden and Gun*, October–November 2011. Reprinted by permission of the author.

"Hogzilla," by Dan Baum. Originally published in *Gun Guys: A Road Trip* (New York: Knopf, 2013). Reprinted by permission of Knopf.

"A Taste for the Hunt," by Jonathan Miles. Originally published in *Garden and Gun*, October–November 2011. Permission courtesy of the author.

"Eat Dessert First," by Robb Walsh. Originally published in *Barbecue Crossroads: Notes and Recipes from a Southern Odyssey* (Austin: University of Texas Press, 2013). Reprinted by permission of the author on behalf of University of Texas Press.

"Anyone and Everyone Is Welcome," as told to Francis Lam by Sue Nguyen. Oral history conducted for the Southern Foodways Alliance, July 27, 2008.

"The Great Leveler," by Julia Reed. Originally published in *But Mama Always Put Vodka in Her Sangria! Adventures in Eating, Drinking, and Making Merry* (New York: St. Martin's Press, 2013). Reprinted by permission of the author.

"The Post-Husk Era," by Robert Moss. Originally published in *Charleston City Paper*, August 8, 2012. Reprinted by permission of the author.

"Ode to Gumbo," by Kevin Young. © 2008 by Kevin Young. Originally published in *Dear Darkness* (New York: Alfred A. Knopf, 2008). Reprinted by permission of the author. All rights reserved.

"Mother Corn and the Dixie Pig: Native Food in the Native South," by Rayna Green. Originally published in *Southern Cultures* 14, no. 4 (Winter 2008). Reprinted by permission of the University of North Carolina Press / *Southern Cultures* and the author.

"Every Ounce a Man's Whiskey? Bourbon in the White Masculine South," by Seán McKeithan. Originally published in *Southern Cultures* 18, no. 1 (Spring 2012). Reprinted by permission of the University of North Carolina Press / *Southern Cultures* and the author.

"When the Queso Dripped Like Honey," by Sarah Hepola. Originally published on *Gilt Taste*, June 13, 2012. Reprinted by permission of the author.

"Willie Mae Seaton Takes New York," by Lolis Eric Elie. Originally published May 10, 2005, by the *Times-Picayune*, LLC. All rights reserved. Reprinted with permission.

"Mississippi Chinese Lady Goes Home to Korea," by Ann Taylor Pittman. Originally published in *Cooking Light* 26, no. 10 (November 2012). Reprinted by permission of the author.

"An Oyster Named Dan," by Jack Pendarvis. Originally published in *Lucky Peach*, no. 7 (Spring 2013). Reprinted by permission of *Lucky Peach* and the author.

"Coconut: The Queen of Cakes," by Jeffrey Steingarten. Originally published as "Sugar High: Baking the Perfect Coconut Cake" in *Vogue*, January 2013. Reprinted by permission of the author.

"The Vicksburg Lebanese Supper," as told to Amy Evans by Mary Louise Nosser. Oral history conducted for the Southern Foodways Alliance, September 1, 2010.

"Soul Food? What Is That?" by Langston Hughes. Originally published in *Simple's Uncle Sam*, by Langston Hughes, compilation by Arnold Rampersad and Ramona Bass. Copyright © 1965 by Langston Hughes. Copyright renewed 1993 by Arnold Rampersad and Ramona Bass. Reprinted by permission of Hill and Wang, a division of Farrar, Straus, and Giroux, LLC.

"We Shall Not Be Moved," by Jessica B. Harris. Originally published in *High on the Hog: A Culinary Journey from Africa to America* (New York: Bloomsbury, 2012). Reprinted by permission of the author.

"Fixing on the Next Star," by Patricia Smith. Originally published in *Shoulda Been Jimi Savannah* (Minneapolis: Coffee House Press, 2012). Reprinted by permission of the author.

"The Brixton: It's New, Happening, and Another Example of African American Historical 'Swagger-Jacking,'" by Stephen A. Crockett Jr. Originally published on *The Root*, August 3, 2012. Reprinted by permission of the *Washington Post*.

"I Placed a Jar in Tennessee," by John Jeremiah Sullivan. Originally published in *Lucky Peach*, no. 6 (Winter 2013). Copyright © 2013 by John Jeremiah Sullivan. Used by permission of The Wylie Agency LLC.

"A Love Letter to North Carolina's Red Bridges Barbecue," by Monique Truong. Originally delivered as a talk at the Southern Foodways Alliance Symposium, October 2012. Printed in the *Washington Post*, November 30, 2012. Reprinted by permission of the author.

"The Missing Link: Donald Link Opens Second Cochon in Lafayette," by Brett Anderson. Originally published in the *Times-Picayune*, October 2, 2011. Reprinted by permission of the author.

"Of Pepperoni Rolls and Soup Beans: On What It Might Mean to Eat like a West Virginian," by Courtney Balestier. Originally published in *Gastronomica* 13, no. 2 (Spring 2013). Reprinted by permission of the University of California Press.

"Pasquale's Hot Tamales," as told to Amy Evans by Joe St. Columbia. Oral history conducted for the Southern Foodways Alliance, March 31, 2006.

"cutting greens," by Lucille Clifton. From *Collected Poems of Lucille Clifton*. Copyright © 1987, by Lucille Clifton. Reprinted with the permission of The Permissions Company, Inc., on behalf of BOA Editions, Ltd., www.boaeditions.org.

"Remembering Pitmaster Ricky Parker," by Joe York. Originally published on the Southern Foodways Alliance blog, May 3, 2013. Reprinted by permission of the author.

"Grace," by Jake Adam York. Originally delivered at the Southern Foodways Alliance Symposium, October 2012. Printed in the *Washington Post*, November 20, 2012. Reprinted by permission of Sarah Skeen and Nicky Beer.

The Southern Foodways Alliance

The Southern Foodways Alliance, founded in 1999, documents, studies, and celebrates the diverse food cultures of the changing American South.

We set a common table where black and white, rich and poor—all who gather—may consider our history and our future in a spirit of reconciliation.

A member-supported nonprofit, based at the University of Mississippi's Center for the Study of Southern Culture, we collect oral histories, produce documentary films, sponsor scholarship, stage symposia, and publish great writing.

DOCUMENT

Documentary projects are central to the SFA's mission. Oral history interviews and documentary films not only capture the stories of our region for future generations, they illuminate people and place. Since the formal inception of our documentary initiative in 2005, we have collected more than eight hundred oral histories—tales about barbecue and boudin, tamales and tupelo honey.

We catalog our oral history archive online. Additionally, we share these stories through podcasts, smart phone apps, and various social media platforms.

Each year, the SFA produces several films in concert with the University of Mississippi's Southern Documentary Project.

Our subjects range from goat cheese artisans to fried pie cooks, from buttermilk producers to barbecue pit masters. All films may be streamed through our website.

STUDY

The SFA is the foremost national resource focused on the study and living history of Southern foodways. As an institute of the Center for the Study of Southern Culture, at the

University of Mississippi, we take seriously our charge to contribute to academic dialogues about food.

Academic rigor underscores our work. We host a lecture series that focuses on foodways topics. We aid students by offering internships and graduate assistantships. In the fall of 2011, we welcomed our first postdoctoral teaching fellow. In the fall of 2014 we welcome a tenure-track professor to campus.

CELEBRATE

By way of symposia on food culture and other public programs, the SFA celebrates the diverse food cultures of the American South.

For a look at our coming calendar, visit www.southernfoodways.org.

SFA FOUNDING MEMBERS

Ann Abadie, Oxford, Miss.
Kaye Adams, Birmingham, Ala.
Jim Auchmutey, Atlanta, Ga.
Marilou Awiakta, Memphis, Tenn.
Ben Barker, Durham, N.C.
Ella Brennan, New Orleans, La.
Ann Brewer, Covington, Ga.
Karen Cathey, Arlington, Va.
Leah Chase, New Orleans, La.
Al Clayton, Jasper, Ga.
Mary Ann Clayton, Jasper, Ga.
Shirley Corriher, Atlanta, Ga.
Norma Jean Darden, New York, N.Y.
Crescent Dragonwagon, Eureka
    Springs, Ark.
Nathalie Dupree, Social Circle, Ga.
John T. Edge, Oxford, Miss.
John Egerton, Nashville, Tenn.
Lolis Eric Elie, New Orleans, La.
John Folse, Donaldsonville, La.
Terry Ford, Ripley, Tenn.
Psyche Williams Forson, Beltsville, Md.
Damon Lee Fowler, Savannah, Ga.
Vertamae Grosvenor, Washington, D.C.
Jessica B. Harris, Brooklyn, N.Y.
Cynthia Hizer, Covington, Ga.

Portia James, Washington, D.C.
Martha Johnston, Birmingham, Ala.
Sally Belk King, Richmond, Va.
Sarah Labensky, Columbus, Miss.
Edna Lewis, Atlanta, Ga.
Rudy Lombard, Chicago, Ill.
Ronni Lundy, Louisville, Ky.
Louis Osteen, Charleston, S.C.
Marlene Osteen, Charleston, S.C.
Timothy W. Patridge, Atlanta, Ga.
Paul Prudhomme, New Orleans, La.
Joe Randall, Savannah, Ga.
Marie Rudisill, Hudson, Fla.
Dori Sanders, Clover, S.C.
Richard Schweid, Barcelona, Spain
Ned Shank, Eureka Springs, Ark.
Kathy Starr, Greenville, Miss.
Frank Stitt, Birmingham, Ala.
Pardis Stitt, Birmingham, Ala.
Marion Sullivan, Mt. Pleasant, S.C.
Van Sykes, Bessemer, Ala.
John Martin Taylor, Charleston, S.C.
Toni Tipton-Martin, Austin, Tex.
Jeanne Voltz, Pittsboro, N.C.
Charles Reagan Wilson, Oxford, Miss.

John T. Edge (www.johntedge.com) is the director of the Southern Foodways Alliance. He writes a monthly column, "United Tastes," for the *New York Times*, is a contributing editor at *Garden and Gun*, and a longtime columnist for the *Oxford American*. His work for *Saveur* and other magazines has been featured in six editions of the *Best Food Writing* compilation. He has been nominated for four James Beard Foundation awards, including the M. F. K. Fisher Distinguished Writing Award. In 2009, he was inducted into Beard's Who's Who of Food and Beverage in America. He is a coeditor of the *Southern Foodways Alliance Community Cookbook*.